Geopolitics and the (the Twenty-first Century

This book argues that in the twenty-first century Eastern Eurasia will replace Europe as the theater of decision in international affairs, and that this new geographic and cultural context will have a strong influence on the future of world affairs.

For half a millennium, the great powers have practised what might be called "world politics," yet during that time Europe, and small portions of the Near East and North Africa strategically vital to Europe, were the "centers of gravity" in international politics. This book argues that the "unipolar moment" of the post-Cold War era will not be replaced by a US–China "Cold War," but rather by a long period of multipolarity in the twenty-first century. Examining the policy goals and possible military–political strategies of several powers, this study explains how Washington may play a key role in Eastern Eurasian affairs if it can learn to operate in a very different political context.

This book also considers the rapid pace of technological change and how it will impact on great power politics. Considering India, China, the United States, Russia, Japan, and other countries as part of a multipolar system, this book addresses the central questions that will drive US policy in the coming decades.

This book will be of great interest to students of international security, military history, geopolitics, and international relations.

C. Dale Walton is Lecturer in the Department of Politics and International Relations at the University of Reading (UK) and managing editor of the journal *Comparative Strategy*.

Geopolitical theory series
General editors: Geoffrey Sloan and Mackubbin Owens

Geopolitics and the Great Powers in the Twenty-first Century

Multipolarity and the revolution in strategic perspective

C. Dale Walton

Routledge
Taylor & Francis Group

LONDON AND NEW YORK

First published 2007
by Routledge
2 Park Square, Milton Park, Abingdon, Oxon, OX14 4RN

Simultaneously published in the USA and Canada
by Routledge
270 Madison Ave, New York NY 10016

Routledge is an imprint of the Taylor & Francis Group, an informa business

Transferred to Digital Printing 2009

© 2007 C. Dale Walton

Typeset in Times by Wearset Ltd, Boldon, Tyne and Wear

British Library Cataloguing in Publication Data
A catalogue record for this book is available from the British Library

Library of Congress Cataloging in Publication Data
A catalog record for this book has been requested

ISBN10: 0-415-35853-1 (hbk)
ISBN10: 0-415-54519-6 (pbk)
ISBN10: 0-203-00473-6 (ebk)

ISBN13: 978-0-415-35853-8 (hbk)
ISBN13: 978-0-415-54519-8 (pbk)
ISBN13: 978-0-203-00473-9 (ebk)

For Amy,
My unrelated little sister

Contents

Acknowledgements

A multitude of friends and colleagues have contributed to this work, but Colin S. Gray deserves special mention for the enormous contribution that he has made to my education in matters geopolitical over the years. In addition, J.D. Crouch and Bill Rood contributed much to my perspective on geopolitics, as did many of the students in the postgraduate geopolitics course I taught at Missouri State University. I would also like to thank the numerous friends and fellow academics who have enlightened me on various issues, particularly Steve Cimbala, Chris Harmon, Tom Kane, James Kiras, Peter Pham, John Sheldon, Steve Rosefielde, Larry Serewicz, and Brad Thayer. Also, I thank Bill Van Cleave, a friend, mentor, and my longtime department head, for his support and encouragement over the years. He has contributed enormously not only to my own intellectual and career development, but to those of a seemingly-endless number of other academics and policymakers

Able research support was provided to me by several highly capable assistants: Caleb Bartley, Sage McLaughlin, Jackie Moseley, Steve Peterson, and Dave Walgreen. I also would thank Andrew Humphrys, my editor at Routledge, for his support throughout the publication process, as well as Geoff Sloan, who is both an editor of this series and a colleague at the University of Reading. Claire Dunstan has my thanks for her help in the editing, typesetting, and printing of the book. My kind-hearted wife, Shelley, not only accepted the annoyances intrinsic to being an author's spouse, but also contributed her skills as a proofreader.

As always, any errors solely are my own.

Introduction

New powers and old politics

The chief purpose of this work is to argue that the world political system is presently undergoing a fundamental transformation. This change has two distinct, but related, aspects: the end of the era that the great geopolitician Halford Mackinder termed the Columbian Epoch to a Post-Columbian Epoch and the shifting of the geographical center of gravity in international politics from Europe to an area referred to herein as Eastern Eurasia. This book explores the broad implications for world politics of these tectonic changes, with particular attention to how the United States might cope with them and maintain its position as the preeminent power in the world despite the passing of its ephemeral "unipolar moment."[1]

In a paper presented to the Royal Geographical Society in 1904, Mackinder argued that the era of exploration, which he termed the Columbian Epoch, was ending, and that the world was becoming a "closed political system."[2] At the same time, he warned, technology (particularly the development of intricate rail networks) was again making it possible for the Heartland – the core of Eurasia, the place from which, in previous centuries, wave after wave of nomadic invaders threatened the European Rimland – to menace the seapowers of Western Europe. In short, Mackinder believed that a long era was coming to an end, and that a new age, filled with peril, was being born.

This author contends that Mackinder was largely correct in his broad analysis, even if he was mistaken in certain specifics, and that his warning about the passing of the Columbian Epoch provides a good starting point for a geopolitical analysis of how world politics will likely develop in coming decades.

Mackinder and the Cold War

In retrospect, one might argue that there were two small but significant flaws in the analysis that led Mackinder to believe that the Columbian Epoch was imminently coming to an end, and that it would likely be followed by a period of Heartland supremacy over the European seapowers. First, he perhaps underestimated the capability of a mighty offshore seapower – the United States – to protect the declining European seapowers from the Heartland power. However, the history of the mid-twentieth century demonstrates just how close Mackinder's fears came to being fulfilled.

Nazi Germany made a very serious, and quite nearly successful, attempt to unseat the Soviet Union as the Heartland tenant and make itself the master of Europe from the English Channel to the Urals. This vast superpower would have commanded the majority of the world's industrial production, a very sizable chunk of its manpower, and all the natural resources necessary eventually to establish itself as the hegemon of the entire planet. Berlin failed catastrophically in this enterprise, and as a result the Red Army was able to flow out of the Heartland fortress and fill the power vacuum created in East–Central Europe by the destruction of Germany and exhaustion of France and Britain. As it consolidated its control over its new colonial possessions, Moscow kept its economy on a war footing and appeared poised to expand westward. The United States, however, effectively chose to abandon permanently its usual isolation from Continental politics and act as the protector of those European countries that had not yet been absorbed into the Soviet imperium. The result, of course, was the Cold War, and the United States successfully held Moscow at bay until the Soviet Union expired and the bulk of the Heartland was inherited by a reborn, but relatively weak, Russia.

Mackinder's second omission is intimately related to the first: he paid insufficient attention to the possibility that, while technological developments had placed the seapowers in a vulnerable position, further advances might serve to provide them with new and powerful defenses. A number of critical technological advances occurred in the mid-twentieth century: nuclear (and later thermonuclear) weapons, long-range bombers, and, eventually, intercontinental ballistic missiles (ICBMs) and submarine-launched ballistic missiles (SLBMs) were all developed and fielded. For the first time, immense damage could be done to the interior of the Heartland without a single soldier setting foot on its soil. The fact that it was the United States that enjoyed a technological lead during the early part of the Nuclear Age likely is highly significant; one shudders when contemplating how world history might have developed if the USSR had held an atomic monopoly during the critical years of the late 1940s. Again, if Mackinder was wrong, it was only by a little, and it is very easy to imagine how a Hitler or a Stalin might have been able to leverage control of the Heartland and thus gain mastery over the world.

Mercifully, however, the West survived, and even thrived. Despite its traditional reticence to involve itself in Eurasian affairs, the United States proved to be a surprisingly competent protecting power. However, it should be remembered that it was not merely the competence of the United States that determined the outcome of the Cold War; the shortcomings of the Soviet Union were equally important. Despite their Leninism, and even after they had built an awesome nuclear arsenal while still maintaining an overwhelming conventional advantage against the North Atlantic Treaty Organization (NATO), Soviet leaders never could quite bring themselves to do that for which they were supremely well-prepared, invading Western Europe. Moreover, despite possessing the resources of the Heartland, the Soviet Union proved unable to compete over the long term with a superpower foe possessing a far more efficient free market economy.

Although the militarily overmuscled Soviet state collapsed internally, this was not foreordained. There is no iron rule of history holding that empires must stand idle while more nimble foes beat them – indeed, such behavior is unusual, especially for a polity as well-armed and unashamedly aggressive as the USSR. Under proper circumstances, the Cold War might have been nothing more than an interwar period akin to that between the first two world wars; indeed, it is likely that in the months before his death Stalin was laying the groundwork for an eventual war against the United States.[3] American leaders do deserve credit for implementing a containment policy that proved successful, but it would be naïve to assume that because their policy *did* work that, therefore, it *had* to work. Soviet leaders *chose* not to initiate a third world war, just as surely as Hitler decided to launch World War II, under conditions that arguably were far less favorable to Germany than those that Moscow enjoyed in, say, the late 1970s.

Of course, it is also possible that a Soviet adventure in Europe would have ended in Moscow's defeat or a nuclear exchange so great as to shatter the two superpowers, as well as many other states. The purpose, herein, is not to argue that Heartland dominance of Eurasia was well-nigh foreordained, but somehow, miraculously, avoided. Rather, the seapower-oriented NATO alliance triumphed thanks to some combination of specific economic, military, and other advantages, the wisdom of its leaders, and simple good luck. The key point is that even before World War I Mackinder saw a threat emanating from the Heartland that was very real; his concern that a motivated Heartland tenant might emerge as the hegemon of Eurasia was valid, and the fact that he understood this threat before Germany even had made the first of its two bids for Heartland dominance, and long before the Cold War, showed extraordinary foresight.

The death of the Columbian Epoch

Because the seapowers proved more resilient than Mackinder thought likely, the Columbian Epoch did not end in a disastrous *Götterdämmerung*, and a cruel new era of German or Soviet world hegemony did not emerge. Instead, the period from approximately 1914 to 1991, particularly the years from 1945 onward, should be seen as one of Epochal decline – the slow degeneration of the Columbian Epoch and the transition to a new era, which is referred to herein as the Post-Columbian Epoch, a term that Mackinder himself used (albeit with a slightly different timeframe in mind). During these years, a long-enduring Euro-centric multipolar great power system finally disintegrated, the victim of a series of political earthquakes that resulted from tectonic pressures that had been building for centuries.

The first of these events was World War I. Despite the damage that it inflicted on the continental powers, the war itself did not destroy the multipolar system. The war and its aftermath did, however, lay the groundwork for the collapse of the old order (of which multipolarity was a critical aspect). The war killed, outright, two relatively weak, but nonetheless important, players in the European order, the Austrian and Ottoman Empires, and indirectly replaced the Heartland tenant with a new and more dangerous one, as the Russian Empire transformed into the Soviet Union. The latter transition is particularly notable. Russia was always somewhat of an odd duck in the European system, Christian and thus more-or-less recognized (unlike the Ottoman Empire) as a "proper" European power, but with a culture and history strikingly different in many respects from that of Central and, especially, Western Europe. Yet, with the transfer of power to the Bolsheviks, Russia became, paradoxically, both more and less "European." It was more European in the sense that it had thrown off its rather outmoded monarchal autocracy and replaced it with a system based on the supposed cutting edge in Western thought – Marxist scientific socialism, a mode of socio-political organization that, in the eyes of its many proponents, was the inevitable (and enticing) future. Russia had, however, become less European in the sense that it had now clearly set itself against the institutions and governments of the West, creating a Soviet Civilization intended to supplant its Western predecessor.

In the aftermath of the Great War, other "new modes and orders" (to borrow Machiavelli's phrase) developed. Fascism, which is often presented as the antithesis of Communism but more accurately is described as its intellectual first cousin,[4] emerged in Italy, and National Socialism, a particularly malevolent fascist variant, developed in Germany.[5] In the ensuing World War II, control of the Heartland was contested by two powers of the very kind that Mackinder most feared. Previously, he had expressed his concern that the Heartland would fall under the control of a power sufficiently competent to organize the Heartland's resources efficiently, and ruthless enough then to use those resources to gain hegemony over all Eurasia.[6] Both the USSR and Germany potentially fitted this description. Although Germany presented the greater immediate threat to the states of Western Europe, the outcome of World War II was hardly reassuring. Throughout the Columbian Epoch, a mutipolar system had endured on the European continent; despite occasional changes in the lineup of players (Spain and the Netherlands dropping from the ranks of the great powers, for example) the system remained fundamentally unchanged. The events of the first half of the twentieth century, however, smashed this apparatus beyond all repair. The war catastrophically damaged the international status of the Axis Powers. An invaded and partitioned Germany obviously had been removed from the ranks of the great powers; Italy, which had never actually been a great power but had pretended to that status, was reduced to a punchline for jokes about military incompetence; and Japan, the only non-European great power other than the United States (and, in any case, never more than a marginal player in events in Europe) was forced to renounce war as an instrument of state policy. The irreversible decline of Britain and France was not immediately and overwhelmingly obvious – a reality attested to by the fact that both powers have permanent seats on the UN Security Council – but it soon became clear that both countries were no longer great powers in any reasonable sense of the term.

It should be emphasized that it was not inevitable that multipolarity would be replaced by a bipolar system with two superpowers; there was no geopolitical clock that was predestined to strike midnight in 1945. Throughout (and even before) the period under discussion, human actors made decisions that sped the collapse of multipolarity. If they had made different decisions, it is entirely conceivable that multipolarity would have endured even to today (and, indeed, that the Soviet Union itself would never have come into existence). Any notion that bipolarity eventually *had* to take hold because Washington and Moscow were simply so much larger in population and resources than countries such as Britain, France, and Germany is excessively reductionist. Moreover, such thinking ignores the vitally important ways in which smaller powers can shape the international political landscape. For example, a Germany that had not been exhausted by its mad adventure of 1939–1945 would have been a very different power, as would Britain and France if they had not expended much treasure building oversized colonial empires of dubious strategic value, then proceeded to spend vast resources in two exhausting wars, and followed these decisions by implementing expensive domestic welfare schemes. Indeed, it is all too easy to forget the proximate cause of World War I itself: the Austrian Empire, a great power clinging to that status by the tips of its fingernails, felt it necessary to make war on Serbia in order to protect its interests in the Balkans and its national prestige. The actions of such lesser powers as Romania, Italy, Serbia, Bulgaria, and the Ottoman Empire played a considerable role in shaping the international security environment during and after 1914,[7] a fact that should be kept in mind when pondering the dynamics of a multipolar environment.

Nevertheless, the destruction of the multipolar order was the outcome of the cataclysms of the early twentieth century, and the resulting bipolar Cold War is best understood as the "deathbed era" of the Columbian Epoch. *Central and Western Europe remained, strategically speaking, the geographical center of great power competition, but the most powerful polities no longer were inhabitants of that region – they were outside powers, not of the European Rimland, but acting on it.* The struggle over Europe was still the struggle for the world (a theme explored in greater detail in Chapter 2), but the age of Central and Western European primacy had passed.

The Post-Columbian Epoch

It is argued, herein, that the Columbian Epoch ended in a rather bizarre anticlimax on Christmas Day 1991, when the USSR was officially dissolved; the Communist Heartland tenant, which throughout its existence had been paranoid about the danger that outside powers presented to it, committed suicide. Using this precise date as a cutoff admittedly is arbitrary; Epochal shifts are not instantaneous. Italian sculptors and painters did not all wake up one morning and begin creating beautiful art because the Renaissance officially had begun; similarly, in many respects the international security environment changed little with the formal collapse of Soviet power. Nonetheless, the 1991 date is a good boundary line for two reasons. First, the Soviet Union made a serious bid to become the sole global hegemon, but its Russian successor cannot plausibly accomplish such a goal (although Russia conceivably may be part of a future coalition that will seek world hegemony). This is a geopolitical change of no small import – at least for the time being, the Heartland power presents little threat to any Western industrialized country, much less to Eurasia as a whole, when it is acting alone. Second, the end of bipolarity opened the way for American dominance in world politics – a period of unipolarity.

This unipolar system will not long endure. The Cold War was a time of transition out of an Epoch generally marked by multipolarity; the current unipolar era is a transition period into another Epoch that will also, generally, be multipolar. Moreover, American unipolarity will not last nearly so long as the Cold War did; already it is crumbling (witness the international opposition to the war in Iraq), and in no more than a couple of decades the international system again will be marked by a robust multipolarity. The Post-Columbian Epoch will, however, in some respects be radically different from its predecessor.

First, and central to the argument of this work, the geographic center of world politics will be Eastern Eurasia, a region (or, perhaps more accurately, a "meta-region") which includes both the Asia-Pacific and South Asia. Its western border can be envisioned as a line running from Pakistan to China's border with Kazakhstan, and then dividing the Central Siberian Plateau from the Western Siberian Plain; to the east, it is easiest to imagine its border as the 180°E longitudinal line (save for a small piece of Siberia east of this line, which should also be considered part of the region). Thus, Japan, Indonesia, Australia, and New Zealand are contained in Eastern Eurasia.

This population of Eastern Eurasia and its commercial importance (which continues to grow rapidly) alone would make it vitally important, but the region's geopolitical significance results from more than demographic and economic statistics. Critically, it is emerging as the core of world political struggle – the home to a majority of the great powers,[8] and the place where the most vital political struggles of this century will occur. It was not coincidental that the two world wars (and before that, the Seven Years' War and other conflicts of worldwide significance) were centered in Europe, as events in that region shaped those worldwide – to achieve hegemony in Europe was a prerequisite to world hegemony.

At this point, it is useful to consider the intellectual contribution of the great Dutch-American geopolitician Nicholas J. Spykman, whose ideas differed from Mackinder's in several key respects. Most importantly, for the purposes at hand, Spykman reversed Mackinder's assumption that control of the Heartland was the prerequisite to control of the world. In this conception, control of what Spykman referred to as the Eurasian Rimland (roughly analogous to Mackinder's Inner or Marginal Crescent), was in fact the key to world power. Spykman was ahead of his time; he very likely overestimated the power potential of the Rimland at the time that he was writing, while underestimating the significance of the Heartland. When Spykman died, in 1943, Western and Central Europe was approaching strategic exhaustion, while the Asia-Pacific region (with the obvious exception of Japan) was not yet a major center of world political power. The Soviet collapse and the rise of China and India, however, have made Spykman's vision increasingly relevant, while diminishing the salience of Mackinder's.[9] In this century it is quite likely that the former's response to the latter's arguments regarding the struggle between the Eurasian heartland and its periphery – "If there is to be a slogan for the power politics of the Old World, it must be 'Who controls the rimland rules Eurasia; who rules Eurasia controls the destinies of the world' "[10] – will be a guiding geopolitical principle.

The Heartland certainly is still geopolitically significant, but it is now most unlikely that control of that area can be leveraged into control of the world. Rather, we are entering a period akin to the early part of the Columbian Epoch in several respects. A number of great powers will compete in a very fluid political arena; for reasons subsequently described in detail, one should not expect "hard" alliances of the kind that marked the Cold War. Moreover, sheer mass will not guarantee success in the new political environment; as in the early Columbian years, intellectual nimbleness and a willingness to adopt new technologies (and accept the risks that accompany those technologies) will be vital. Indeed, one might describe the emerging era as "the Columbian Epoch on fast-forward" – powers will have to be enormously versatile and ruthless to compete successfully in an environment in which technological, social, and economic change will occur far more rapidly than at any previous time in human history. History's scrap heap will grow taller in the coming decades as flawed ideas and failed polities are piled onto it. Those powers that compete successfully, however, will receive the rewards of security, prosperity (on a scale that most humans living today barely can conceive), and an opportunity to shape the future of humankind.

The center of the action

As Europe was in previous centuries, Eastern Eurasia will be *the* major center of geopolitical activity in this one. It is here that states will struggle for regional dominance and, ultimately, world power. Eastern Eurasia is the most economically, geographically, and strategically significant area of the world, and the only one of the three most important global geographic centers of power that is politically "up for grabs."

Of the two other centers of world economic and political power, one is overwhelmingly dominated by the United States and the other is consolidating both politically and economically. The North America Free Trade Area (NAFTA) is strategically stable, save for relatively minor issues, such as guerrilla violence in southern Mexico and the possibility that Quebec will secede from Canada; in any event, these and similar problems do not threaten Washington's dominant position in North America. The institutions of the European Union (EU), on the other hand, increasingly dominate Europe. Recent setbacks to the European project notwithstanding, it is entirely possible that Brussels *eventually* will succeed in its long-term goal of consolidating economic and foreign policy authority. However, even if the EU should collapse entirely (a most unlikely prospect), that still would not necessarily undermine European peace: its peoples appear to lack the stomach for another great war, and those states that could conceivably vie for power, such as Germany, France, and Britain, are not violently antagonistic toward each other. At the same time, Russia, presently, is too weak to threaten EU members and appears to have abandoned Soviet fantasies of conquering Europe outright. It is only in the Balkans, at the margins of Europe, and to the south, in simmering North Africa, that serious violence threatens in the foreseeable future. Nevertheless, turmoil in those areas would not fundamentally undermine the strategic order that reigns in Western and Central Europe.

Many of the countries in other regions of the world – sub-Saharan Africa, Latin America, Central America, Central Asia, and the Middle East – contain important resources, straddle trade routes, or are otherwise strategically noteworthy. However, none of these areas has the compelling combination of wealth, population, and strategic geography that would make them likely arenas for great power competition with the highest stakes.[11] Obviously, much of the world's energy reserves are contained in the Middle East and Central Asia, but great power competition in central Eurasia will be of a different character than on its eastern rim.

In the central and south-central portions of Eurasia, outside powers attempt to influence the availability, movement, and price of energy resources; additionally, the United States takes a special interest in the continued survival of a close ally (Israel) and the development of stable, America-friendly governments in Iraq and Afghanistan. These are important questions, but they are secondary to the struggle over hegemony in Eastern Eurasia – the relative place of great powers at the high table of international politics will be decided in the latter contest. If China emerges as the undisputed hegemon of Eastern Eurasia (a far-from-certain outcome, for reasons discussed in detail in Chapter 4), it will not only be the predominant power in Asia, but clearly the greatest power in the world.

Eastern Eurasia today includes four countries that plausibly might be described as great powers (India, Japan, China, and Russia),[12] as well as a panoply of medium powers, several of which are wealthy and technologically advanced (including South Korea, Australia, and Taiwan). Many of the world's goods are produced, and much of its energy and food consumed,[13] by the billions of people who live there, and the region certainly is not receding in importance.

In the Columbian Epoch, the character of the international system and the status of its individual players were decided in Europe. In the current age, Eastern Eurasia will be the geopolitical center of the world. The struggles that occur there will determine which states grow more powerful and which weaken, or even die. *It is here that any great power wars in this century will likely be centered*; the Stalingrads and Waterloos of tomorrow will be in Eastern Eurasia rather than Europe. Moreover, it should be considered highly, if not overwhelmingly, probable that great power wars in fact will occur.[14]

Optimists would consider this viewpoint misguided, if not heretical –

certainly, it is not the sort of thing that one says during a cocktail party at the UN Secretary General's apartment (at least if one wishes to be invited back). However, the arguments for enduring great power peace are less than compelling. One of the most popular is the assertion that the proliferation of weapons of mass destruction (WMDs) has made war between parties possessing such weapons so risky that they will avoid armed struggle. Alternately, one can argue that trade and the complexity of the international supply chains on which today's multinational corporations rely makes war so patently unwise that major states will avoid it, or that various international institutions so constrain the behavior of such polities that they may rattle sabers but will go no further. The truly ebullient might even argue that democratic states never go to war and that within a few decades all of the significant powers will be democratic.

Any of these arguments *may* be true, but skepticism is advisable, as they are all unproven. The simple fact is that, regardless of how much data political scientists may marshal in the defense of their theories or how elegant their analyses may be, the history used to support them is a short and atypical one. It is true that the Cold War era was a "peaceful" one in the sense that the United States and the Soviet Union did not go to war with each other, but – as noted above – bipolarity itself is unusual in recent centuries. Moreover, from 1914 to 1953 Russia/the Soviet Union experienced two world wars, a civil war, and very vigorous internal oppression, planned famine, and purges; the cost of all this will never be known, but numerous tens of millions of Russian/Soviet lives were cut short in these years. This decades-long horror show surely had some influence on subsequent Soviet decisionmaking (though, notably, it did not prevent the USSR from undertaking actions, such as the secret deployment of nuclear weapons to Cuba, which carried a substantial risk of war with the United States). The other superpower was essentially defensively oriented – despite occasional bold talk of Communist rollback, Washington never mustered the will necessary, for example, to support self-liberated Hungarians in 1956 or Czechs in 1968 – and inclined to accept the existence of the Soviet Union as at least a semi-permanent strategic condition. Though their political philosophies were diametrically opposed, for an enormous variety of reasons neither superpower ever made the decision to launch a war against its counterpart. While one might like to draw from the Cold War the lesson that after 1945 great power war became impossible, that conclusion would be based on perilously thin evidence. A simple thought experiment illustrates the point: supposing that Party Secretary Stalin had lived for an additional ten years, or even five, would one be *very confident* that there would never have been a third world war?

If the United States is to retain its superpower status, rather than declining into a "regional power on steroids," potent in the Western Hemisphere but possessing little influence over the most critical international questions, Washington must not only remain active in Eastern Eurasia, but also successfully adapt its foreign policy to emerging realities. However alluring the notion of permanent American unipolarity may be, it is an illusion. Multipolarity is reemerging, and if the United States should attempt to deal with major allies as it did in the Cold

War, it will marginalize itself. The most important potential American allies in Eastern Eurasia will not be supplicants, as were the deeply wounded states of post-war Europe, but polities with a variety of alliance options. This does not imply, however, that the United States must, as some Americans appear to believe, tremble at the thought that some allies may disapprove of a given US policy. Indeed, as an outside power, in many cases Washington will enjoy a greater variety of strategic options than any Eastern Eurasian power will possess. American policymakers cannot expect to ensure the continuation of unipolarity, but, if they are wise, they may ensure that the Old World remains in balance and that no power can threaten the United States' position as the greatest of the great powers.

The revolution in strategic perspective

A number of technological revolutions are ongoing that will have an enormous impact on economics, society, and military affairs in this century. However, the impact of these technological changes will be far greater than most students of international affairs appreciate – greater, even, than a revolution in military affairs (RMA). As Chapter 5 argues, there is an ongoing RMA, which is referred to, herein, as the Second American RMA (the first having been the nuclear RMA that began in 1945). However, another, more fundamental and ultimately more important, revolution is taking place, an event referred to, herein, as a revolution in strategic perspective (RSP). While several RMAs may occur in a century, RSPs are far rarer – the last one occurred at the beginning of the Columbian Epoch as the concept of a unified world political system began to take hold in Europe.

The emerging RSP is intimately connected to the shift in the geographic center of world politics from Europe to Eastern Eurasia; indeed, the latter is an aspect of the RSP. This RSP should not, however, be understood chiefly as a matter of physical geography. The last RSP, as we shall see, was the result of the interaction of technology, which made regular transoceanic voyages practical, and the "mental universe" of European political elites, who came to see politics as global in character. This, in turn, resulted in the Columbian Epoch, and the establishment of Europe as the strategic center of the world. This RSP also relates to both geography and technology, perhaps in an even more complex fashion.

The aforementioned decline of the Eurocentric and multipolar international systems and the resulting move to bipolar, and then unipolar, systems, combined with the rise of several Eastern Eurasian powers, is a process that is inextricably tied to technological, social, and economic change. These various kinds of change themselves are deeply intertwined, of course, with developments in one area impacting the others. Technological development, however, will be a particularly critical catalyst for change of other kinds, including in the international political system. States will struggle to adapt to the enormous and very rapid technological changes that will occur in the early twenty-first century, and those that are most successful in doing so will reap outsized rewards.

In the last RSP, farsighted leaders integrated the fact that technology had fundamentally changed the structure of the international political system and adapted their paradigms accordingly, shifting mentally from a world of "regional international systems" to one with a single global international system. Leaders who did not make this shift consigned their polities to long-term decline. Twenty-first century leaders will be faced with a similarly daunting challenge, adapting their paradigms and policies to a period of "wild technology" that may overthrow seemingly reliable "formulas" for military success, economic prosperity, and social cohesion.

It should be remembered that Ottoman bureaucrats, Ming Mandarins, and other grandees who did not alter policy to account for a newly global political environment were not simply foolish – they merely continued to apply a *previously* successful strategic prescription, unaware of the fact that failure to adapt would have disastrous long-term consequences. Today, an American policymaker might, apparently quite wisely, argue that the United States has enjoyed an enormously successful "run" for more than sixty years, and that it would be far too risky to alter either domestic or international policy radically. In another time, this might well be sound advice. However, given the changing international political environment, such a cautious course would, for reasons discussed herein, virtually ensure long-term decline. The international political system is dynamic, and developments that are not directly related to high state policy and military affairs nonetheless may prove, over time, to be of enormously great import to the health of individual powers and the structure of the system itself.

The argument

No author who endeavors to discuss issues of the sort studied in this book can address them in fine detail. In attempting to delve into, for example, the domestic politics, foreign policy, military potential, economic development, and other specifics of every country – or even of every great and medium power – in Eurasia, a recklessly brave writer would soon be buried under a mountain of detail. Thus, this work avoids, insofar as is practical, discussions of current foreign policy controversies, the present military capabilities of various Eastern Eurasian countries, and similar questions. For the most part, discussion of specific polities, other than the United States, has been limited to Chapters 3 and 4, and even then only some key countries are discussed in an effort to illuminate certain critical issues.

This work attempts to provide an overview of the geopolitical dynamics of this century, and thus the general characteristics of the international system are more important to the subject at hand than are the political developments specific to any given country. Even if, for example, China were to split into two states, or a large-scale nuclear conflict occurred between India and Pakistan, the *general* geopolitical analysis, herein, would still be valid, because even such major events would not change underlying geopolitical trends, even though it would alter profoundly the fate of specific states. Again, the purpose, herein, is not to predict future events in detail, but merely to use geopolitical reasoning to sketch the outlines of the emerging international system.

Chapter 1 offers a brief discussion of the development of "classical" geopolitics, explaining why geopolitical tools are still useful in this century and defending geopolitics from some of the charges made against it – chiefly, that it is an overly deterministic and inherently imperialistic pseudo-science. It also makes the case that geopolitical analysis should not be seen as limited to physical geography; rather, geopolitics should incorporate all manner of knowledge related to human geography, and that, therefore, an understanding of broad socio-cultural, religious, technological, and other trends is critical to geopolitical understanding.

The purpose of Chapter 2 is to explain the concept of RSP, using the last RSP, the global European political ascendancy that marked the Columbian Epoch, as a case study. This chapter builds on concepts first introduced by Sir Halford Mackinder over a hundred years ago, but uses the benefit of hindsight to propose modifications to his theory that account for why the previous century did not develop precisely as he might have expected. It argues that the Columbian Epoch in fact did not end in the early twentieth century, but rather underwent a long-term period of decline that concluded with the fall of the Soviet Union and that it is only in recent years that humanity has entered a Post-Columbian Epoch.

Chapter 3 discusses the reemergence of global multipolarity and its implications. Most importantly, the chapter explains why unipolarity is rapidly degrading and should be replaced by an environment in which numerous great powers vie for position. It provides a brief outline of the challenges facing some significant actors and of how great powers are likely to interact in a multipolar environment. In particular, Chapter 4 addresses China's place in the emerging world political environment. It is argued that although it is probable that China will be the most muscular of the Eastern Eurasian great powers, it would be mistaken to assume that Washington and Beijing necessarily will face off against each other in a second cold war. While it is likely that the two powers will maintain an uneasy relationship, and it is entirely possible that eventually they will go to war, the chapter explains why the political-diplomatic environment in Eastern Eurasia will be far more complicated than the one that prevailed in Europe during the Cold War. The chapter also briefly notes the importance of interactions among great, medium, and small powers.

Chapter 4 draws on the previous analysis to present an Eastern Eurasian strategy for the United States in the early decades of the twenty-first century. In essence, the chapter argues that it is not practical, given the emerging multipolar character of international politics, either to maintain its present unipolar position or pursue a strategy based on a permanent, American-led multilateral alliance, similar to NATO, whose chief purpose would be to contain Chinese power. Rather, Washington will have to adapt to a strategic environment containing numerous strong powers, and should dedicate itself to ensuring that multipolarity continues to develop in a healthy fashion, and that no single state or coalition becomes excessively powerful. If it does so, the United States may continue for many decades to be the most powerful individual state even as it lays down the burdens that it today carries as a global quasi-hegemon.

Chapter 5 focuses on the role of terrorists and other "strategic entrepreneurs" in the strategic environment of the twenty-first century. Most importantly, it addresses how the horizontal spread of technology is creating conditions in which seemingly weak and minor actors increasingly will have the capability to inflict enormous damage on great powers. In certain respects, this is nothing new – many powers have been damaged or even destroyed by movements led by pre-viously-obscure rebels and prophets – the horizontal spread of highly lethal weaponry clearly creates new dangers with which the great powers must cope, and, most importantly, has implications for their mutual relationships. The chapter, far from displacing states as the most significant strategic players, argues that the most critical factor governing the importance of violent non-state actors in the world system will be whether and/or how great powers choose to use such actors against other.

Chapter 6 addresses the "next RMA" and how that RMA and the RSP are connected. It explores the significance of emerging technologies to the political and military landscape, and discusses why those technologies have enormous implications for global politics. Most importantly, it explores how technological development will be interwoven with social, political, economic, military, and other changes in this century, and explains why these changes are creating an environment ripe for an Epochal transformation in the strategic environment.

It should be emphasized that this work is one of "diagnosis," not "treatment." The book endeavors to describe the RSP and the conditions that created it; although its conclusion does outline some general "rules of thumb" for success in the Post-Columbian Epoch, it does not propose to offer precise solutions to the complex challenges that policymakers will confront. This author's crystal ball is far too cloudy to permit such specificity. Certainly, the argument that an RSP is aborning is a bold one, but this book's discussion of the strategic future is not calculatedly outrageous. It is argued that developments in biotechnology, robotics, nanotechnology, computer science, and other areas will have an enormous impact because, in the author's judgment, that is the most prudent conclusion based on the available evidence. Given what is known today about these technologies and what can be inferred from that knowledge about their likely future development, the argument for massive change in human civil-ization, and thus on international political life, appears, at least to this observer, well-nigh invincible. Sir Halford understood very well indeed that technological change and geopolitical conditions were eternally interconnected, and if the technological "super-revolution" is as colossal as a reasonable observer might expect, it will alter geopolitical conditions profoundly.

1 Geopolitics in an uncertain world
The case for classical geopolitics

The importance of physical and political geography to international politics is self-evident. The influence of climate, access (or lack of access) to resources, national agricultural potential, and similar factors have an obvious influence on the development of polities. It would, for example, make no sense to discuss Icelandic history without reference to the facts that Iceland is an island, was accessible to Vikings in longboats, and today is strategically significant to any polity that wishes to control access to the Atlantic.

The characteristics of a country's neighbors are of great importance. Different geographic "neighborhoods" have unique histories and face very different issues – and, just as with residential areas in a city, some neighborhoods are far more violent than others. It should, however, be noted that which geographical neighborhoods are violent and which are not can change radically over time. This is not to deny, because of enduring geographical reasons, that some territories are more likely to experience military activity than are others, but rather to note that changes in the international political environment can impact enormously the likelihood of military activity in a given area. For example, for many reasons, most definitely including geographic ones, the Low Countries region was a theater of frequent military activity for centuries, but today it is at peace because the European political environment has changed greatly in recent decades. If one were to be crudely deterministic and assume that neighboring countries invariably seek to expand territorially at the expense of relatively weak neighbors it would be very difficult to explain how Canada survived the twentieth century, but if one takes other considerations into account – particularly the foreign policy of the United States and its character as a polity – the fact that Canada continues to thrive is not at all surprising.

A region may be home to several great powers, as Europe was on the eve of World War I, or none – at present, there are no Latin American, African, Middle Eastern, or Central Asian great powers. The states that occupy a territory may be weak or powerful, populous or few, and culturally similar or dissimilar. The latter fact is notable – although geographical proximity *generally* correlates to cultural similarity it is possible for neighbors and near-neighbors to have little in common culturally. For instance, Israel and Saudi Arabia are far less distant geographically than are Israel and the United States, but, speaking broadly, the

Israelis share many cultural similarities with Americans while they are very different indeed from Saudis.

An unearned infamy: the reputation of classical geopolitics

Although most observers agree that geography is a significant factor in the development of polities and the interactions between them, the legitimacy of geopolitical analysis *per se* is frequently questioned. Geopolitics has long been derided as being overly deterministic and simplistic, if not inherently violent. This narrow view of geopolitics is unjust both to the field and its theorists – it represents a stereotype rather than an analysis. As in any field related to politics, geopolitics is populated by a variety of individuals who build theoretical paradigms, all of which presumably are flawed or incomplete in some respects. However, geopolitical thinkers, and particularly those from the Anglo-American school of thought described below, have made a contribution to our understanding of international politics far out of proportion to their modest numbers, and their work provides insights that can greatly assist those who seek to understand the broad trends that will drive international politics in the twenty-first century. The best geopoliticial writing – like the works of a Sun Tzu, Thucydides, or Karl von Clausewitz – is valuable to students of international politics in any age.

Much of the hostility to geopolitics is the result of the association of the field with General Karl Haushofer and German *Geopolitik*, and some of the common criticisms of geopolitics are accurate when specifically aimed at *Geopolitik*.[15] While the degree to which Haushofer and his associates influenced the foreign policy of the Third Reich is still debated, *Geopolitik* certainly was imperialistic in its orientation and Haushofer himself was willing to distort his analysis so as to maintain influence with the government that he served. Overall, *Geopolitik* lacks value as a method for understanding international politics,[16] and Haushofer and his associates had little influence on Anglo-American geopolitics in his own time, much less today. Anglo-American geopoliticans never embraced Haushofer's work – even in the 1930s, *Geopolitik* was much-criticized outside of Germany and rejected as an intellectual fig leaf for military aggression.[17]

It would be difficult indeed to argue convincingly that Anglo-American geopolitical thought is infected by Nazism when two key "founding fathers" of twentieth century Anglo-American geopolitics, Sir Halford Mackinder and Nicholas J. Spykman, were explicitly anti-Nazi, while a third, US Admiral Alfred Thayer Mahan, was a professed democrat who died before the creation of the National Socialist movement. Haushofer's geopolitical views were clearly influenced by Mackinder's work, but Mackinder cannot justly be indicted for the intellectual excesses of a German counterpart who was never even his student in any formal sense. (Indeed, largely because of its association with Haushofer and his disciples, Mackinder disliked the term "geopolitics" itself, preferring instead simply to refer to his field as political geography.) Although there have been many attempts to toss the Anglo-American geopolitical tradition along with

German *Geopolitik* into a common category,[18] there are critical differences between them, one of which is that Haushofer's work explicitly favored German territorial aggrandizement – essentially a prescription for great power war.[19]

In addition, the fact that the Anglo-American geopoliticans were offering council to democratic governments and were explicitly attempting to undermine the power of tyrannical states surely must weigh in their favor. (The British Empire and the United States, imperfect though they were, were unquestionably the moral superiors of Haushofer's Nazi Germany.) Most major twentieth-century geopoliticians had strong ideas about policy and wished to see their ideas implemented by government policymakers. This is certainly true of Mahan, Mackinder, and Spykman, perhaps the three most significant figures in early twentieth century Anglo-American geopolitics, who were all active members of the policy/academic elite. Mahan was a career officer (although most of his voluminous literary output was penned after his retirement from the US Navy) with very strongly held beliefs about both military preparedness and foreign policy. In addition to his active academic career, Mackinder served the British government in various positions at different times, including service as a Member of Parliament (1910–1922) and British High Commissioner to South Russia (1919–1920).[20] Writing during World War II, Professor Spykman, a faculty member at Yale, sought to shape American policies related to the peace that should emerge out of the conflict. Thus, all three authors were deeply invested in the great political events of their time and sought to give advice that could be translated into international political power.

Geopolitics as counsel

Whether the fact that geopolitics, generally, has not been a disinterested scholarly endeavor undermines its usefulness as an analytical tool is itself important – but the answer to the question very much depends on one's viewpoint. If one takes the perspective that scholarship must be entirely neutral – and leaving aside the obvious question of whether human beings can be truly unbiased when writing about controversial matters and defending their viewpoints against those with whom they disagree – then most geopoliticians clearly fail this test, as would the overwhelming majority of political philosophers, foreign policy analysts, and other political writers. No one who was not heroically naïve would assume that John Locke did not care whether England maintained a parliamentary system of government or adopted despotic autocracy, or that George Kennan was entirely blasé about which bloc would win the Cold War.

Given the times in which they composed their influential works on geopolitics – Mahan in the late nineteenth and early twentieth centuries, Mackinder throughout the first half of the twentieth century, and Spykman in the middle of that century – it is unsurprising that the three authors, like most of their contemporaries, espouse many views that are today unfashionable in many quarters.[21] Most importantly, their vision of political intercourse assumed that strong polities will tend to take advantage of weakness in their peers and that if it is to ensure its survival and prosperity a state must be willing to act in a manner that some observers might consider ruthless or even thuggish.[22]

One plausibly could contend that geopolitics does not concern itself sufficiently with questions outside the traditional understanding of power politics and therefore has a stilted worldview. Critical geopolitical analyst Gearóid Ó Tuathail boldly argues that:

> The old conceptual maps of geopolitics do not work in a world of speeding flows, instantaneous information, and proliferating techno-scientific risks. Nevertheless, the urge to arrest this teeming complexity of our age by returning world politics to certain "fundamental axes" or "timeless truths" remains, merely the latest version of a long-standing countermodern impulse to (re)invent certainty in a world where the vertiginous "creative destruction" of transnational capitalist modernity dominates. . . . Like orthodox geopolitics, critical geopolitics is both a politically minded practice and a geopolitics, an explicitly political account of the contemporary geopolitical condition that seeks to influence politics. Unlike orthodox geopolitics, critical geopolitics has a much richer understanding of the problematic of "geopolitics" and a better conceptual grasp, I wish to argue, of the problems facing states in conditions of advanced modernity.[23]

Criticisms of this character do not make a readily disprovable charge – they in essence argue that orthodox – or, to use the term preferred herein, classical – geopolitics offers an old-fashioned and blinkered view of the world, and one can just as easily argue that critical writings offer little that is of practical use in the understanding of relationships between states and their relation to geography. Ó Tuathail himself contends that, "Eschewing explicit interest in providing 'advice to the prince,' critical geopolitics critiques the superficial and self-interested ways in which orthodox geopolitics 'reads the world political map' by projecting its own cultural and political assumptions upon it while concealing these very assumptions."[24] While one should note that the cultural and political assumptions of critical geopoliticians quite effectively can be hidden behind a Great Wall of jargon impenetrable to all but a tiny handful of initiates, Ó Tuathail does make an interesting distinction between the cultures of critical and classical geopolitics.

Despite a professed interest in "praxis," critical geopoliticians thus far have had a negligible influence on policy. In contrast, the most significant Anglo-American classical geopoliticians succeeded, at least to a degree, in influencing policy.[25] Generally, it is quite clear when reading classical geopoliticians that the authors have strong views about the practical use of political and military power and that they wish policymakers to adopt their specific recommendations. Far from being a shadowy process, this is a straightforward attempt to influence the actions of the government officials and other opinion leaders addressed in the scholarship. Therefore, the major Anglo-American geopoliticians generally have used language accessible to the leaders of their day and offered suggestions they believed to be practical given the political culture and economic, diplomatic, and military potential of the state to which they were offering advice. Thus, there is a major chasm between classical and critical geopoliticians: the former are engaged in an essentially practical enterprise – the advising of policymakers and other men and women of affairs – while the latter are engaged in a theoretical project whose logic and language is highly self-referential.

It should be, noted, however, that even many students of international affairs who describe themselves as "Realists" or "Neorealists" nonetheless believe classical geopolitics to be of little use as a tool of international political analysis. Indeed, in *Politics Among Nations* – the defining book for the "classical" or "human nature" school of Realist thought[26] – Hans Morganthau is merciless in his criticism of geopolitics. He treats geopolitics, along with nationalism and militarism, as examples of what he calls "the fallacy of the single factor." Morganthau contends that:

> Geopolitics is a pseudoscience erecting the factor of geography into an absolute that is supposed to determine the power, and hence the fate of nations. Its basic conception is space. Yet while space is static, the peoples living within the spaces of the earth are dynamic. According to geopolitics, it is a law of history that peoples must expand by "conquering space," or perish, and that the relative power of nations is determined by the mutual relation of the conquered space.... Geopolitics only tells us what space is destined, because of its location relative to other space, to harbor the master of the world. It does not tell us to what particular nation that mastery will fall.... Geopolitics, as presented in the writings of Mackinder and [James] Fairgrieve had given a valid picture of one aspect of the reality of national power, a picture seen from the exclusive, and therefore distorting, angle of geography. In the hands of Haushofer and his disciples, geopolitics was transformed into a kind of political metaphysics to be used as an ideological weapon in the service of the national aspirations of Germany.[27]

Morgenthau's definition of Haushofer's geopolitical project is not unreasonable, but his description of Mackinder and Fairgrieve is very misleading and his overall estimate of geopolitics is a caricature.

Mackinder notes in his 1904 lecture and article *The Geographical Pivot of History* that: "I recognize that I only arrive at one aspect of the truth, and I have no wish to stray into excessive materialism. Man and not nature initiates, but nature in large measure controls. My concern is with the general physical control, rather than the causes of universal history. It is obvious that only a first approximation to truth can be hoped for."[28] This certainly is not the argument of a crude geographical determinist.[29] It is fair to say that Mackinder, like other responsible geopoliticians, considered geography to be a key factor in the development of human societies, but did not believe that it was the sole important factor in international politics or that a proper understanding of political geography would allow entirely accurate prediction of future political events.[30]

If geopoliticians actually claimed that the historical development of all societies and their institutions is simply and solely a matter of geography, geopolitics indeed would be a useless tool for understanding international politics because its premises would be reductionist to the point of absurdity. However, that is a far-from-accurate perspective whose pervasiveness highlights the "public relations" problem that classical geopolitics has faced for over half a century. Geopolitics has been defined by its opponents, with predictable results.

The usefulness of classical geopolitics

As one moves from a constricted view of geopolitics as a geographic pseudo-science to a consideration of the connection of geography to international politics it is important to acknowledge that the term "geopolitician" should not be restricted to a handful of individuals who explicitly or implicitly declare themselves to be such. Rather, it is appropriate to widen the term to encompass any political-strategic thinker who both acknowledges the importance of geography to international relations *and* whose work addresses in detail the interaction between the two. Thus, because his work demonstrates a deep awareness of the importance of geography and geographical relationships are central to his thought, a figure such as Admiral Mahan should be considered a geopolitical thinker even though he was not self-consciously a "geopolitician."

By contrast, it would be misleading to refer to many strategic thinkers as geopoliticians because, regardless of the overall quality of their thought, their work does not dwell on the general importance of geography to the relationships among polities. It therefore would be inappropriate to consider thinkers such as Karl von Clausewitz, Sun Tzu, and Niccolò Machiavelli to be geopoliticians, though they all, in some fashion, address geography in their works. One might ask whether, if geography is vital to the development of polities and geopolitics provides a useful prism for the study of international politics, this necessarily implies that the works of non-geopoliticians are critically flawed. The answer is that this is not necessarily the case, as there is a distinction between a work that more-or-less is silent on the importance of geography in shaping the international political system over long periods of time and one that actively *denies* that geography is an important factor in international politics. For example, issues related to the impact of geography on power politics were peripheral to Clausewitz's great project of describing the character of war and its place in international relations. Thus, when he discusses geography it generally is in the context of military operations.[31]

The contention herein is that an appreciation of geography is necessary, but not alone sufficient, to a proper understanding both of how polities develop over time and how they interact in the international system. Geography is central to international relationships for the simple reason that polities occupy, struggle over, and interact across space; there are, however, great issues of international relations that have little *direct* reference to geography, even if geography always is silently shaping the international system. Geopolitics is a useful tool for understanding certain aspects of international relations, but it is certainly not a substitute for all other discussions of international politics – Sun Tzu's attempt to enunciate core strategic principles and Machiavelli's musings on the uses of power and the nature of *virtu* are outside the realm of geopolitics proper even if human affairs cannot be divorced from geography.[32]

Very little of the analysis that crowds under the broad tent of international relations theory is essentially geopolitical in character or even informed significantly by the work of any of the major geopoliticians. This is unfortunate. Clearly, most modern international relations theorists generally have been resistant to geopolitics. First, the aforementioned issues regarding the reputation of geopolitical thought has been a significant barrier. Second, in recent decades there appears to have been relatively little cross-fertilization between geopolitically-minded thinkers and international relations theorists except in critical theory and related realms. (Indeed, geopolitics remained sufficiently obscure that Morganthau was still caricaturing geopolitics in the fifth edition of his *magnum opus*, the last version that he edited before his death.) Third, dynamic geopolitical worldviews do not fit well with many of the conventions of international relations models. For understandable reasons, international relations theorists often are more concerned with theoretical elegance and general applicability than with the nuances of international political life. Geopolitical thought thus tends to fall between two stools: a very rigid geopolitical model might be theoretically elegant, but surely would have the reductionist vices that critics such as Morganthau attribute to all geopolitical theories. Conversely, it would be difficult to fit a geopolitical discussion that attempted to account for the nuances of international political life, such as the impact of ideology and strategic culture on decisionmaking, into a "black box" general theory that can be equally applied to all states.

Geography clearly is an important factor shaping world politics, but for the reasons noted above, its role in shaping the international political environment has not received sufficient attention. The study of geopolitics is a vital "niche field," and it is to be hoped that classical geopolitical thought will enjoy an increased influence on the study of international relations, particularly on the ongoing development of Realist theory. Only classical geopoliticians combine the core assumptions of *Realpolitik* with an abiding interest in how geography impacts world politics. Thus, they have access to an enormously rich vein of thought literally ranging over millennia – figures ranging from Thucydides to Herman Kahn all have strategic insights that a classical geopolitician can apply to his or her analysis.

The enduring relevance of geography

As the US military demonstrated by operating very successfully even in so distant and inhospitable a place as Afghanistan, geography today does not offer a reliable protective barrier to any state fighting a first-rate opponent. Those who believe that geography is becoming less meaningful may cite this fact as powerful evidence for their argument. There are, however, several facts that should be considered when assessing the defensive value of favorable geography.

Even geography that is enormously favorable to defense has never guaranteed success against powerful foes; the conquest of Peru, for example, was effected at very little cost to Spain. (Conversely, thirteenth century Muscovy was located in a very vulnerable location, but took advantage of its position and built one of the largest empires in world history.) Geographical considerations most often are critical in closely matched strategic contests, or in cases where the more powerful polity might be convinced that victory only would be attainable at a prohibitive cost. In the latter case, a less powerful state on the defensive may be able to leverage advantageous geography to its advantage and thus compensate for its disadvantage in overall military power.

The most precipitous decline in geography's defensive utility actually did not occur recently, but happened with the development of long-range bombers, nuclear weapons, and ballistic missiles. Even before the completion of the Manhattan Project, the United States and Britain already had developed the ability to inflict very substantial damage on the Axis powers *despite not having control of the ground*, a critical change from previous military experience, when gravely damaging an enemy's homeland required armed men on the ground who enjoyed setting fires. With the development of air-delivered nuclear weapons, it became possible to inflict truly devastating damage on a foe without a single soldier's foot touching enemy soil, and by the mid-1950s, if not earlier, the United States possessed the ability to inflict state-shattering damage on its Soviet counterpart. Ultimately, the deployment of intercontinental ballistic missiles in great numbers allowed their wielders not only to overcome geography, but to compress time further – while it took six years to conduct World War II, the enormous superpower ICBM arsenals made it possible to conduct an even more devastating conflict in an afternoon.

It should be noted, however, that, even today, geography clearly has not lost all its military importance. While geography might have had little meaningful impact on a US–Soviet central nuclear war, it certainly is not irrelevant to most conventional engagements.[33] Conventional military operations have not yet moved "beyond geography," and will not do so in the foreseeable future; this embarrassingly obvious fact sometimes is lost in current discussions of the RMA.[34] It is true that long-range conventional strikes with bombers and cruise missiles now are more accurate and effective than ever before, and it is probable that developments in computer technology mean that sophisticated "cyber-campaigns" will become an important feature of future wars. Nonetheless, soldiers still slog through mud, ships still cross oceans, and severe storms still prevent aircraft from flying.

A twenty-first century geopolitics

In recent years there has been increasing discussion of broad technological trends that many observers believe will change international politics, and human society in general, fundamentally. Technology indeed is advancing rapidly; in the last several decades there have been parallel and overlapping telecommunications, computer, and transportation revolutions, any one of which would be a matter of great import for human civilization. These revolutions (along with their attendant military revolution) do not, however, render traditional geopolitics irrelevant – space, and the question of who controls it, remains central to international affairs.

The majority of the earth itself is not organized into states. The oceans (other than territorial waters), the Arctic, and the Antarctic are in this sense unorganized; they essentially are considered the common property of humanity. However, only a tiny number of humans live outside of states at any given time and groups of people live in defined territorial entities and are classified as citizens of a state regardless of whether they feel any emotional connection to that political unit. This, of course, does not mean that every state is represented by a functioning government capable of effectively administering all of its territory. "Failed states" are nothing more than legal fictions, and even many "real" states are unable to control all of their territory. There is, for instance, a functioning government of Columbia, but it does not command those parts of the country that are under the control of the *Fuerzas Armadas Revolucionarias de Colombia – Ejército del Pueblo* (FARC-EP) guerrilla group. The organization of world politics is not so simple that one can look at a map and find precisely how the international political system is organized, even if world politics cannot be understood without reference to geography.

Many geopoliticians have stressed the importance of economic factors to state power, particularly addressing the importance of geography to economic development.[35] Factors such as natural resources, access to the ocean, position along land trade routes, and agricultural potential are all important to a state's economic development. Relatedly, geopoliticians also have considered how geography impacts population, while the latter factor of course is also relevant to economic development. Additionally, to a great extent geography determines which cultural influences a society will be exposed to, although this is admittedly less true today, as near-instantaneous audio-visual communications allow individuals in free (and even partially free) societies to enjoy access to eclectic cultural influences.

Given that these interrelated factors are all relevant to the study of international politics, it is clear that geopolitics must address far more than physical geography alone. Although critics allege that geopoliticians attempt to use geography deterministically to discover simple immutable truths, a useful geopolitics must seek to uncover the *connections* between geography and the political culture, society, and economic life of polities and, more broadly, interpret how geography disciplines the interaction among polities. This, in turn, may assist an observer in discerning *general* trends in international politics (although a degree of humility is always in order when addressing the future, as unanticipated factors can have an enormous impact on unfolding history) and discussing the developing security environment.[36]

Nonetheless, physical geography continues to play a critical role in international, including great power, politics, and recent examples of this fact abound. For instance, geography was central to the long American struggle with Saddam Hussein's Iraqi regime.[37] Regardless of whether one is considering the politics of European unification, the world market price for crude oil, or the question of whether Beijing can claim primacy in the South China Sea, physical geography is a critical part of the discussion.

There is, however, much more to geopolitics than just physical geography. One of the most important factors influencing twenty-first century geopolitics is human geography – the distribution of peoples over the earth, the languages they speak, how they identify themselves ethnically and religiously, and so forth. Even if one does not accept Samuel Huntington's contention that a "clash of civilizations" is unfolding, the human aspect of geography is surely not a factor of diminishing importance. A useful geopolitics for the twenty-first century, far from being geographically deterministic, must be built on the understanding that individuals are independent historical actors. Political interaction takes place in a geographical context, but leaders are not automatons; geographical realities limit the options available to policymakers, but do not render socio-cultural and other factors irrelevant.

To remain a useful tool, geopolitics must continue to assess the influence of technology on world politics. Geopolitical theory has never been blind to the significance of technology, and several great Anglo-American geopolitical theorists have paid close attention to the interaction of geographical and technological factors. Most notably, Mackinder's own ideas were explicitly connected to technology[38] – he believed that breakthroughs in naval technology had created the conditions in which Western European sea powers might thrive, and feared that rail lines might enable a land power that controlled the Eurasian Heartland to grow so strong that it could threaten gravely the political fortunes of the European sea powers.[39] Given the extraordinarily rapid rate at which technological development has occurred in recent years, the need to consider the impact of technology on international political interactions is obvious. Indeed, this work argues that the world is presently in the midst of the most significant geopolitical shift in roughly 500 years – a movement from the Columbian Epoch of geographical exploration and European dominance to a Post-Columbian Epoch in which the center of political gravity will be in Eastern Eurasia and massive technological change dramatically alters both the great power system and human society more broadly.

The ongoing development of various information, biotechnological, robotic, and other technologies has potentially enormous implications for world politics. While it is impossible to predict precisely how these and other technologies will mature in coming decades, continuing rapid technological development appears certain. In the past, technological breakthroughs repeatedly have served to advance the interests of some powers and damage the prospects of others – indeed, the very concept of technological (as opposed to doctrinal) military revolutions implies that some polities are able to leverage technology to their advantage in warfare, a zero-sum endeavor. As in the past, one may expect that powers capable of effectively harnessing one or more key technologies will enjoy critical advantages over less-adaptable rivals.

The Post-Columbian Epoch

Although any attempt to date the beginning or end of a historical Epoch is necessarily somewhat arbitrary, the death of the Soviet Union provides as good a marker for the end of the Columbian Epoch as the voyage of Columbus does for its beginning. With the end of the Cold War and the collapse of the Heartland superpower, new possibilities in world politics have emerged. Most importantly, the Cold War standoff in Europe is no longer the central struggle in great power politics, and this change, along with the related collapse of the Soviet state (an unusually powerful and dangerous Heartland tenant), marked the closing of the Columbian Epoch.

The two world wars of the twentieth century served as the catalyst for a dramatic shift in great power politics: Russia/the Soviet Union, a late developer among the European powers and, at least arguably, not Western, [40] and the United States, a geographically non-European but culturally Western polity, emerged as superpowers that dwarfed countries such as France and Britain that, only a short time earlier, had been regarded as first-rate powers. Thus, the Cold War was the "deathbed scene" for the old Europe-based great power system – Western and Central Europe remained the primary geographical locale for great power competition, but the countries actually located there were no longer the primary movers in world politics. This final period lasted for a bit under fifty years (*c.*1945–1991), meaning that it constituted a bit less than a tenth of the entire Columbian Epoch (*c.*1492–1991). Although Europe certainly will not become irrelevant to international politics – indeed, in all likelihood a unified Europe will be one of the world's most influential polities – it no longer will be the international political center of gravity.

In the years since 1991, history has moved remarkably quickly and, for reasons discussed throughout this work, it likely will further accelerate. The current age will be particularly remarkable for two, previously noted, reasons: the emergence of Eastern Eurasia as the central arena of world politics and ongoing rapid advances in a broad variety of technological fields, including robotics, biotechnology, genetics, computer science, and nanotechnology.

At least for the next several decades – one would not presume to guess the structure of the international system a century from now – this Post-Columbian Epoch will continue to have many of the characteristics of the preceding age: great power politics will be organized in a recognizably Westphalian fashion, with states as the most critical actors in the international system, although the actual roster of great powers will be different than it was in the twentieth century. Describing the general character of the Post-Columbian Epoch is the main purpose of this work. However, aside from the shift in the center of world political competition from the western to the eastern portions of Eurasia, the key characteristic of the successor to the Post-Columbian Epoch is its unpredictability – an attribute that will, for reasons that are discussed subsequently, become progressively more prominent with time. Technological development will continue to encourage rapid economic and social change, and all of these will impact the struggle for great power supremacy.

At least since the development of the first agricultural societies, technological change has been intimately connected to political history, and, just as in many past instances, the ability of polities to adjust to technological change will have an enormous influence on their international status. Unlike in earlier periods, however, the sheer weight of looming technological advances mean that this process of technological adaptation will require *extremely* nimble adaptation on the part of societies striving to maintain and enhance their international political status; in comparison to the ongoing technological revolution, the Industrial Revolution was a glacial process. Examples of this fact are already myriad; one need only consider how deeply desktop computers have penetrated the American workplace in the last two decades, a much shorter period than the average worker's career. Subsequent chapters will investigate this revolutionary environment in greater detail and explore how rapid technological change will create an environment favorable to massive political change whose ultimate results will be highly unpredictable.

Conclusion: capturing the new Epoch

For the reasons described above, it is the contention of this work that the international system has already moved beyond the Columbian age into a Post-Columbian Epoch. In this new era, which began *c.*1991, the arena of decision in great power politics will move away from Europe, where it was located for approximately half a millennium, to Eastern Eurasia. However, the work of the eminent classical geopoliticians still provides a template that is useful in explaining this momentous shift; they have gifted us with tools that can be applied to aid in understanding how geography, in all its forms, shapes international political discourse even as we enter a new geopolitical era.

Attempting to make very precise predications about the mid- to long-term future would be folly. From the perspective of 2050 most predictions made today will appear as silly as the mid-twentieth-century claims that within a few decades Americans would commute to work in flying automobiles – thoughtful geopolitical analysis can assist policymakers in preparing for the future, but the geopolitical toolbox does not include a crystal ball. Yet regardless of what unforeseeable events occur in the future, humans will continue to occupy physical space and have needs that can only be met by interacting with geography. Food must be grown, energy harnessed, goods manufactured, and all these things must be transported to their ultimate consumer, sometimes passing through a large variety of middlemen in several countries along the way. So long as humans exist, the physical world will continue to be relevant to them and will shape the development of their polities.[41] Moreover, so long as human nature remains unchanged,[42] polities will continue to strive for dominance. Over the next several decades, everything in international politics will change, yet everything will remain the same.

2 The geography of universal empire

The geopolitics of the Columbian Epoch

As the introduction noted, Halford Mackinder defined his era as one that had begun, approximately, with the voyages of Columbus and was, he believed, coming to a close in his own day. In the period between the Renaissance and Mackinder's own time, European maps of the world were progressively filled in as the geographical knowledge of their makers increased.[43] Although Mackinder himself was a geographer, he derived little satisfaction from this accomplishment because he worried that with the closing of the Columbian Epoch, the effectiveness of British sea power as a strategic tool was also waning. This, he surmised, could have disastrous consequences both for the British Empire and Western civilization in general. Mackinder foresaw that in the new "post-Columbian age," the West would have to contend with a worldwide "closed political system," a condition that bore some resemblance to the age before the Columbian Epoch, when "mediaeval Christendom was pent up in a narrow region" and acutely threatened from outside. In the Columbian Epoch, Western civilization had the good fortune to break out of its trap by sea and enjoy a strategic golden age in which it expanded its influence explosively.[44] However, there would be no escape from the new closed system.

Mackinder's key fear, that a precipitous decline in the strategic utility of seapower would occur as railroads provided huge landpowers with a new and efficient means of transport on interior lines of communication, and that this, in turn, would likely lead to Western and Central Europe's domination by the Pivot (or, as he later called it, the Heartland) region of the Eurasian interior,[45] did not become reality. There were a number of reasons for this, both technological (such as the rise of airpower and, later, the mating of long-range ballistic missiles with nuclear weapons, developments which made the Heartland "fortress" vulnerable to devastating deep strikes) and political (once the United States chose to act as the arbiter of European politics, Britain and other states had a potent offshore ally against menacing Heartland powers).[46]

Mackinder's analysis contained many essential truths. This author would argue that the Columbian Epoch concept is profoundly useful, but that this period lasted rather longer that Mackinder envisioned. When Mackinder assumed that the filling in of the map meant the death of the Epoch, he merely skipped a step: a period of decay in which Western and Central Europe would remain the center of world politics but would no longer contain the world's two most powerful polities, with the European seapowers being saved from the tender mercies of the Heartland by an offshore power, the United States.

Certainly, Mackinder's observation that European powers made a great strategic breakout from Eurasia during the early Columbian Epoch is both correct and insightful. Increasing awareness of the world resulted in a critical change in the geographical viewpoint of Europeans. Indeed, one could even adapt a concept from the strategic-historical debate on the existence of RMAs, and say that it led to an RSP. It required time for the revolution in European thinking about the character of world politics to take root. Political paradigms were not fundamentally altered immediately after knowledge of the New World reached Europe, but over time increasing geographical awareness led to a tendency to see the *entire* world as a *single* political stage, and this was a new way of thinking about politics.

Unlike RMAs, which are, essentially, technological or tactical/doctrinal in character even if they are often the result of broader social changes, the "Columbian RSP" was a change in viewpoint on international politics itself, a crucial difference but not one that automatically rendered the RSP marginal to military affairs. The fact that Europeans, particularly Western Europeans, came to see the world as a single system had a major effect on their strategic decision-making, both encouraging an emphasis on the development of strong navies and other military forces deployable far from the home country and shaping their perception of *what* is important.

Until the Columbian Age, there was no such thing as true *world* politics. Significant polities such as the Aztec and Inca Empires and the major European states coexisted without being aware of the existence of their counterparts across the Atlantic. Thus, by any reasonable definition, they were not all units in a unified world political system. However, as Western Europe increasingly became involved in the African coast and the eastern parts of Eurasia, and were aware of the existence of the Americas, the European political system rapidly transformed into one in which great powers had truly worldwide interests.

Throughout most of human history, political leaders have tended, correctly, to see an inverse relationship between the distance between their country and a foreign land, and its political relevance to their own polity. Faraway countries might be exotic and intellectually interesting, but most often, more-or-less, were seen as being politically irrelevant. Of course, there was more to distance than the absolute number of miles separating polities. Well-established trade links over water could greatly increase the profitable economic intercourse between polities and increase the likelihood that they would be allies – or deadly enemies. Mountains and other geographic obstacles would generally have an opposite result, increasing the travel time between polities and decreasing their economic and political relevance to each other.

Most of the great pre-Columbian empires were, from a global perspective, rather diminutive – the Roman Empire was centered on the Mediterranean, the Chinese world on China's great rivers and its coast. Although coexisting historically, the two had relatively little knowledge or intercourse with each other aside from the movement of silk and other luxury goods from east to west. Truly enormous empires did not tend to last for very long: Alexander's Macedonian Empire shattered with his death, while the gargantuan Mongol Empire began the process of dividing into separate polities even as it was still expanding. Given technological limitations, realistically there could not be a single world political system. Political leaders effectively defined "the world" as that region of the geographic world which mattered politically in their own eyes. The occasional exception like Alexander the Great, who wanted to conquer all of India, a subcontinent that surely had previously been seen by only a tiny number of Greeks, were eccentric, a reality underlined by the fact that Alexander's men – who had ably followed him in the Egyptian desert and across the length of Persia – eventually refused to cross the river Hyphasis (Beas). Alexander had long since proven his genius to them, but apparently they could not see the point of troubling themselves with the conquest of all India. Most Macedonians probably could understand their king's desire to conquer the Persian Empire, but India was simply irrelevant to the political world as they conceived it and Alexander's army saw no point in undertaking the hardships necessary to conquer it in its entirety.[47]

Seeing one world, whole

It is impossible to precisely date the transition of the regional international political systems to a unified system, but for the purposes at hand it is sufficient to use Columbus' first voyage to the New World in 1492 as a convenient marker. Although, for long thereafter, European great powers had little knowledge of and minimal interest in substantial parts of the world – such as the interiors of Africa and the Americas – and were still ignorant of many places where humans lived (including the Australian continent), they were engaged in what can reasonably be described as world politics.[48]

Over centuries, the world political system developed to the point where no large polity anywhere in the world was truly tangential to European affairs. Moreover, the struggle for power within Europe was shaped by the activities of Europeans abroad. The example of Portugal is instructive: by the mid-sixteenth century, the national fortunes of this small European state were intimately tied to its imperial and trading interests in such varied locales as Africa, India, Southeast Asia, China, and South America.[49]

The Columbian Epoch was marked by European multipolarity with a vigorous competition among states for power and prestige. However, in a system of vigorous competition there is always a tension between the desire of individual states for more power and the tendency of other states to resist would-be hegemons. In Europe, the most muscular polities attempted to accumulate sufficient power to establish continental hegemony. However, in the Columbian Epoch none of these succeeded in *fully* establishing hegemony over Europe. Thus, none could climb to the next rung of the ladder and become a world hegemon, as European hegemony was a necessary precondition for world hegemony.

One should not, however, assume that European hegemony would have automatically resulted in world hegemony. During most of the Columbian Epoch there were at least three major regional centers of power on Mackinder's "World Island": Europe, the Middle East, and China.[50] Of the three, China was the most isolated from the others;[51] as a result of geography and, perhaps more importantly, national policy, China was generally content to limit its interaction with the distant parts of the world. (Although after China had weakened greatly relative to European great powers, falling behind technologically, militarily, and economically, the latter states were able to impose their presence in that country.) Although the European powers came to have a worldwide geopolitical perspective, no major polity in the other regional centers of power truly developed such a view during the Columbian Epoch. This is an extraordinary and intriguing fact: given an opportunity to expand their political horizons (and national power) far beyond their current territory, non-European policymakers usually showed little interest in doing so.

Strategic culture and geography

It is easy to underestimate the importance of ideology in shaping the strategic culture and action of a polity, and one of the perils of Realism is that it can discourage one from examining carefully the prevalent intellectual currents in a given polity at a particular time. Thus, the theoretical "black box" that to the dedicated Realist can represent any state at any time can distort analysis; vital cultural and intellectual factors may be ignored by those who too vigorously apply theory to actual historical cases. On the other hand, however, it is imprudent to ignore the reality that states will often choose to act in ways that are perceived to be strategically advantageous even if it requires that they go against the prevailing ethical and social mores of their society.[52]

Yet the strategic perception of leaders is to a very great degree determined by their cultural biases. They may not undertake actions that objectively would be strategically advantageous because they do not perceive how they would profit, or even consider a particular action so outrageous that they do even contemplate it.[53] Thus, it is worth examining whether there was an identifiable strategic cultural factor – a "showstopper" – that made it implausible for non-European great powers to pursue a worldwide role.

China's rejection of an overseas role is an unusually stark example of a conscious, and ultimately very important, strategic choice by a policymaking elite. Not long after the voyages of Admiral Zheng He's great treasure fleet,[54] the Mandarin policymaking class elected as a matter of national policy to turn away from the sea and focus on internal matters. This was a clear shift in policy, a turning away from a budding *weltpolitik* that would have an enormous impact on world history. If Ming China – a sophisticated and wealthy sea power – had chosen to continue its overseas empire-building activities, it quite possibly would have both prevented its eventual dynastic decline and extended its sway over much of the Pacific and Indian Ocean as well as Africa and possibly even the New World. In such circumstances, the political and exploratory history of the Columbian Epoch obviously would have been altered enormously.

Ming policymakers instead chose to treat overseas activities as a distraction from more important matters of imperial governance. Thus, they instituted policies diametrically opposite to those so successfully pursued by Western European sea powers such as Portugal and Spain. After Zheng He's voyages, Ming officials actively discouraged exploration, allowing the great national fleet to rot in harbor, refusing to fund further seagoing exploration, and closely regulating (and for the most part forbidding) ocean-going commerce. Thus, did the power perhaps best-positioned in the fifteenth century to achieve world preeminence enter onto a course that undermined its economic vitality and allowed a number of comparatively tiny and poor states in the European Rimland to far surpass it in national power. The reasons for this ultimately disastrous policy choice, and for the staunchness with which Ming and later Qing officials continued to cling to it tenaciously despite its increasing obvious defects, are complex. Clearly, however, interrelated sociological, political, fiscal, and other issues together resulted in the long Chinese rejection of the sea.[55]

For purposes of the present discussion, two factors relevant to the Ming Dynasty's strategic choices should receive particular note. First, Ming officials already governed an enormous inland empire that required one of the most sophisticated bureaucracies that any polity had yet devised. Moreover, this empire had inherently vulnerable borders, and was constantly threatened with "barbarian" invasion from outside, a fact that was all-too-obvious to Ming rulers who had replaced China's previous Mongol overlords. Large Eurasian powers such as China invariably have vulnerable frontiers that demand attention and defense of the Chinese northern frontier was enormously costly. The tendency to see frontier protection as the most serious strategic issue confronting the state and all other military and exploratory activities as distractions followed naturally from this border problem. Second, China's attitude in regard to questions of universal empire was not one that necessarily strongly encouraged or discouraged distant imperial adventures. In the Chinese geopolitical conception, China was, essentially, the center of true civilization and the only legitimate empire. All other territories perhaps should, ideally at least, have been indirectly ruled by China through leaders subordinate to the emperor, but those areas that were not always could be dismissed as barbarian polities. Thus, Chinese policymakers did not have a strong ideological imperative to extend their imperial authority over the entire world, as the emperor enjoyed legitimacy as the one true ruler on earth regardless of whether he de facto ruled over the entire planet, although vigorous dynasties did expand the frontiers very far indeed and universal empire plainly was justifiable intellectually.[56]

The revolution in strategic perspective that occurred in Europe and the expansion of regional politics to a world stage only affected the Islamic world indirectly – and ultimately for the worse, as polities that were, during the early years of the Columbian Epoch, small and poor relative to the great Islamic states, came to surpass them militarily and economically. For the purposes at hand, the

Ottoman Empire is the most interesting of the Islamic polities, as it had the greatest degree of strategic interaction with European states, and, given its economically and technologically advanced society and enormous national power during the early Columbian Epoch, likely had the best overall opportunity to break out of its regional status to become a world power.

Generally speaking, the leaders of major Islamic and Christian states had a somewhat similar conception of their religio-ideological mission. The two faiths shared several commonalities relevant to imperial legitimacy; most importantly, they were both universal in their orientation. Although practitioners of either faith might see outsiders as barbarians (and the view of Europe prevalent in the Ottoman ruling class for most of the Columbian Epoch certainly reflected such an attitude), no human – civilized or barbarous – was irrelevant in a religious sense and thus, at least theoretically, no individual was altogether politically irrelevant.[57] Thus, both Muslim and Christian political leaders generally believed they had an obligation,[58] insofar as was practical, to spread their religion to all mankind.[59]

Given these attitudes, both Christian and Islamic great powers, unlike China, had a fairly compelling religio-ideological justification for universal expansion. Although the notion of a religious duty to expand always fit somewhat uneasily in the more-or-less secular world of European dynastic politics, some states relied on it fairly heavily. Yet a truly universal political perspective never emerged among Ottoman leaders during the Colombian Epoch and, despite the fact that the Empire possessed a potent combination of land and sea power during the early years of the Epoch, it never decisively broke out of the Mediterranean to become a global presence.[60]

While there is no one single reason why the puissant Ottoman Empire was unable to break out of Eurasia, its geographical position clearly was a factor of great importance. The Ottomans of the early Columbian Epoch were possessed of a religio-ideological perspective that would have been favorable to further expansion. Indeed, the Ottomans were very active militarily in Southern and Central Europe, laying siege to Vienna for the first time in 1529. Although the operation did not succeed, "[t]he failure to capture Vienna on that occasion was seen by both sides as a delay, not a defeat, and opened a long struggle for mastery in the heart of Europe."[61] Indeed, by examining the pattern of conflict in the first centuries of the Columbian Epoch it is clear that during these years, and despite notable naval activities, the integrity and expansion of the Empire's land borders remained the latter's primary Ottoman concern.

When the Empire's location is considered, its focus on border defense and expansion is unsurprising. The Byzantines faced many of the same challenges as their Ottoman successors, and given the character of these problems, it is impressive that each empire survived for centuries: a great empire centered in Anatolia easily could have collapsed in a generation or two if it was governed without strategic acumen. Indeed, in the seventh century the Byzantines experienced a quick and enormous strategic disaster: the Muslim armies exploding out of the Arabian Peninsula conquered much of the Empire,[62] and thereafter

Constantinople's military history in the Middle East might be described essentially as an ultimately unsuccessful attempt to break out of Asia Minor and regain its lost territory.

Like the Byzantines before them, the Ottomans had to maintain great land and sea power if they were to guard their imperial interests properly; unlike a true land power or sea power such as, respectively, the Russian or British Empires, it was risky to slight one form of geographic military power, as this could place the polity at considerable risk over the long term. However, the waters surrounding the Empire's borders, particularly the Mediterranean, were of immediate strategic importance; the Atlantic Ocean was not, and this impacted both shipbuilding techniques and naval policy. Moreover, the Ottomans had several vulnerable frontiers, while centrifugal forces were always a potential threat, particularly in areas far from Anatolia. In short, the Ottoman sultans faced a panoply of issues that sapped the treasury and distracted their energy away from novel, long-range strategic projects. By contrast, Ferdinand and Isabella commissioned Columbus' first great voyage as the *Reconquista*, the grand strategic challenge with which Spain had long grappled, was ending.

The Ottomans did have one very substantial advantage in terms of overseas expansion: a strong Persian Gulf presence. Operating from the Gulf, the Ottomans conceivably could have made themselves the permanent dominant presence on some of the richest shipping routes in the world. European, North African, and Middle Eastern trade with India, the East Indies, and East Africa could have been almost completely dominated if the Ottomans had conducted a suitably vigorous naval policy. However, they instead allowed their presence in the Eastern portion of Eurasia to atrophy. A handful of naval engagements – none anywhere near as disastrous as the Battle of Lepanto in the Mediterranean[63] – sealed the Ottoman surrender of influence in this area. Although they sometimes inflicted damage on their opponents, the sixteenth century Ottomans were unable, even, to expel Portugal from the Indian Ocean area,[64] much less the English and Dutch, who became progressively more active in the waters south of Eurasia.

Having failed to make a great strategic breakout in either Central Europe or via the sea, the Ottoman Empire continued to play international politics much as it always had, and often with considerable success. Yet in a global political environment, its comparative power progressively declined relative to the major Western European states. Much of this, no doubt, is attributable to economic factors – both sophisticated intercontinental trade networks and access to New World specie (an infusion of wealth vital to Spain) could be immensely valuable. However, it would be simplistic to attribute Ottoman decline wholly to economic factors, much less solely to international trade issues.

On balance, it appears that there was not an unbreachable intellectual wall that would have stopped non-European great powers from engaging in overseas expansion. This would have required a very strong cultural factor: a taboo against crossing water, for example, or an absolute conviction that all unexplored lands surely were hellish and utterly unfit for human habitation. It appears that there were potent strategic cultural and practical factors militating against the overseas expansion of Ming China, but it is entirely plausible that a number of strategically creative policymakers working over time – or perhaps even one exceptional and long-reigning emperor – could have launched China onto a course that would have led it to accentuate its sea power and engage in large imperial enterprises abroad. Moreover, the religiously-derived ideology of the Ottoman state elite would easily have been adaptable to provide support for overseas expansion. The Ottomans, at least in ideological terms, were very convincing contenders for global power.

In both the Chinese and Ottoman cases, it is clear that geography played a central role in the decision to reject a worldwide role. Both powers faced considerable challenges that resulted from their geographic location, and although either might well have benefited enormously from undertaking large-scale overseas expansion, neither chose to accept the risks that would have accompanied doing so. Both China and the Ottoman Empire, thus, were unwilling to make the intellectual leap necessary to become global powers. Broadly speaking, the leaders of these polities still thought in regional terms, and this is demonstrated by their actions. Even if there was a universal aspect to their state ideologies, the actions of Chinese and Ottoman leaders did not reflect a belief that the entire world was strategically relevant.

Mackinder's decision to call the 400-year period of European expansion the Columbian Epoch was quite appropriate. Clearly, various European seapowers (and mixed sea and land powers like France) enjoyed a period of unique strategic prosperity. Of the European great powers of the period, probably only Prussia/Imperial Germany and the Habsburg/Austrian and Russian Empires can be described as classic land powers, but all were very much a part of the European great power system and their rise reflects the power potential of the regions in which they were located – Northern, Central, and Eastern Europe all possessed considerable natural and human resources – and, as Mackinder no doubt would note, it was difficult for seapower to have a direct and decisive military impact in those parts of Eurasia. Thus, these powers were full and active participants in a great power system shaped by the sea powers even if they were continentally-oriented – while they did not have quite the global interests of France and Britain, they nonetheless played by the "rules" of the great power system, and fully accepted that, for example, events in India and North America were strategically/diplomatically relevant to the distribution of power and territory in Europe itself.

Strategic learning and the Post-Columbian Age

The Colombian RSP was, at its heart, an intellectual revolution, a breakout of the Western European seapowers from a regional to a world perspective on politics that in turn shaped how the European great power system operated. Thus, the European great power system came to function at two levels: as a device for the distribution of power in Europe itself and also as a mechanism for the distribution of world power. From the perspective of European states (particularly the sea powers), *the world became their strategically relevant region.*

This abstract view, in turn, shaped policy and strategy, as it made overseas colonial concerns critical for the sea powers, and this in turn affected European politics. (Certainly, the Seven Years' War merits the title of "world war" as much as the conflict referred to as World War I does.) This does not mean that every sea power prospered – after their explosive strategic success in the early Columbian Epoch, the Iberian powers declined, while the Netherlands proved too small and vulnerable to invasion to long maintain its position as a great power of the first rank – or that no land powers made great gains: most notably, Prussia/Germany and Russia became and remained major international players. Yet a global political perspective shaped the European political system. Even though precisely how each great power maneuvered within that system was determined by its own unique geographical, socio-economic, cultural, and other circumstances, they all essentially were playing the same game on the same board. Even if Russia had little direct interest in whether Britain or France commanded the Caribbean, while Britain had no immediate stake in which polity controlled the Caucasus, all the powers believed that such issues were indirectly relevant to their vital national interests.

During the early centuries of the Columbian Epoch, the only non-European power to participate substantially in this Eurocentric international political system was the Ottoman Empire, and it did not successfully adapt to it. This does not mean that it could not have done so – there was no economic, technological, military, or similar factor that made the leap to global power implausible. Moreover, it had a credible religio-ideological justification for a worldwide imperial mission. Yet it proved unwilling to adapt intellectually to the new world political system, and ultimately suffered as a result.[65]

This survey underscores a great irony of the Columbian Epoch. While it is common for scholars to discuss the threat of imperial overextension and attribute political decline to the excessive conquest of territory – and there is no doubt that there are many cases where overextension was at least partially responsible for imperial collapse[66] – there is a compelling argument that *the non-European great powers that did not successfully adapt to the global character of world politics actually suffered from underextension.* By choosing to retain their traditional character as large land empires with little interest in distant overseas conquests, they also unknowingly insured their relative decline. The overwhelming dominance of the European powers in the Columbian Epoch was not foreordained. There were other Eurasian great powers that might, if they had acted more boldly, have retained their status as great powers of the first rank and even, potentially, have bid for world hegemony.

The stakes: why the politics of Eastern Eurasia are of global importance

It would be most imprudent to simply assume that in the twenty-first century the nations of Eastern Eurasia will make the same errors as the Ottoman and Chinese Empires did in previous ones. Yet all too often even the largest Eastern

Eurasian states are dismissed as having merely "regional" interests, the underlying assumption being that they do not have worldwide interests because they do not presently have global influence comparable to that enjoyed by the United States. This attitude represents a fundamental misunderstanding of the geopolitical character of great power competition. In a world war different theaters will vary in importance to the great powers involved – the Third Reich, for example, easily could survive losing decisively in North Africa, but its inability to conclude Operation Barbarossa successfully ultimately proved fatal – and the same principle applies to peacetime as well.

Although there will be three critical regional power centers in the twenty-first century, two of them are largely "out of contention" – the United States enjoys hegemony in North America, while the future of Europe presumably will largely be determined by non-violent intra-European political processes. This leaves only the most populous of the three power centers – the home to roughly half of humanity – as a zone for political clashes among the great powers that will be metaphorically, and most likely also literally, violent. Thus, to dismiss the struggle for Eastern Eurasia as mere regional politics is as profoundly wrong-headed as describing World War I as a regional war. In a literal sense, this description might be accurate – the great majority of the bloodshed in the latter conflict occurred in Europe, and much of that was spilled over a long, thin line running through northern France. However, it was a world war in the most important sense: the fate of the world political system was decided in the trenches of the Western Front, and thus, in certain respects, the outcome of Verdun and the Somme were as important to Africa, the Middle East, North America, and Eastern Eurasia as they were to Europe.

If, to take just one example, Ludendorff's desperate gamble of 1918 had paid off and the Allied trench line had been breached catastrophically, twentieth century political history surely would have been enormously different. The Allies probably would have agreed to an armistice that confirmed Germany's gains in the east, hobbling the young Soviet Union and perhaps setting the stage for an eventual German intervention to eliminate the ideologically obnoxious Bolsheviks; Britain and, particularly, France would have been humbled and Berlin would have emerged as the greatest power on the Continent, if not its hegemon; the Austrian and Ottoman Empires, sickly though they were, would have ensured their continued survival, at least for a time – a fact that would have great implications for, among other things, the politics of the Middle East;[67] the United States would not have been confirmed as the arbiter of European politics, though Washington might have felt compelled to take on a permanent role in Europe as a guarantor (alongside London, no doubt) of France's survival, becoming part of a "mini-NATO" focused on Germany; and Corporal Adolf Hitler probably would have went on to an obscure career, likely as a street corner artist, at most as a fringe politician with an exasperating tendency to lecture his dinner guests.

These are only the most obvious ways in which the political landscape would have been altered, and one can speculate on other issues, such as the fate of

European colonialism. After all, a strange "accidental alliance" of Wilsonians and communists planted many of the intellectual seeds for the twentieth century's anti-colonial movements, and the success of the Allies was widely interpreted as an ideological victory for self-determination and democracy. A victory by the Central Powers, however, would have done much to make the world safe for emperors and to bolster the notion that imperialism was an inevitable, and perhaps desirable, part of human political life. As events actually did unfold in the mid-twentieth century, China only barely escaped partition, if not complete colonization; the British Empire disintegrated largely because the belief in a Wilsonian natural right to self-rule took root both in London's academic and policy class and among intellectuals from throughout the Empire who spent their youth in British public schools and universities;[68] and the French Empire collapsed despite the desperate efforts of a metropolis that had been impoverished and proven less-than-puissant by World War II.

It, of course, is impossible to say definitively whether or not the European colonial empires would have survived the mid-twentieth century (and perhaps even thrived) if the Central Powers had emerged victorious in World War I, but even if they did not, they would have died under specific circumstances that would have been quite different from those that actually prevailed. One cannot know what would have replaced the imperial recessional and the "long twilight struggle" between the Americans and Soviets for ideological and geopolitical victory in the Third World, but in any case the details of history would be quite different, and that fact would have great ramifications for the strategic environment worldwide.

The stakes at play in Eastern Eurasia are, in the most general respects, not very different from those at play in France in 1918, but one can hope (though perhaps it is a faint one) that the international political environment has changed sufficiently that this particular struggle will be resolved without recourse to state violence on such a vast scale. In short, Eastern Eurasia is *the* critical political theater in the early twenty-first century, and the future of humanity as a whole will largely be guided by the events in that region *in ways that are not necessarily comprehensible at the present time* – although historical hindsight is far from perfect, one is much more likely to understand the importance of events in retrospect.

The comparison between this era of geopolitical tussling and World War I is perhaps appropriate for another reason – the Post-Columbian Epoch is, like the world wars, a time of intense transformation in the international system. Mackinder was not quite correct in his belief that the Columbian Epoch was coming to an end *c.*1900, yet, he was right about the larger fact that it was coming to a close. Mackinder overestimated the political impact of railroads and other modern means of transportation and underestimated both the potential of airpower and Washington's ability to keep the old political order on life support, but given the boldness of his thesis these were small errors indeed.[69]

Eastern Eurasia is where the emerging struggle for international primacy will occur, but, as in the world wars, a powerful offshore superpower can potentially, and perhaps decisively, throw its weight into the struggle. Unlike in the era of the world wars, however, a corroded multipolar system is not in its death throes and, absent catastrophic strategic decisions by both the United States and China's neighbors, a new bipolar one is not being born. Rather, for reasons argued throughout this work, a short-lived unipolarity is most likely giving way to a new multipolarity. Moreover, as this multipolar world system takes shape, another factor will also become increasingly relevant – various technological fields that are presently in an early stage of development will mature to the point that they will collectively have a key influence on the international struggle for power. Just as Mackinder's prediction that the Columbian Epoch was coming to an end was slightly premature but nonetheless revealed an essential truth, his beliefs regarding the ability of transportation technology to transform the balance of power between landpowers and seapowers were not correct in their specifics, but illuminated critical questions.

As the Post-Columbian Epoch unfolds, technology increasingly will redefine the grammar of war and other forms of international political discourse. Properly leveraging any of several critical technologies would allow polities to enjoy critical advantages over their competitors, but precisely how this might occur is not readily predictable. Certainly, traditional categories of power potential will not become irrelevant, but a lead in one or more key technological areas may allow a state that is relatively weak in most respects to enjoy an enormous short-term military advantage over otherwise stronger foes, if it can harness that technological advantage militarily.

Given the nature of scientific research and the reluctance of many societies to explore certain technological avenues aggressively (American policymakers, for example, tend to be rather nervous about cloning and genetic engineering of humans),[70] it is probable that no one power will enjoy permanent and comprehensive superiority in technologies that may be militarily useful, although Washington may well continue to field the most impressive military force overall. While previous RMAs, including the current one, have taken decades (and sometimes centuries) to reach fruition, the forthcoming period of military revolution will be one in which many "mini-RMAs" could occur and these petite revolutions may allow states to enjoy temporary but massive superiority in a limited area such as biological weapons or artificially-intelligent unmanned aircraft and other robotic systems. (This issue is explored in greater detail in Chapter 6.)

Conclusion

For great powers, and would-be great powers, the lesson of the Columbian Epoch is clear: enormous wealth, abundant human and natural resources, access to cutting-edge technology, and other capabilities do not, by themselves, guarantee effectiveness at the grand strategic level. While such assets certainly increase the margin for error for policymakers – as Adam Smith wisely said, "There is an awful lot of ruin in a nation," and that is particularly true of a great one – even the most impressive advantages can be eroded over time if leaders do not "get the big things right." By contrast, weak powers can enhance their status enormously if their leaders surf the tides of history effectively; while it did enjoy a favorable geographical position, it was hardly preordained that tiny Britain eventually would rule the largest empire in the world. Indeed, it was not predetermined that Europe would rise to become the strategic center of the world. Polities such as the Ming and Ottoman Empires *could* have leveraged their advantages to pursue policies that would have made them competitive, and perhaps dominant, throughout the Columbian Epoch; indeed, Japan did precisely this in the latter nineteenth century and very quickly ascended to great power status. If a comparatively small and impoverished Japan was able to achieve such a feat so late in the Columbian Epoch, it is difficult to overstate what the Ming Empire might have accomplished if it had not turned away from exploration and the sea. Yet it chose a different course, and suffered the consequences.

The strategic lessons of the previous Epoch are deeply relevant to the current one. The present era of rapid technological, social, and political change presents challenges that, in some respects, are quite similar to those of the early Columbian Epoch; in this century all manner of innovations will challenge the worldview of policymakers, and some polities will adapt successfully to emerging strategic conditions while others will fail to do so. Powers that prove adaptable in a rapidly changing international environment will enjoy a critical advantage over those that are excessively conservative in their attitudes.

Yet it would be a mistake to reduce the discussion of twenty-first century international politics to a simple bumper sticker slogan admonishing policymakers to "embrace change." The fundamental character of international politics has not changed radically because human nature has not changed. The international system – what might be called the machinery of world politics – is, however, undergoing an Epochal shift and a multipolar world system centered on Eastern Eurasia is coming into being. To understand that fact is the first prerequisite for strategic success in this century; it is as important to comprehend this as, during the Columbian Epoch, it was vital to see that a Eurocentric world system was taking shape. Moreover, in the Post-Columbian Epoch there will be little time for strategic "slow learners" to adapt – for reasons discussed subsequently, history will move at a rapid pace, and, as a result, even the United States could find itself marginalized if it fails to take the measures necessary to ensure its ability to compete successfully over the long term in a profoundly competitive strategic environment.

3 The Grand Casino reopens

Multipolarity and international politics

For the majority of the Columbian Epoch, global politics was marked by multi-polarity and the vigorous competition among states for power and prestige. However, in such a dynamic international system there is always a tension between the desire of individual states for more power and the tendency of other states to resist would-be hegemons. In Europe, very powerful polities continually attempted to accumulate sufficient power to establish continental hegemony and, therefore, assume the role of preeminent world power. However, in roughly 500 years of the Columbian Epoch none of these *fully* succeeded in establishing European hegemony.

Even after the multipolar world system collapsed as a result of World War II, neither the United States nor the USSR enjoyed full hegemony over all of Europe. Certainly, Moscow enjoyed hegemonic (indeed, even outright imperial) control over the Warsaw Pact states, but Washington's sway over its allies was more limited. The United States certainly was preeminent in NATO, but many of its allies were willing to distance themselves from the Americans on issues ranging from Vietnam to SDI. Most importantly, neither Moscow nor Washington succeeded in establishing itself as the world hegemon.

The short half-life of unipolarity

The closest that a state has come to the attainment of universal hegemony is the United States, in the period from approximately 1991 to the present. However, it would be more accurate to see the present world order essentially as a "unipolar plus" world system, which has only one superpower but numerous great and medium powers and international organizations actively working to shape, constrain, and/or undermine Washington's foreign policies. Moreover, this should be but a brief transitional stage that will quickly be replaced by a new multipolar system. Indeed, as the international controversy surrounding the overthrow of the Saddam Hussein regime demonstrated, unipolarity already is in an advanced stage of decay – many entities, including several of Washington's formal allies, along with international bodies such as the United Nations Secretariat, cooperated to constrain American behavior, thus delaying the invasion of Iraq and attempting to prevent it altogether. After the invasion occurred, the members of this "coalition of the unwilling" changed tack and proceeded to complicate the American occupation of Iraq, calling on Washington to hand over power in that country quickly and regularly criticizing all manner of US decisions (and, of course, the notorious Abu Gareb prison abuses). These are not the actions of polities and international institutions cowed by a towering superpower and deeply fearful of the punishment that would result from opposing it.

Clearly, the United States is unable reliably to enforce its will in international diplomatic bodies such as the United Nations Security Council, while in the global economy there is no one dominant state. While it is powerful, Washington is unable to control outright international political-economic bodies such as the World Bank, the World Trade Organization (WTO), and the International Monetary Fund (IMF). Also, of course, individual states (and the state-like EU) do not sit idly and allow the Americans to dictate the terms of trade; they vigorously protect their own interests and, in many cases, feel compelled, for domestic political reasons, to advance the goals of powerful interest groups, industries, and individual corporations.

It is only in the military realm that the United States indisputably is preeminent and can be expected to remain generally superior to any other individual power for the foreseeable future. Certainly, other polities will increase their military power relative to that of the United States, and some may even achieve niche superiority over Washington in specific areas, but it would be very surprising indeed if any competitor were able to conjure a "blindside RMA" that would change entirely the grammar of war and critically undermine overall American military superiority.

The character of multipolarity

As unipolarity degrades, several states (and the presently difficult-to-define EU) can be expected to play an increasingly influential role in world affairs. Most of these are, in essence, young powers; this is particularly true of the EU, which is still very much under construction (and whether it will become a "superstate," collapse, or settle somewhere between these two extremes certainly remains debatable). The governments of India, China, and Japan represent three very old civilizations, but themselves are all little more than half a century old – India's democratic government emerged with the British withdrawal from South Asia, the People's Republic of China resulted from the Communist victory in the Chinese Civil War,[71] and Japan's democracy was crafted during the American occupation of that country. Only one, Russia, was a superpower in the twentieth century, and it also is a special case for another reason: although the Russian Federation, technically, is very young and Moscow has rejected Marxism–Leninism, there is, arguably, a much greater degree of continuity between the government of the USSR and the pseudo-democratic regime of Vladimir Putin than that between British-ruled and post-colonial India, Nationalist and Communist China, or militarist and democratic Japan.[72]

These polities – China, the EU, India, Japan, and Russia – are, along with the United States, the most plausible potential "poles" in the developing multipolar international political system. This does not, however, mean that their rise is inevitable; for any number of reasons, one or more of these powers may prove incapable of acting as a great power. Russia's economic and social health is dire, and both Moscow and Tokyo command relatively small (and aging) populations. The future of the EU itself is very uncertain, and even if it "deepens" and a truly unified foreign policy comes into being, one cannot be certain that Brussels will be willing to accept the military risks and obligations that are inseparable from "real" great power status – after an exhausting Columbian Epoch, Europe seems to long for semi-retirement. The same could be true of Japan (although the Japanese have the misfortune to live in a neighborhood full of thugs who are likely to view affluent retirees as potential prey). China and India presently appear to be developing robustly, but at this point in their economic development, both are highly vulnerable to global economic events (one can only imagine the damage that a world depression comparable to that of the 1930s would do to the export-driven Chinese "miracle economy") and, on a per capita basis, both are much poorer than the developed countries. Moreover, China already may be in early stages of a painful political transformation that will continue over the next few decades (the end result of which is unknowable), while India suffers from all manner of centrifugal forces – regional, ethnic, religious, socio-economic, and otherwise. Only the United States is almost certain to remain a strong pole, but even it could prove unwilling to defend its claim to being the greatest of the world's powers, if it appears that the enterprise would be very costly in blood and treasure.

Assuming that most or all of these polities continue to act as great powers, a very active multipolar power system will develop. Such a system would be flexible, with the ever-present possibility of alliance shifts, and therefore entirely different from the alliances of the Cold War. In the latter period, it was possible for marginal players (such as Egypt, for example) to shift their allegiance, but the alliance structure as a whole was very rigid. In any case, one would expect a bipolar alliance structure to be less flexible than a multipolar one, but, because of the military aspect of the struggle and deep ideological divide between the two superpowers, this characteristic was particularly pronounced during the Cold War: European liberal democracies were not willing to ally with a totalitarian Soviet superpower whose intentions they could not trust and whose political values were antithetical to their own. (Warsaw Pact countries of course did not have the option of turning away from Moscow's breast, as Hungarians and Czechs discovered.) In the multipolar system of the future, the military situation will be dissimilar from that prevailing in Europe during the Cold War, and at this point it appears unlikely that ideology will play a strong role in shaping the strategic environment, although this could change with surprising rapidity if new and strident ideologies develop. The most pressing medium-term question confronting the various players in Eastern Eurasia is China's rise, but Beijing is not poised to conquer its neighbors (except, obviously, Taiwan) and displays little desire to spread its present state ideology, which is brewed for domestic consumption: unlike full-strength Maoism, today's mixture of pseudo-Marxism and assertive Chinese nationalism could hardly be expected to set hearts afire worldwide.

To understand the developing international system, it is important to see the rise of China in context. In 1945, the Soviet Union and United States were colossi bestriding a broken Europe. The major states of Eastern Eurasia are not broken – indeed, most of them are developing economically and militarily at a rapid clip. China is the largest of these states, but – unlike in the Europe of 1945 – Eastern Eurasia is not a strategic vacuum ready to be filled by single power, a fact that many analysts – including, perhaps especially, American ones – fail to comprehend.

Beyond bipolarity: the balancing of China

Many of today's analysts place China in the regional context of "East Asia" or "the Asia-Pacific." As a matter of convenience, this is understandable, but it puts the People's Republic of China (PRC) in a framework that is unduly restrictive geographically; China is not a regional power as that term is generally conceived. First, there is the obvious fact that China's most important provinces are located on its coast, but it also borders Central Asia, Southeast Asia, South Asia, and Siberia. In addition, it is a country with a long coastline and a clear interest in the long-term development of more substantial naval capabilities.[73] In short, China's geographic location and national aspirations virtually ensure that its future actions will have important repercussions throughout the Asia-Pacific, South Asia, and the world as a whole. Beijing is well-positioned economically and militarily to be one of the most potent players in the struggle for preeminence in Eastern Eurasia, a contest with, for the reasons outlined above, global strategic implications. If it were to succeed in becoming unquestionably preeminent in Eastern Eurasia, China would displace the United States as the most powerful country in the world.

Nonetheless, in Washington there is still a tendency to see China's emergence as a struggle between a regional power striving for local hegemony and a geographically distant superpower attempting to balance that would-be regional hegemon and provide for the security of its East Asian allies. In this vision, the key potential prize for China would be hegemony over the Asian Rimland, with perhaps small territorial adjustments in the Spratly Islands and elsewhere, but no major changes in borders except for the elimination of Taiwan as a distinct political entity. It is generally assumed, probably correctly, that even a rancorous China would not be overweening in its ambitions – at least for now, Beijing has little apparent lust for *lebensraum* and, presumably, would be quite happy to tolerate Finlandized neighbors who showed proper deference to the Middle Kingdom.[74] One should not, however, ignore the global strategic implications of Chinese hegemony in Eastern Eurasia – a China preeminent in Eastern Eurasia tomorrow would be in a position not unlike that of Imperial Germany yesterday, if the latter had emerged triumphant in World War I.

Yet there are very substantial barriers to Chinese hegemony over the Asian Rimland. Some of these are noted frequently: the country's continuing poverty in per capita terms and the inefficiency of certain sectors of its economy, as well as the problems presented by tens of millions of Chinese who are filtering from the countryside into the cities; its military backwardness and the resulting inability of the PLA to project power regionally; and the potential for internal political instability that could undermine foreign policy and threaten the ability of the Chinese Communist Party (CCP) to maintain power. These indeed are daunting problems, and they cannot be solved quickly. The PRC's transition from a poor to an affluent country is an ongoing process that even in the most optimistic scenarios will require decades. In the meantime, China's relative poverty hinders its ability to conduct a consistently aggressive foreign policy successfully, as this would require huge military and related expenditures, but, at the same time, surely would damage economic relationships with the United States, Japan, and other key trading partners.[75]

There is also an additional factor that is very powerful, especially when considered along with the aforementioned ones: it is enormously easier for a country to establish hegemony – or, for that matter, outright imperial authority – over polities that are incapable of effective self-defense (either singly or collectively) than to browbeat strong foes into submission. By applying "traditional" balancing techniques of the sort that were practiced very successfully by European states for most of the Columbian Epoch, it should be possible for China's neighbors (with help from the United States), to constrain Chinese power. Allowing command of Eastern Eurasia to simply drop into China's grasp would require suicidal incompetence on the part of China's great power peers;[76] while this certainly is possible, it is rare for many illustrious polities simultaneously to be inflicted with appalling strategic judgment.

It is true that many of the countries in Eastern Eurasia are too small and/or too poor to defend their interests effectively against China, *if* the latter can bring significant military power to bear against them (and in the case of those countries that do not share a border with China, and perhaps even some that do, that might be a very significant caveat). Numerous countries, including Brunei, Nepal, Cambodia, Bhutan, Burma, and Laos would fit this description. Other states, such as Thailand, the Philippines, and Vietnam, which has a technologically unimpressive military but an imposing martial tradition (indeed, in 1979 Hanoi inflicted very substantial casualties on a Chinese punitive expedition),[77] have somewhat greater military potential, but might be easily intimidated if forced to stand alone against the Chinese giant. However, it should be remembered that some relatively small powers have relationships with outside powers that would make it risky for Beijing to attempt frank intimidation.

Other Asian states possess significant real or potential military power: Japan, Australia, South Korea, and Taiwan are all militarily competent powers; Indonesia's military capabilities are relatively modest, but could grow and improve as that country develops economically; Russia is in decline but still possesses a large military with pockets of quality and a huge nuclear arsenal; and, in time, India may even emerge as a "second China," huge, increasingly prosperous, and convinced of its right to a major international role and sphere of influence.[78]

The American factor

A key element in the developing strategic situation in the Asia-Pacific is the United States. Over the last decade a clear consensus has emerged in the American policymaking establishment that it would be detrimental to the vital interests of the United States for China to become the arbiter of international politics in the Asian Rimland. This is an eminently reasonable assumption, and, given the fact that China's current government is authoritarian, deeply suspicious of the West, and espouses values antithetical to those supported by the United States, it would be most unwise for Washington to stand idly by while Beijing seeks to maximize its power. If it is assumed that China possesses the resources and will to achieve hegemony in Eastern Eurasia, the parallel with the Cold War is clear: an outside superpower (the United States) must defend its interests by preventing an ambitious continental superstate from establishing hegemony over an immense and strategically vital portion of Eurasia.

The potential strength of numerous Eastern Eurasian states, however, undermines the Cold War parallel. The PRC, indeed, may come to possess the military resources to defeat any one of its neighbors in a limited, non-nuclear war, but competent leaders do not stand idly by waiting to be picked off individually. (The great states of Western and Central Europe found themselves in a very vulnerable position in the early Cold War period, but this was the result of World War II and the associated final destruction of the old multipolar balance-of-power system.) If China acts in an increasingly provocative manner toward its neighbors they may be expected to react, increasing their own military budgets and forming various informal partnerships, or even formal bi- or multilateral alliances.

Moreover, Chinese aggression would tend to encourage countries that presently do not have a cooperative relationship with the United States to cultivate one. By attempting to bully its neighbors, the PRC probably would cause the American military-diplomatic presence in Asia to expand – an outcome that Chinese policymakers surely would find most disconcerting. Indeed, one of the quandaries that Beijing faces in any march to hegemony is that, given China's physical location and sometimes thuggish ways, the United States is a desirable partner simply because it is far away and generally not inclined to interfere grossly in the domestic politics of its friends. If the United States continues to demonstrate its commitment to containing Chinese power, any state that feels threatened by Beijing will likely be attracted to Washington.

It is, however, improbable that a formal multilateral alliance between the United States and a generous number of Eastern Eurasian states will be constructed,[79] as China does not present a threat sufficiently menacing to compel the creation of such an entity (indeed, if such an alliance did form it would provide compelling proof that multipolarity was not developing in a healthy fashion). However, this does not preclude the broadening and deepening of American diplomatic and military ties in Eastern Eurasia.

American policymakers should not assume that Washington will cope with a bipolar diplomatic atmosphere in Eastern Eurasia in the twenty-first century. China has no universal ideological pretensions, no equivalent of the Soviet Union's Warsaw Pact empire, and does not enjoy a massive military advantage over various possible coalitions of neighboring states. At the same time, the United States cannot – and need not – play a role similar to that which it fulfilled in Europe in the twentieth century. The major states of Eastern Eurasia are capable of self-defense; they merely need the United States to act as a broker of coalitions, a provider of defense technology, and an arbiter of great power politics if the security environment should become unbalanced and one state, or coalition of states, becomes powerful enough to threaten the health of the multipolar system.

During the Cold War, Washington made the most important policy decisions and carried them out, often despite the misgivings of key allies. Any effort to contain Chinese power will not be so simple, and it is unlikely, for the reasons noted above, that the actions of the United States would solely determine its outcome. However, American actions will have a considerable impact on how easily this task can be successfully carried out, and any of three errors would grievously damage the effort: first, undue reluctance to face the fact of Chinese ambitions; second, attempts to force unenthusiastic partners to undertake unpopular measures; or, third, an obsession with preventing alliance defection.

The first issue essentially is intellectual – indeed, it is at the core of today's "China debate" in the United States – and will be determined within the US policymaking establishment. The second matter is diplomatic; Washington must not make diplomatic calculations using a "Cold War slide rule." Realistically, NATO-Europe had to accept American leadership; states in Eastern Eurasia will have a wider diplomatic menu from which to choose. A hamhanded diplomatic posture simply would encourage these states to cooperate among themselves without reference to Washington. Third, American leaders should realize that a major difference between the Cold War and the containment of China is that alliance defection is likely in the latter case. No NATO member defected from the organization and allied with the Soviet Union; indeed, the very idea seems slightly absurd. The multipolar diplomatic situation in Eastern Eurasia may be quite different and it is not difficult to imagine that some states will be willing to ally themselves with Beijing if the latter offers sufficient inducements. It is important, however, that such defections remain minimal and, particularly, that China remains unable to convince a major power such as India or Russia to join it as a junior partner (an issue discussed in more detail below).

If it wishes effectively to support its interests in the twenty-first century, it is vital that Washington first acquires a clear conception of the nature of the contest in Eastern Eurasia and recognizes that it will be fundamentally different structurally from the previous century's Cold War. If that understanding is incorporated into the strategic worldview of American strategists, it will be possible to begin the construction of a realistic strategy for the containment of Chinese power.

Nightmare: the possibility of a great power axis

There is one very substantial potential threat to the development of a healthy multi-polar system in Eastern Eurasia. As we have seen, acting alone, China is unlikely to be so potent as to establish itself as a hegemon over the objections of its great power neighbors. However, this very muscular state could serve as the senior partner in an alliance with one or more other great powers. The creation of such a coalition would be a very negative development, as it would increase substantially the likelihood of major war. Although China initially might see such an alliance as a mechanism to balance the "excessive" power of the United States, the Americans and the other states of Eastern Eurasia would be very foolish indeed to treat it as a defensive entity. China, flush with the successes in recent decades and, by all appearances, quite convinced that a glorious destiny lay before it, cannot be trusted to act with moderation any more than Napoleonic France, Wilhelmine Germany, or Lenin's Soviet Union could be. Acting as the senior partner in a great power alliance surely would reinforce Beijing's worst instincts. Moreover, the junior partner(s) in such an alliance might prove to be even more dangerous, acting recklessly while hoping, like the Austrians of the early twentieth century, that their puissant ally could shield them from the possible negative consequences of their actions.

Who might such a junior partner be? The future twists and turns of world politics of course are unknowable, but one state, Russia, stands out as a particularly likely candidate for a number of reasons:

- The Russian Federation is in obvious long-term decline,[80] struggling desperately merely to maintain its great power status, much less again become a superpower. Pooling its resources with China would allow Russia to be a "virtual superpower," a partner in an alliance with superpower-level military, economic, and diplomatic resources.
- Moscow has very good reason to fear the growth of Chinese power, particularly given the emptying out of its Far East of ethnic Russians and migration of Chinese nationals into that same area and the fact that the Chinese could make plausible historical claims to considerable tracts of Russian territory. Russian leaders could decide that bandwagoning with Beijing is more prudent than keeping it at a distance.
- Russian and Chinese strategic capabilities and requirements have substantial complementarities. For example, Russia has, despite the economic shocks following the Soviet collapse, maintained a very considerable military-industrial complex. It has worked particularly assiduously to maintain its research and development capabilities. However, there has been a steep post-Soviet decline both in Russia's quantitative military needs and arms sales abroad. China, in contrast, has ample cash on hand, an underdeveloped military-industrial complex, and a voracious appetite for cutting-edge military equipment. Also of note is the fact that preferred access to Russian energy resources would be most attractive to the Chinese, who clearly are concerned about the possibility of supply interruption.

• Russia and China already united in the creation of the Shanghai Cooperation Organization (SCO), a multinational grouping in which they are the
key states.[81] The SCO is a rather amorphous entity that is not yet – and
likely never will be – a military alliance similar to NATO. However, the
mere fact that the SCO was created (in 2001, as the successor to the
"Shanghai Five," which was organized in 1996), is indicative of a desire on
the part of Moscow and Beijing to partner on security issues. Moreover,
Russia and China conducted joint military exercises in 2005.[82]

It is by no means a certainty that China and Russia will partner together in the
future, much less that they will be both inclined and able to create a broader
alliance which might include states such as Iran. However, the possibility of
such an alliance should not be dismissed casually,[83] as the threat that it would
present to the balance of power in Eastern Eurasia would be very substantial
indeed.

In the worst case, such an alliance could form an immediate and gargantuan
menace to the interests of the United States, endeavoring to organize Eurasia,
destroying or "Finlandizing" all other significant Old World powers and making
the supercontinent's resources (natural, industrial, and human) available to the
conquering powers. Even if such a "super-threat" did not come about, however,
a hostile great power alliance still could place American vital interests in grave
danger. At the least, it would be a potent diplomatic and military bloc likely to
attract smaller bandwagoning allies. In addition, it should be noted that it may
be difficult to assess accurately the political intentions of a great power alliance
– allied great powers may contend publicly that their national goals are limited
when, in fact, they are very expansive. Indeed, even if the goals of an alliance
are initially modest a series of political-military successes might encourage the
partners to seek ever-greater gains.

A China–Russia axis at least temporarily would undermine radically the
development of a healthy multipolarity in Eastern Eurasia, inviting – indeed,
necessitating – the creation of a counterbalancing combination, its probable
"anchors" being India, Japan, and the United States. This condition of "artificial
bipolarity," with most (perhaps even all) of the world's great powers lined up
into two gangs warily eying each other, itchy fingers tapping holsters, would be
far more likely to degenerate into violence in any given year than was the relatively stable Soviet–American standoff. It was, of course, in similar conditions
that both of the twentieth century's world wars erupted.

Great and small power interactions

Medium and small powers played a key role in the vibrant multipolar system of
the Columbian Epoch, and it is to be expected that they will be similarly important in this century. Decisions by such countries to cooperate or conflict with
great powers can greatly affect the balance of power in Eastern Eurasia and the
struggles between great and lesser powers can even be the catalyst for war – the

immediate causes for the world wars of the twentieth century, after all, were Austria's pressure on Serbia in the wake of Archduke Franz Ferdinand's assassination and Germany's invasion of Poland. A number of issues that may be relevant to great power politics in the early decades of the twenty-first century are considered in Table 3.1. This list by no means is intended to be exhaustive; it merely notes some possible issues and illustrates how events occurring in, or driven by, small and medium powers may be relevant to the great powers.

When one considers the likely role of small and medium powers in the developing international political system, it becomes all the clearer that a reversion to bipolarity is highly unlikely. The rich variety of states located in Eastern Eurasia and their enormously varied national goals creates a security environment with many "cross-pressures": as the great powers jostle for position, small polities will have many opportunities to play them off each other and leverage whatever advantages they possess. Bipolarity and rigidity in the international system tend

Table 3.1 Small/medium and great power interactions

Event	Broader importance
The Socialist Republic of Vietnam (SRV) moves closer to the United States or the PRC	Impact on the US–China relationship; possible US naval or other bases in the SRV and thus implications for the defense of the ROC; repercussions throughout SE Asia as other countries feel a diminished or enhanced incentive to align with the PRC
Worsening Islamist extremism in countries with large Muslim populations, including Pakistan, Indonesia, Bangladesh, and Malaysia	Relevant to American counterterrorist efforts and US relations with these countries; enhanced threats to India and other states; likely support for Islamists by great powers wishing to directly or indirectly harm competitors; possibility that part of the Pakistani nuclear arsenal will fall into terrorist hands
The central government of Indonesia is unable to manage successfully centrifugal pressure and the country splinters	Possible civil war that may draw in great powers; conceivable rise of one or more Islamist states; safe passage of ships through the Straits of Malacca endangered; likely spillover of violence to Malaysia and elsewhere; power vacuum provides opportunities for assertive great powers to expand their influence in SE Asia
North Korea uses nuclear weapons against South Korea	Possible American use of nuclear weapons against North Korea; likely involvement of Japan in the conflict; clash of interests between Washington and Beijing
Taiwan declares independence	Likely Chinese invasion of Taiwan, resulting in a great power war between the PRC and United States

to reinforce each other: the unique conditions of the latter 1940s encouraged a bipolarity that undermined the freedom of action of the small and medium powers and this, in turn, buttressed the bipolar system itself. Efforts to break bipolarity – of which the Non-Aligned Movement was the most notable – enjoyed little success. The end of the Cold War, however, shattered this rigid system. The states of Eastern Eurasia are enormously varied in size, culture, economic development, military capability and many other respects; as the center of global politics shifts to this meta-region, the result will be the development of a very vibrant multipolar system.

Conclusion

The decay of today's "unipolar plus" system, in which the United States is pre-eminent, is inevitable. Washington lacks both the will and resources to maintain its primacy indefinitely, and various great powers would not forever tolerate it. Unipolarity already is on its deathbed, while a revitalized multipolar system is being born. It is likely that unipolarity will be mourned belatedly, for, whatever its imperfections, the American superpower is as benevolent a hegemon as one reasonably could demand, and Washington's ascendance made large-scale international war, much less manic aggression by major states of the kind that occurred repeatedly in 1930s, very improbable. Nonetheless, the patient is slipping away, and bringing a healthy new multipolar system into being is of critical importance, because that would likely be the most stable and least war-prone alternative to the current international regime.

Obviously, it is of vital importance to the United States that the PRC does not become the hegemon of Eastern Eurasia. As noted above, however, regardless of what Washington does, China's success in such an endeavor is not as easily attainable as pessimists might assume. The PRC appears to be on track to be a very great power indeed, but geopolitical conditions are not favorable for any Chinese effort to establish sole hegemony; a robust multipolar system should suffice to keep China in check, even with only minimal American intervention in local squabbles. The more worrisome danger is that Beijing will cooperate with a great power partner, establishing a very muscular axis. Such an entity would present a critical danger to the balance of power, thus both necessitating very active American intervention in Eastern Eurasia and creating the underlying conditions for a massive, and probably nuclear, great power war. Absent such a "super-threat," however, the demands on American leaders will be far more subtle: creating the conditions for Washington's gentle decline from playing the role of unipolar quasi-hegemon to being "merely" the greatest of the world's powers, while aiding in the creation of a healthy multipolar system that is not marked by close great power alliances.

4   Leviathan slimming
Guarding American interests in a multipolar environment

For the reasons discussed previously, the United States presently is in a unique historical position. In the five centuries preceding 1991, no power attained unquestionable preeminence worldwide, but the United States presently has the world's largest economy, easily the most powerful military, and Washington effectively acts as the chief arbiter of international affairs. It would be a considerable exaggeration to say that Washington rules the globe, but, to use Colin S. Gray's metaphor, it is the international sheriff – a capable gunslinger and the only actor capable of organizing "posses" that maintain world order.[84]

Although unprecedented, this state of affairs is not altogether surprising when one considers the unique circumstances under which the United States emerged as a preeminent power. As noted above, the Cold War was the Columbian Epoch's period of dotage. The World Wars shattered a multipolar international system that was, in retrospect, extremely fragile, and this was followed by bipolar competition between two radically different powers. One of the Cold War superpowers was the wealthiest country on earth, a populous and culturally vibrant state that was the world's center of technological and financial innovation and easily capable of fielding and maintaining an impressive military establishment and constructing an ever-more-costly welfare state while still enjoying consistent economic growth. By contrast, its competitor was a grim totalitarian empire whose chief cultural product was stultifying propaganda that was inflicted on citizens who (aside from a small elite) lived in conditions that were, by the standards of their American contemporaries, squalid. Given that its state philosophy was based on fundamentally flawed economic principles and that its lust for military power seemingly was unquenchable, the Soviet Union chose to place its economy on what amounted to a permanent wartime footing. As Moscow was eventually to discover, this was not a recipe for long-term success.[85] The Soviet enterprise slowly ground to a halt, its leadership having failed to do the one thing that potentially could have resulted in hegemony over Eurasia and long-term strategic supremacy: initiating an invasion of Europe, thereby starting a third world war.

In retrospect, one can see that Soviet superpower status was in certain respects illusory. Soviet military power was disturbingly real, and Soviet leaders were deadly serious about "burying" the West,[86] but the USSR was a unipolar superpower, a strategic "one-trick pony" that attempted to compensate for its limitations through exorbitant military spending and sheer ideological will. It was far from the first such power – indeed, Germany, Japan, and Italy had similar problems at mid-century, although military overspending was less of a threat to the long-term health of these states than was the extraordinary aggressiveness of National Socialist, Italian Fascist, and Japanese militarist ideology. Soviet Marxist-Leninists were rather more subtle than their Axis counterparts, insofar as they posited that history was on their side and that patience could be a virtue. This allowed them the luxury of only undertaking military aggression when they were highly confident of victory – as against unlucky Lithuanians, Latvians, Estonians, and Finns, for example – and of being cautious when faced with nuclear-armed Americans and other foes capable of effective self-defense. The Soviet leadership's critical miscalculation, ironically, resulted from the very patience that allowed the USSR to outlast many other twentieth-century totalitarian regimes. Unlike the Axis states, which were obsessed with military adventurism, regardless of whether they were properly prepared for such undertakings,[87] the Soviets prepared assiduously for their great drive to conquer Western Europe and yet never quite mustered the will to carry it out.

Ancient powers sometimes enjoyed great overall superiority in their strategic neighborhood, but even in more recent times powers sometimes have been able to achieve preeminence in one aspect of military power; the long period of the British dominance of the sea is the clearest example of the phenomenon. No power has enjoyed gross superiority on land for such a long period, but the Soviet Union clearly was the greatest landpower for several decades, while Revolutionary/Napoleonic France was, for a brief but brilliant period, far superior to any one of its continental foes. A more arguable case of landpower preeminence would be Germany early in World War I, a state that – although, like Napoleonic France, ultimately defeated on the battlefield – was able to cope with an overall economic–industrial disadvantage relative to the Allied Powers and nonetheless inflict enormous damage simultaneously on Russia, France, and the British Expeditionary Force.

The Second American RMA

For over a decade, there was a very active debate in American academic and policy circles over whether an RMA was presently ongoing. Today, the RMA essentially is taken for granted in policymaking circles, though the terminology has changed somewhat, as the term RMA now generally is used more-or-less interchangeably with the Rumsfeldian notion of "transformation."[88] Both concepts, particularly the latter, remain somewhat slippery. Pentagon analysts debate whether particular technologies and weapons systems are "transformational," while former US Secretary of Defense Donald Rumsfeld referred to Operation Enduring Freedom's Battle of Mazar-e Sharif as a "transformational battle."[89]

A small library of books, articles, and speeches already has been dedicated to RMA/transformation and the purpose, herein, is not to rehash this long-running controversy.[90] The author would, however, contend that the concept of RMA is a generally useful one, even if much of the recent debate over RMA has not been. Dramatic improvements in operational art and/or the proper use of a key technology can make a very important difference indeed in combat and can, as a result, have a massive strategic effect. Furthermore, there is a very good case to be made that over the last century the United States has been outstandingly resourceful in applying technology (and, in recent decades, doctrine) to create conditions conducive to military revolution. This work argues that the current transformation so strongly endorsed by Rumsfeld in fact is characteristic of the closing period of the Second American RMA, and that a *new* RMA will occur in the early decades of this century.

The First American RMA was a conspicuous one, and it was the very model of a technology-driven revolutionary change in warfare: the invention of nuclear arms.[91] On July 16, 1945, the existence of a new weapon, capable of inflicting far more immediate destruction than had any explosive device previously devised, was confirmed. This is as clear a division – in this case, between the pre-nuclear and nuclear eras – as one could wish for. After the initial nuclear test, the United States, and soon, the USSR and other polities, built on the foundation laid at Los Alamos, most importantly by developing thermonuclear warheads and, later, mating nuclear weapons with ballistic missiles of ever-increasing range, but these were incremental improvements to the revolutionary weapon that was developed at Los Alamos.

The ongoing Second American RMA is much subtler than the first, as it is dependent on the development of technologies that are, for the most part, unrelated or only marginally related to nuclear weapons. Indeed, the Second American RMA is in some respects a repudiation of the first. Despite having invented nuclear weapons and even used two of them in warfare, Washington very quickly grew uneasy with the prospect that such devices again might be used in anger, a fear that grew more acute as the Soviet arsenal expanded in size. Increasingly faced with the possibility that a nuclear conflict in Europe could escalate into a general nuclear war that could threaten the survival of the United States as – to use Mackinder's language – a "Going Concern,"[92] policymakers attempted to devise military options that would allow for the successful non-nuclear defense of Europe. While there was, and is, very serious reason to doubt that Moscow would have consented to fight a third world war by "gentlemen's rules" and refrained from nuclear use if Washington did likewise,[93] the effort to construct a non-nuclear defense option for Europe was nonetheless beneficial because it both inspired useful doctrinal reform – AirLand Battle doctrine, devised in the 1980s, is the forefather of today US operational art[94] – and encouraged the development and acquisition of highly capable non-nuclear weapons systems.[95] The first large-scale "road test" of the transforming US military was the Persian Gulf War of 1991, and the results were impressive.

The US military *c.*1991 was, however, rather different from that fielded in Iraq twelve years later. The 1991 force essentially was still a Cold War military establishment – large (though already considerably downsized from its Reagan-era peak), muscular and prepared to fight Soviet armored and motor rifle divisions, and, as a result, distressingly difficult to move and support logistically. Fortunately, for the United States, the Iraqi dictator, whose chances of being elevated by historians to the ranks of history's great warlords appear slim, watched idly as months passed and Washington moved its military from other continents, unloading it at conveniently located and capacious ports on the eastern Saudi coast.

Over the next twelve years the US military continued to transform, partly for positive reasons (a generous stream of research and development funding continued to flow to the Pentagon) but also for negative ones. Until its closing years, the 1990s was a decade of ongoing downsizing despite the fact that the military was continuously asked to perform a variety of duties around the globe. It was clear that creativity would be required if the military, particularly the Army, was to be able to do all that was asked of it: the armed forces were expected somehow to be able to maintain the capability to dispatch Iraq-sized regional foes, perhaps even two simultaneously, with minimal casualties while also parceling out combat units to discipline Haitian, Somali, and other thugs. As the Clinton era progressed, ever more of the fruits of the (largely civilian) ongoing revolution in computer science and related fields were adopted by the US military, often with considerable enthusiasm,[96] and the divergence between the US military and the armies fielded by many US allies, including most NATO countries, became increasingly stark.

The gap between the United States armed forces and other military organizations is now so large that it is not uncommon for authors to speak of Washington as though it were not just the sole superpower, but even the only great power. This is an exaggeration, but it is notable that the gap between the United States and the rest of the world is sufficiently substantial that no power – except Russia, should it choose to risk undertaking a nuclear strike against the American homeland – can credibly threaten to defeat the United States militarily if the latter truly is dedicated to achieving victory. Indeed, even a coalition of two or three great powers could not, under most circumstances, expect victory in a conventional conflict. This still leaves the possibility that a polity could defeat the Americans by developing "niche" capabilities and then leveraging those areas of competence to convince Washington that military victory would be so expensive as to be Pyrrhic. However, that is an inherently dangerous game for the lesser power – and, if Washington chose not to be "reasonable," the result potentially would be catastrophic for the attempted blackmailer.

Some authors have argued that the ongoing military improvement actually is an evolutionary, rather than a revolutionary, process.[97] It is true that, unlike the First American RMA, the current revolution did not occur instantaneously as a result of the deployment of a new weapon. However, it is, nonetheless, important to note that the Second American RMA has occurred rather speedily: it arguably began in the latter stages of the Vietnam War with the introduction of early precision-guided munitions (PGMs) and was demonstrably mature at the time of the 1991 Persian Gulf War. In this short time, the difference between

American conventional military capabilities and those of its nearest potential competitors became very large indeed.

When one discounts the effect of exceptional generalship unrelated to tactical/operational innovation per se, the American advantage over its enemies is much larger than that enjoyed by Revolutionary and Napoleonic France over other European great powers, or by Germany over its enemies during the brief, and debatable,[98] "*Blitzkrieg* RMA."[99] This is not a minor point. Napoleon, as well as several German generals active in World War II, did not only create and implement tactical/operational innovations that were revolutionary in their effect; they were also very talented battlefield commanders, and this permitted them to leverage their innovations to greater effect. The current RMA, by contrast, was built on the assumptions implicit in the current promotion policies of the US military. The American general officer corps is populated by well-educated and competent men and women, but most likely there are few true military geniuses among them; many brilliant but difficult or eccentric officers never attain even one star under the current system,[100] and most individualists no doubt prefer to steer clear of the officer corps and instead avail themselves of the tolerance that Silicon Valley and even (albeit to a lesser degree) Wall Street and Washington's civilian sector have for talented oddballs. Today's United States does not need Napoleons or Guderians to successfully execute its military operations – competent, experienced managers are adequate to the task.

Although the current RMA was shaped by the US military establishment and defense contractors employed by Washington, the technologies and tactics that have resulted in this RMA progressively will be adopted by other polities. Whether operational/doctrinal or technological – and the Second American RMA contains elements of both – the knowledge that makes any RMA possible, eventually will spread to, and be adopted by, other states. Of course, not all of the weapons systems used so successfully by the US military will be copied by other countries. It is unlikely, for example, that in the next few decades any state will attempt to field a manned heavy bomber as sophisticated as the B-2 Spirit; the costs of developing and building similar bombers is simply too high for almost all countries, and it appears that the few that could afford such an instrument would prefer to spend their scarce resources on less expensive weapons systems that can perform many of the same functions. Polities will adapt the current RMA to their own circumstances, and foreign states can mitigate high research and development costs by using commercial off-the-shelf technologies and procuring (and often adapting) weapons developed by other countries. As the technologies characteristic of the current RMA spread to more countries, PGMs, sophisticated sensors, tactical ingenuity, and computer networking will allow many states to field forces that bear a partial resemblance to the American military of today.

The Second American RMA is, however, unusually difficult to imitate, insofar as it relies on a broad array of technologies wielded by highly-trained personnel in joint operations, which creates difficulties for would-be imitators. Even very wealthy and sophisticated states would find it very difficult to replicate the combat effectiveness of the 101st Airborne Division or Third Marine Expeditionary Brigade, even if they were to outfit their own units with equal or better equipment. Strong officership, *esprit d'corps*, combat experience and the resulting "lessons learned," and similarly intangible assets cannot be purchased at an arms fair. Simply put, the American military is now very good indeed at fighting wars; even in the conflicts which it finds most difficult – urban guerrilla wars, as in Iraq – it inflicts punishing losses on its enemies. There are only a few other military establishments worldwide – such as the Israeli and British Armies – that plausibly might claim to have an overall quality of personnel as high as that of the Americans, and most of the current great powers lag far behind in this regard. The Russian, Chinese, and Indian militaries may have pockets of excellence, but their overall personnel quality, clearly, is far below that of the United States, while the EU of course does not yet have a unified military establishment – and even if it did, the British Army is an exception on a continent where military excellence has been allowed to atrophy since the end of the Cold War. Japan's Self-Defense Force is quite respectable, but small – and Tokyo has not fought a war for over sixty years. Clearly, the Americans will be at the forefront of overall military prowess for some time.

This does not, however, mean that the US military is invulnerable. In the normal pattern of RMAs, the advantage enjoyed by the United States would be expected to progressively dissipate as competitors became increasingly competent at countering the (presently enormous) advantages enjoyed by Washington. The present situation is unusual, however, because the current RMA is, essentially, a repudiation of the previous RMA, yet the previous one has not lost its potency. Nuclear weapons remain an immensely powerful military technology and provide states with an affordable and practical route by which to build a force that can negate many of the advantages that the United States today enjoys.

The notion that the end of the Nuclear Age was imminent was quite popular in the years immediately following the fall of the Berlin Wall, but the rosy hypothesis that the decline in Soviet–American tension and a resulting decrease in the size of superpower nuclear arsenals would cause a "trickle down" rejection of nuclear weapons by other actors has not reflected the reality of the last decade. The nuclear arsenals of the Cold War superpowers indeed have declined radically, and in the 2002 Moscow Treaty, Russia and the United States agreed that each will have no more than 1700–2200 aggregate warheads by December 31, 2012.[101] Yet the problem of horizontal proliferation has worsened – in recent years India, Pakistan, and North Korea have conducted nuclear tests, the latter despite the 1994 Agreed Framework, which allegedly froze its nuclear weapons development.[102] (The fact that Pyongyang cheated on the Agreed Framework was a surprise to no one save for the spectacularly naïve, a category that apparently includes a number of former Clinton Administration officials.) Meanwhile, Iran almost certainly is well on the road to acquiring its own "Shia bomb."[103]

Nuclear weapons potentially are a a very useful political instrument for any state facing major security challenges, but they can be particularly beneficial to those which cannot afford to construct a large and advanced conventional military force. While developing nuclear weapons is expensive, the cost of maintaining a small nuclear arsenal is very modest compared to the direct and indirect costs of maintaining an American armored division or carrier battle group. Two very lopsided victories over the Iraqi Army convincingly demonstrated that qualitatively much inferior conventional force cannot cope with today's "postmodern" American military any more effectively than the Aztecs could address the threat presented by the Spanish conquistadors.[104] Playing by "American rules" results in defeat, but countries can, if they dare, introduce nuclear weapons into a conflict and potentially alter the strategic equation radically.

Ballistic missile defenses (BMD) impact the strategic utility of nuclear weapons, complicating first-strike planning enormously, for example, but do not entirely negate the usefulness of nuclear weapons for several reasons. First, no defense is perfect and this fact gives pause to leaders confronting a nuclear-armed opponent. Second, ballistic missile defense only addresses one mode of nuclear delivery. While ballistic missiles are the best means currently available for delivering nuclear weapons quickly, across great distances, they are not the only possible tools for transporting such devices. Strategic and tactical aircraft, as well as cruise missiles, can deliver warheads with great precision, and during the Cold War the superpowers developed warheads that could be carried in backpacks, fired from artillery tubes, and so forth. If BMD undermines the usefulness of ballistic missiles, it is probable that many would-be proliferators simply will shift their delivery strategy rather than altogether abandoning their effort to obtain nuclear weapons. Also, the possibility that a state will attempt to smuggle a nuclear weapon onto a foe's territory cannot be dismissed. While this is far from the militarily preferable fashion in which to deliver a warhead, a polity willing to accept the enormous risks that would accompany such a tactic may find that a "hidden bomb" would provide enormous diplomatic leverage in a crisis.

The United States currently is in a unique historical position, as it enjoys a technological lead in all forms of geographic military power – air, sea, land, and space. This advantage is the fruit of decades of research and development spending combined with the collapse of the USSR, Washington's chief competitor in the development of military technology. The United States is a military colossus, the only state that can project significant military power worldwide; other great powers are, militarily speaking, second-rate.

This overwhelming dominance cannot endure.[105] Some observers contend that the United States will continue to enjoy military preeminence because no other power can match its enormous military spending, but this assumes that current trends will continue – a very hazardous conjecture when discussing the future of world politics. It is quite probable, during the next decade or two, that ambitious powers will attempt an "end run" around the Second American RMA by combining certain of its technologies with nuclear weapons. Even more importantly, however, it is highly probable that within two or three decades, developing technology (and resulting doctrinal) developments should result in the full flowering of a new RMA that builds on the Second American RMA but is clearly distinct from the latter.

The latter RMA, however, will only be one product of a technological revolution that will be Epoch-shaping. The next RMA will result from new strategic circumstances; successfully adapting to these novel conditions will require an RSP. The underlying phenomenon that will create an RSP is far more significant than the next RMA itself. Only those states that can adapt to global, political, and military realities that have altered radically will prosper.

The danger of resting on laurels

The fact that the United States is preeminent in land, sea, air, and space power makes it unique in the modern world (and, of course, in the ancient world only land and sea dominance were at issue). However, this will not necessarily always translate into military, much less political, victory for Washington. Today, the truly overwhelming military advantage that the United States enjoys over any single potential opponent is sufficiently large that reasonable observers might be tempted to dismiss the imminent demise of unipolarity. Why, after all, should unipolarity disappear if one state is preponderant militarily? This is a strong point, and it surely is true that *overall* the United States will remain the most powerful country in the world, militarily, for some time. However, Washington cannot expect to maintain today's crushing military dominance for much longer, and it certainly will not be able to translate raw military power into permanent global dominance.

The subtlety of the changes presently occurring in world politics, itself, presents a key problem. The United States has never been notable for it foresight in strategic matters – generally, when Washington has faced critical strategic problems it has done so only with great reluctance and after failing for some time to acknowledge the magnitude of the threat that it faced; American indifference to the challenges presented by Germany in the 1930s and the USSR in the latter 1940s are classic examples of this point, but it applies equally well to Osama bin Laden and his al Qaeda network.[106] Unless one enters the realms of fantasy and imagines that the United States executive and legislative branches somehow came under the control of a cabal of Machiavellis and Richelieus who combined strategic acumen, ruthlessness, and a willingness to spend virtually unlimited resources on military power, it is very difficult to imagine how Washington could maintain its present overwhelming military lead. Certainly, the United States could do much more than it presently does to maintain and improve its armed forces, but the political circumstances in Eastern Eurasia are such that Washington cannot realistically prevent the rise of states whose leaders are intent on actively shaping their strategic environment and who, therefore, will desire to enhance their military power.[107] Indeed, the possibility that a challenger will develop novel military capabilities that the United States could not readily counter is also not to be dismissed lightly. Although "wonder weapons" have, on the whole, an unimpressive history in changing the outcome of a specific war, biotechnology, robotics, and other fields of scientific research may hold great promise for polities seeking specific military advantages over the United States. (This possibility is explored in greater detail in the next chapter.) One should not forget also the possibility, noted in the previous chapter, that two or more great powers could form a military-political alliance.[108]

This does not, however, mean that the United States progressively will be sidelined from the great power system in Eurasia and demoted from a superpower with worldwide interests to an unusually muscular regional power. Indeed, such an outcome is extremely unlikely; there have been many cases where states have abandoned *Weltpolitik* and been reduced to the status of regional or even minor powers – notably, many European states followed this course in recent centuries – but there is no strong reason to believe that the United States is inclined to turn its back on the world outside the Western Hemisphere or that it will be compelled to do so because (as was the case for Britain after World War II) the cost of maintaining its status would be ruinous. The United States should continue to be a major actor in Eurasian politics for decades to come. Indeed, if it pursues prudent policies Washington may emerge as the arbiter of great power politics and play a role in twenty-first century Eastern Eurasia, not dissimilar from that of nineteenth century Britain in regard to Europe – a rather enviable position, overall.

Eventually, it will be necessary for the American government to cooperate with allies who are near-peers, or even true peers. If the United States is to achieve its national goals, it will have to treat such powers as equals – not in the strictly formal sense that, for example, all the NATO allies are "equals," but with the understanding that these partners are actors of considerable weight who will not always be easily categorized as "allies" or "enemies" and who cannot simply be ignored when they disapprove of American policy. This may appear to be simple enough, but it in fact would require a fairly significant shift in American strategic culture.

Rogues and suckers: the challenges of preeminence

A hearty perennial that reappears regularly in academic journals and the opinion pages of newspapers is the debate concerning American "arrogance" toward allies. Critics of American alliance management frequently complain that Washington is making key decisions that are opposed, or at least not warmly supported, by its allies and warn that unless greater deference is shown to allied sensibilities the United States will suffer when the insulted allies withdraw their support for US policies. Worse still, allies may be completely alienated as they become convinced that the United States is a foolish, irresponsible, and/or homicidal power. Thus, Washington will be left (to use a currently popular phrase) as a "rogue superpower," feared and disliked by the wider world, isolated and unable to act as a leader on the world stage.

Variations of the "rogue superpower critique" have been used by those wishing to influence American nuclear weapons policy, US actions in Vietnam, the BMD debate, and Washington's policy toward a bevy of polities – including Iraq, Afghanistan, the Palestinian Authority, North Korea, and Iran. The basic argument that the United States must constrain its own actions if it is to be a respected power is almost infinitely adaptable. Regardless of the issue, one can always argue that the United States must be humble and circumspect if it is to avoid the animus of other states. However, these broad warnings generally are not helpful in determining policy.

It is true that countries should expect that their actions will impact how allies act toward them in the future and, indeed, whether they will continue to be allies; this fact was intuitively understood thousands of years before game theorists created sophisticated models demonstrating the relevance of "tit-for-tat" in international affairs. The rogue superpower critique, however, tends to overstress the emotional aspect of international interaction, expressing anxiety over whether other countries and their citizens trust and have goodwill toward the United States.[109] This reduces international interaction to a popularity contest and results in a one-dimensional solution to any international question: never anger one's allies (or even, perhaps, enemies), as this will rebound to one's own disadvantage. Such a course obviously is untenable for the United States or any other great power. Those countries wishing to shape profoundly the world security environment sometimes *must* undertake actions that will be to the perceived disadvantage of certain of their allies (and if they are not regularly causing their antagonists considerable discomfort they are doing something wrong). Moreover, the United States has many allies, and their interests often are not in concert; thus, actions frequently will be endorsed by some partners and frustrating to others. The foreign policy of the United States is not crafted for the purpose of furthering allied interests; those interests are accommodated so that Washington's goals ultimately will be furthered.

Whether a state is "liked" is largely irrelevant to the efficacy of its foreign policy. Sweden, today, is the very model of a punctilious international actor, highly respectful of international institutions, and relatively generous in its provision of foreign aid; it acts in a fashion that is clearly calculated to garner the quiet respect of the international elite that Samuel Huntington aptly termed "the Davos Culture people."[110] Alas, Stockholm's policy preferences also are safely ignored by the great powers and its actual influence in the international system is quite small. By contrast, the Sweden of Gustavus Adolphus II was utterly different from today's Sweden, and no less predatory than its thuggish peers. However, Sweden then *was* a very active and militarily potent power and prudence required its contemporaries, allied or antagonistic, to take its preferences into account when formulating international policy.

That a state possessing significant power and a willingness to use it, as seventeenth century Sweden certainly did, must be taken seriously by other states when they are calculating strategy, while the preferences of a state having little power, or inclination to use it, usually may be treated as a tertiary consideration, or ignored altogether, is obvious. However, the impact of power on the relationship between allies is more nuanced than a simple formula of "power equals influence"; more raw power does not immediately and invariably translate into more influence over either allies or enemies.

State interactions are complex and there are times that it even may be to the advantage of a polity and its leaders to be feared or thought unreasonable.[111] A state that constantly seeks consensus and strives to cultivate harmony among allies indeed will reap certain benefits, but, because it will be deeply reluctant to take action that would anger its partners, it also will sacrifice a great deal of negotiating leverage with its partners. Allies will come to understand that they can "push the envelope," seeking to maximize gains at the expense of their pliable ally while running little risk of creating a permanent rift. For those allies *not* to do so would be foolish, as they would be surrendering gains unnecessarily.

In contrast, a strong state that regularly bullies partners may obtain many direct advantages if it has the military or economic power to back its threats and assurances. Napoleonic France, perhaps, is the most famous example of this phenomenon, as it constantly demanded money and troops from its weaker "allies," demanded allegiance to the Continental System while largely exempting itself from the rigors of that scheme, and otherwise acted in a thoroughly unreasonable fashion.[112] For a time, this method worked marvelously, allowing France to create a cycle of success in war leading to advantageous relationships with subservient nations that, in turn, would bear many of the financial and human costs of providing Paris with the resources necessary for further military success. Unfortunately for Napoleon, this system did have one critical flaw: most of his nominal allies had every incentive to desert him and cooperate to overthrow his regime. This was especially true for states such as Austria and Prussia, which were faced with the stark choice between defeating France and reclaiming their status as true great powers or being permanently relegated to the status of French satellites.

Based on the US record since 1945, it is clear that Washington is not an international menace that crudely dragoons its allies into supporting reckless policies that undermine international security.[113] While one could argue the merits of various US policies, overall the record demonstrates that Washington is fairly cautious, generally (though not invariably) reluctant to act to alter the status quo significantly, and willing both to consult allies and respect their freedom of action. American leadership in Europe and elsewhere has had a decidedly non-Napoleonic flavor and many allies have elected not to support, or even actively to undermine, the most controversial US initiatives, such as the G.W. Bush Administration's effort to overthrow Iraq's Ba'athist government. Indeed, the latter case illustrates how very cautious the United States tends to be. Attempting to bring about regime change in Iraq was a major departure from previous US policy in the Middle East, but in the global context overthrowing the dictator of a single rogue state is a fairly modest business – a minor tweak to the international system, not an effort to effect fundamental changes that would enormously and permanently impact the well-being of all the great powers.

Although there have been many occasions when the United States, like any alliance organizer, has strong-armed its associates – the most flagrant perhaps being the Suez Crisis, in which Eisenhower placed enormous pressure on France, Britain, and Israel to end their military adventure in Egypt – it generally has employed a light touch. For example, it is notable that despite Lyndon Johnson's desperate entreaties the United States never succeeded in convincing its European allies to send troops to fight alongside the US Army in Vietnam, while the Reagan Administration displayed a generally forgiving attitude toward its Continental allies despite their often merciless criticism of, and occasional attempts to undercut, American foreign policy. Indeed, in 1986 Spain and France refused even to allow American F-111 aircraft to overfly their territory on their way to bomb Libya,[114] a controversy that foreshadowed current allied dissention over the Global War on Terrorism (GWOT).

The history of recent decades indicates that, far from being a mad rogue, the United States arguably has been overly indulgent of some of its dissenting allies. Its reluctance to punish uncooperative European states appears to have so convinced its NATO allies of its pliability that many of them have seen little reason not to oppose American policy initiatives. In regard to the GWOT, some American allies were quite unhelpful even as the United States attempted to build a coalition to overthrow Afghanistan's Taliban regime, an astonishingly obvious state sponsor of al Qaeda, and by the time that the United States attempted to organize a coalition to overthrow Iraq's government many of them, led by France and Germany, were working publicly to thwart Washington.[115] If the United States fails utterly to dissuade them from harsh public criticism of its policy, it can be presumed that allies have little fear that they will pay a high price for their actions. Whatever "tools" are in the American diplomatic kit, they clearly failed to compel France and Germany, among others, in 2002/3.

This is not, however, to argue that the United States should attempt to enforce rigid alliance unity. Even if American domestic political opinion allowed a jackbooted approach, which it surely would not, most European leaders now perceive the Transatlantic link as having little enough value that, surely, they would gladly sever it rather than submit to "party discipline." However, the Iraq example does illustrate a problem that the United States faces in regard to its alliance structure, particularly with reference to its European allies: American policymakers must walk a tightrope, neither driving allies away nor being so indulgent of them that the US alliance structure loses coherence and supposed partners, like France, act as de facto strategic competitors, leveraging their favored position to do greater damage to American national interests than they could if they were simply acknowledged as being less-than-friendly to Washington. This is likely to be an ever-more acute problem with NATO, in particular, as the alliance no longer has a clear purpose and its European members face no threatening Soviet superpower; the Transatlantic relationship is further complicated by the rise of the EU as a potential competitor to the United States for NATO leadership.[116]

Clearly, both an excess and deficit of "niceness" can have undesirable consequences. This observation undermines the rogue superpower critique, but it is also important to recognize the inherent differences between a superpower's relationship with weak allies to whom it provides a security surplus and its inter-action with peers and near-peers in an international security environment in which a "marketplace of power" is flourishing – that is, when states have a panoply of potential allies, partners, and antagonists. During the Cold War, the European states were de facto security dependents of the United States;[117] this gave Washington enormous leverage over them, which it could exercise when it chose to do so.[118] The security environment prevailing in Eastern Eurasia in the twenty-first century will be very dissimilar; the United States will not enjoy a similarly high degree of leverage, and it is not plausible that Washington can construct an alliance in which it acts as a "security patriarch." However, at the same time, it would be undesirable for the United States to display a casual atti-tude toward allied perfidy, as the diplomatic environment will be such that "allies" hostile to US foreign policy aims could be far more dangerous than they are in the current environment. An unwillingness to punish unfaithful allies would undermine Washington's leverage with other partners and encourage them to pursue their own ends without regard to whether they were damaging the interests of the United States.

Lacking the firm blocs of the Cold War period, Eastern Eurasia will be a fluid strategic environment in which there will be a complex network of relationships among states that will evolve over time. This will require more diplomatic acumen than generally was necessary during Soviet–American competition. Merely resolving to either "be nice to" or "be tough with" Eastern Eurasian allies would likely result in grief – every bilateral relationship will be unique, and will solidify or fracture over time according to its own logic.

Leaving the Beltway: moving beyond unipolarity

It was very common for analysts of the post-Cold War period to work from the premise that the issue of whether or not unipolarity would endure essentially would be decided by Washington. The belief that Washington can preserve unipolarity indefinitely if it simply exercises competent alliance leadership remains a common, albeit extraordinarily hubristic, belief inside the Beltway.[119] Such a perspective treats countries other than the United States as though they are simply waiting to be manipulated, prudently or poorly, by American leaders – Washington is thought to be the sun around which all lesser political bodies revolve. (One suspects that Chinese leaders, among others, have a rather differ-ent perspective.) This "Americentric" perspective is contrary to the lessons of history, and even common sense.

One reasonably could posit that there have been several examples of long-lived *regional* unipolarity during and before the Columbian Epoch – for example, the Roman Empire from the Second Punic War onward, several Chinese dynasties at various times, and the Umayyad caliphate.[120] Yet there has never been a long-lived period of global unipolarity since the creation of a unitary world system. Indeed, there has only been one period of clear unipolarity during that time, and thus far it has endured for less than two decades. More-over, this unipolar period resulted from the fall of a bipolar system that had arisen in the unique circumstances surrounding the corrosion and collapse of the previous multipolar world order.

In the latter half of the twentieth century, the United States served as an off-shore balancer in Europe, but did so in a very remarkable way. Rather than acting as a counterweight to a would-be European hegemon threatening the integrity of the great power system, the United States acted as a quasi-hegemon in Western Europe and the peer competitor to a Soviet Union that itself was the hegemon of East-Central and Eastern Europe. This very assertive American presence in Europe was necessary because World War II had delivered the deathblow to the multipolar great power system and created a very real danger that an aggressively expansionist Heartland tenant could achieve hegemony over Eurasia.

By September 1945, there were, with the exception of the Soviet Union, no great powers in Eurasia. Germany and Japan had been authoritatively knocked out of the great power ranks, while the war had demonstrated that Italy never had been more than a pseudo-great power. Great Britain and recently-liberated France continued to cling to a sort of "grandfathered" status, but neither, truly, was a power of the first rank; these countries were shadow powers, ghostly revenants of once-mighty states. Because of American insistence, China was also treated formally as though it was a great power, but it was economically underdeveloped, had been enormously damaged by the Japanese occupation, and still was in a state of civil war.

Moscow and Washington were *the* major players standing at the end of World War II, and the former had been bled white by one of the most staggering demographic and economic disasters in modern times – in less than one thirty-year generation, the Soviet people had suffered World War I, the Russian Civil War, collectivization and state-organized famine,[121] Stalin's purges, and World War II. Indeed, the fact that Moscow absorbed such staggering damage and, nonetheless, attained superpower status and plausibly threatened to achieve hegemony over the Eurasian continent illustrates how badly the great power system had broken down; in more usual historical circumstances, such a pro-foundly damaged polity more likely would be struggling merely to insure the survival of its regime and prevent the catastrophic erosion of its international position.

In terms of national health, the United States of course was quite different from the USSR. Overall, America clearly was a polity on the ascent; while the Great Depression (which was, in any case, a global event) to some degree had undermined confidence in the US economic system, those with an appropriately long-term view could see that the "trend lines" for American power were decid-edly positive. While the United States was relatively weak militarily during the 1920s and 1930s, this was a national choice, not a destiny, as World War II would soon demonstrate. The destruction of the old multipolar order accelerated this ascent, and the United States left World War II in a stronger condition than when it had entered it and even had acquired a temporary monopoly over the most powerful weapon yet devised by humankind.

The tradition of American isolation from European power politics remained strong in the interwar years – indeed, was reinvigorated by the commonly held, though preposterous, belief that US entry into World War I was the consequence of a conspiracy of arms merchants and other malefactors – and was potent enough to compel President Roosevelt to undertake a long and subtle campaign to create conditions under which American assistance to the Allied powers, and eventual outright entry into the war, would be acceptable. However, World War II and the immediate post-war years broke the back of the American isolationist tradition and it never again was ascendant. A good portion of the credit for this sea change must be given to key Truman Administration figures such as Dean Acheson, George Marshall, George Kennan, and the president himself, but the remarkable clarity of the Soviet threat to US interests, itself, was an important factor in the defeat of isolationism. There simply was no other power available to act as the protector of the Western European states, and the fact that the USSR threatened the autonomy, if not the actual physical survival, of these polities increasingly became clear to all but the most deluded observers.[122]

Although international political conditions surely will differ enormously in the coming decades from those of the middle 1940s, it would be grossly irresponsible for the United States to shrug off the burdens of great power status and return to the slumber that it once enjoyed. Almost certainly, if the United States had refused to take an active role in European politics in the middle of the twentieth century, a world would have emerged in which American values would not have flourished – and even their survival on the North American continent would have been profoundly threatened. America's refusal to play a substantial role in the great power struggles of this century likely would have similarly deleterious effects. Importantly, if the United States withdraws to its hemisphere a third world war is far more likely. In a meta-region full of young, rising powers, the presence of a strategically mature superpower can be expected to have a stabilizing effect; the enormous military resources possessed by America compels would-be aggressors to consider carefully before launching a strategic adventure. Even more chillingly, as noted above, it is possible that the multipolar system could become sufficiently unbalanced that it would collapse, with a power such as China building a coalition that would allow it ultimately to emerge as the master of Eastern Eurasia and the greatest power in the world. The United States is the "court of last resort" protecting against such an eventuality.

The latter possibility does not contradict the above argument that US unipolarity is unsustainable – as an extra-Eurasian power lacking the ruthlessness to destroy potential great power competitors preventively, Washington simply cannot sustain unipolarity indefinitely. Nonetheless, while the emerging multipolar system appears robust, it still should receive "care and feeding" – otherwise, it is vulnerable to grossly unbalancing events, such as the creation of a very aggressive coalition dedicated to achieving Eurasian hegemony and willing, if necessary, to fight a third world war to achieve it. Most likely such a coalition would not be able to simply bully its way to hegemony; it probably *would* have to fight, the result being a war enormously costly in blood, perhaps even one that would dwarf World War II in its price. If the aggressive coalition won, in turn, the multipolar system would be destroyed and the United States would face a competitor far more powerful than itself, and, in all likelihood, a world in which democracy and personal liberty would be in eclipse. In any case, *it is a geopolitical imperative for the United States that no power or coalition attains hegemony in Eastern Eurasia*, much less that an explicitly hostile state or coalition succeeds in doing so.

If the United States is to guard its national interests successfully in this century, it is vital that it ensures that the transition from unipolarity to multipolarity occurs in as gentle a manner as possible. In this capacity, it is important to understand that the United States is in long-term relative decline, but, at the same time, to acknowledge that it has very great military, financial, and diplomatic resources at its disposal. If Washington deploys these resources wisely, it can maximize its security over the long term and minimize the probability of a great power war.

Comparing nineteenth-century Britain and twenty-first-century America

When discussing the US role in the world, particularly the question of whether Washington should endeavor to act as an arbiter, comparisons between twenty-first-century America and nineteenth-century Britain are well-nigh inevitable.[123] There are, indeed, considerable similarities, but also some critical differences, between the role that nineteenth-century Britain played in Europe and that which the United States should have in Eastern Eurasia in this century. In both cases, the extra-continental polity: is enormously wealthy; possesses the world's premier navy, as well as other noteworthy military resources; and lacks large-scale continental territorial ambitions (an important consideration, as it diminishes fear of the offshore power and places it in a favorable position to act as an honest broker in territorial controversies). Moreover, both states have a clear and overriding geopolitical imperative: to prevent the rise of a hegemon (or hegemonic coalition) capable of upsetting the continental balance of power. In both the nineteenth- and twenty-first-century cases there is an obvious leading hegemonic candidate – Napoleonic France, and, later, Russia in the past, and China in the future – and the offshore sea powers must insure that there always is a potential combination sufficiently strong to guarantee that the most potent land power is incapable of permanently and decisively altering the balance of power in its favor. To achieve this, the extra-continental state must be diplomatically apt and ready to use economic means and naval power to shape the security environment and be prepared, if necessary, to act militarily on the continent itself.

Key differences between the British and American cases include the fact that the European great power environment was a more mature one. The nineteenth-century international system had a well-developed set of "rules" whose broad outlines were first agreed to in the 1648 Treaty of Westphalia,[124] and which developed further during the ensuing years.[125] Eastern Eurasia, in contrast, is still very much in flux and the emerging multipolar system lacks clear diplomatic and military boundaries.[126] When one considers the number of potential flashpoints in the region – the Taiwan Strait, the Spratly and Parcel Islands, Kashmir, and so forth – this is a most unsettling fact.

The problem of communication among the powers is further exacerbated by the lack of cultural commonality in Eastern Eurasia. Compared to the nineteenth-century European powers – which, with the arguable exception of Orthodox Russia, all were, civilizationally speaking, Western – Eastern Eurasia is a veritable Babel. The countries of the meta-region culturally are very distinct; in Samuel Huntington's civilizational scheme, it contains seven civilizations: Sinic, Japanese, Buddhist, Hindu, Orthodox, Islamic, and Western.[127]

In addition, the United States is different from Britain militarily in significant respects. Washington presently is the greatest land power in the world, while London never was. Moreover, it easily is the greatest airpower, and even in the realm of sea power it enjoys a greater advantage over its potential competitors than Britain did. Although the Royal Navy was *the* force guarding Britain's critical national interests, and even national survival, it never possessed an overwhelming advantage over all combinations of potential foes.[128] By contrast, today, the United States Navy probably possesses more fighting power than *all* of the world's other navies combined. While this advantage will diminish greatly over coming decades, it is nonetheless notable, particularly given that sea power is highly relevant strategically in Eastern Eurasia. In short, the United States is not without some very potent military assets that its leaders can also leverage to diplomatic advantage if they are skillful.

The United States does, however, have one major disadvantage relative to Britain that perhaps will hamper its ability to pursue its interests in Eastern Eurasia effectively: it is a modern democracy whose elite is intensely divided on strategic questions and whose aggressive media tends to be highly critical of government foreign policy. Certainly, members of the nineteenth-century British policy elite did have very substantial disagreements – the differences between the foreign policy views of, for example, Benjamin Disraeli and William Gladstone most definitely were non-trivial – but the very different media environment of the twenty-first century surely makes it more difficult for leaders to pursue a consistent and coherent grand strategy.[129]

The pressures of the "24/7 news cycle" compound an already-substantial difficulty facing the United States: the enormous disagreements *within* the American policy community. While one would not want to understate the degree to which policy views did vary within the nineteenth-century British elite, it would be fair to say that most members of that group shared many general assumptions. For example, all but an eccentric minority agreed that the maintenance of the British Empire was strategically desirable; war generally was accepted as a fact of international life, although there certainly was a divergence between those leaders who saw it as a regrettable business that was best avoided when possible and those who lustily sought organized violence in the belief that it honed the martial virtues that kept a nation strong; even (perhaps especially) when they acted with utter ruthlessness, most policymakers saw Britain as a force for good in the world and believed that by pursuing the national interest they were indirectly benefiting humanity more broadly; and there was a broad consensus that Britain must remain the strongest naval power in the world regardless of the cost of maintaining that status. Importantly, this elite consensus on broad strategic goals ensured that the British government in power at any given time would not desire to tear out, by its roots, the "strategic tree" planted and nurtured by its predecessors – continuity more-or-less was maintained, and, thus, it was possible for Britain to maintain a reasonably coherent long-term grand strategy.

During the early years of the Cold War an elite consensus broadly similar to that in nineteenth-century Britain existed, but by the late 1960s that comity was obviously breaking down, a fact reflected in the increasingly stark differences in national security attitudes prevailing in the two major political parties. From the 1940s until the Vietnam War, the Republican and Democratic parties did share what reasonably could be described as a common vision of containment – there were differences, such as the fact that the Eisenhower Republicans were a bit more frugal than the Truman/Kennedy Democrats in regard to conventional defense spending, but both camps saw the Cold War as an inescapable struggle and held many common assumptions. This included a belief that the American alliance structure that was created in the postwar period, and particularly the NATO alliance itself, was vital to US national security; that the United States must be willing to go to war (even *nuclear* war) to preserve Western European political independence from the Soviet Union, and should go to war in other parts of the world as the necessities of worldwide containment dictated; and that Washington was an indispensable force for good because it protected vulnerable nations from totalitarian Communism (the US president being, in a phrase used without irony by most Americans, the "leader of the Free World"). In essence, the clear and present danger emanating from Moscow welded the American elite together and created a unity of purpose.

Centrifugal tensions were, however, always present within the American policy community. Both parties always had fairly strong "political outliers" – for instance, the Republican Party remained the home to a (progressively dwindling) group of isolationists who rallied around Senator Robert Taft of Ohio, while a fair number of left-wing Democrats never came to see the Soviet Union as a deadly enemy, much less accept that there might be a non-negligible number of American Communists who were spying for Moscow and/or hoping to overthrow the constitutional government of the United States and replace it with a Stalinist regime. More importantly, however, during the Vietnam period, the American policy community split into starkly opposing groups of "hawks" and "doves." After the end of the Vietnam War, the hawk/dove split remained, and even deepened.

The distinction between the two groups is inexact, and in some ways the words are misleading, as they imply that one group is unashamedly predatory while the other always searches for common ground and will not confront even the most thuggish aggressor – characterizations to which most members of both camps would, rightly, object. Within these two major groupings there is an enormous variety of attitudes – today's "doves," for example, include religious and philosophical pacifists; those libertarians who are suspicious of an activist foreign policy; Buchananite "paleo-conservatives" who keenly favored vigorous prosecution of the Cold War but oppose a "neoconservative empire"; liberal internationalists who are highly suspicious of unilateral, but not UN- or NATO-approved, military action; and puppet-wielding street protesters, some of whom heartily defend Palestinian suicide bombings but believe that any military action taken in defense of American interests is *mala in se*. The "hawks" are somewhat less diverse philosophically, as they all agree that, in principle, force is a usable tool in international relations, but they display a wide variety of views on when force actually should be used and how it may be justified. In regard to the latter consideration, they range from *Realpolitikers* in the Kissinger mold, who regard moral considerations as essentially irrelevant to foreign policymaking, to the Wilsonian perspective George W. Bush and those figures in his administration who have (rather inaccurately) been labeled as "neoconservatives."[130]

In recent decades, the two major American political parties have drifted far apart on foreign policy issues. While there are still a few odd cases peppered throughout the policymaking elite, they are now very much the exception, and one can safely assume that when the American executive branch changes hands from one party to the other the foreign policy paradigm prevailing at the top levels of the national security bureaucracy will shift significantly. While the attitudinal differences between the George W. Bush Administration and its immediate predecessor are unusually sharp, and certainly far more pronounced than the differences between the Clinton and G.H.W. Bush Administrations, this is not likely a one-time anomaly: the gap in attitudes toward foreign policy appears to be growing over time, as doves and hawks increasingly flock together under the banners of the Democratic and Republican parties, respectively.

For purposes of this work it is not necessary to explore in detail the intellectual history that led to this division; the important fact for the strategic policy of the United States is that it exists and there is no compelling reason to believe that it is diminishing – indeed, over the course of the GWOT, it appears to have sharpened. This will make it more difficult for the United States to sustain a *consistent* grand strategy that reflects the geopolitical realities of the twenty-first century.

This does not, however, necessarily mean that Washington will fail to achieve its most vital strategic goals; after all, American strategy was far from perfectly coherent during the Cold War. A grand strategy may be successful even if it is somewhat unstable, but abrupt and frequent changes in policy are a form of "self-inflicted Clausewitzian friction" and make it less likely that a polity will achieve its goals.

Even before Halford Mackinder constructed his Heartland theory, most members of the British policymaking elite understood intuitively that all other great powers were potentially hostile and that it was imperative that no single power – whether France, Russia, Germany, or any other polity – be allowed to acquire hegemony over Europe. While the American policy elite similarly would agree that no Eastern Eurasian hegemon should emerge, it is far from certain that its members actually would be willing to take the actions necessary to prevent this.

It is likely that, even with absent American involvement, the powers of Eastern Eurasia themselves would be able to prevent a candidate hegemon (presumably China) from attaining its goals. Yet, although this certainly would be very preferable to hegemonic ascendancy in the region, *such an "internal" balancing would not be optimal from Washington's perspective because it would leave the United States at the margins of the most critical geopolitical contest of the twenty-first century.* The United States would risk becoming the "EU of the Western Hemisphere," predominant in its region but a less-than-full participant in those political events shaping the international security environment. This would allow other, more active, states to set the "rules of the international game" for the simple reason that they would be the ones actually playing the sport – in world politics, it is the players who determine the rules, and the most powerful ones have the greatest say in the matter. The former great powers of Europe provide a vivid example of what happens to polities that willingly withdraw from the rougher side of international life – they are left to stand on the sidelines, demanding, as Robert Kagan argues, that the rules of international interaction be shaped so as to allow them to have a major voice in determining the international environment, with international courts, multilateral organizations, and other entities created to take the place of armies, navies, and air forces.[131] These new organizations are then treated with almost religious reverence – and, of course, ignored by active great powers when it is in their interest to do so. The result, for the inactive powers, is frustration and impotent fury.

A state acting as the arbiter of great power politics on a distant continent, by contrast, is in an enviable position. The United States is unfettered by the historical and geographical shackles that bind states which are located geographically in the Old World. For example, it has only a tangential interest in the cultural/religious and historical aspects of the relationship between Pakistan and India (and, unlike Indians or Pakistanis, most Americans have no opinion whatsoever about the rights and wrongs of the Kashmir dispute and similar questions), and whether or not Russia feels its border with China is secure certainly is more Moscow's concern than Washington's. In short, the stakes for the United States on most questions are relatively small (although it must always keep overarching geopolitical imperatives in mind), but its military power is such that it may intervene decisively in matters that are of deadly importance to specific states within a region. As a result, it enjoys enormous leverage – in an overused catchphrase, an asymmetrical advantage – that can be used to further its own goals.

Whatever the strategic advantages of acting as an outside arbiter, however, it still is plausible that the United States will not prove willing to perform that role consistently. Although some American leaders, perhaps including some presidents, surely will favor a policy of geopolitical balancing, it is just as certain that many will not. Arbitration is, after all, an explicit exercise in *Realpolitik*, and to practice it successfully leaders must be willing to punish recalcitrant allies, assist regimes that may be less-than-desirable in regard to their human rights record and/or democratic credentials, ignore "world opinion" and international organizations when necessary, and otherwise act in a fashion that is not in keeping with political idealism. However, there is a very substantial strain of Wilsonianism in the US-policymaking elite. While this manifests itself in varied ways, it crosses "hawk/dove lines" – for example, it is notable that, despite the very substantial differences between Carter and Reagan, both tended to view with unease the seemingly amoral international maneuvering of their predecessor Nixon.[132]

In fairness, it should be noted that this ambivalence toward *Realpolitik* is not entirely disadvantageous to the United States. Although it complicates the pursuit of the national interest, it also yields benefits such as potentially increasing the level of trust with which foreign governments treat assurances that they receive from US leaders, as this idealism (and the American media's eagerness to enforce its mores) limits the American capacity for perfidiousness. It also offers advantages in regard to public diplomacy: the fact that it stands for a very clear set of philosophical principles does win the United States the admiration of many individuals worldwide. This, however, is a double-edged sword, as it is exceptionally easy to charge the US government with betraying its principles, while brazenly ruthless states such as the PRC are virtually immune to accusations of hypocrisy. These factors present policymakers with challenges that would be daunting under any circumstances: attempting to balance realist considerations with idealism is never simple and most American leaders clearly lean in favor of one or the other. This, however, is nothing new for the United States – the tension between realism and idealism was one of the great themes in the debate over American conduct of the Cold War. More problematic is the fact that many of the dangers to US national interests that the great struggle for Eastern Eurasia presents are indirect, even subtle. Given the great split in worldview within the American-policymaking class, this will make it very difficult to achieve a longstanding consensus on what role the United States should play in Eastern Eurasia.

While the United States will not be able to organize an "East Eurasian NATO" of which it is the unquestioned leader, it is, by virtue of its military power, wealth, and lack of territorial ambition in the region, ideally positioned to act as a broker of coalitions and arbiter of greater power politics. In turn, it may leverage these advantages to serve its own strategic interests – most importantly, maintaining its position as the most powerful state in the multipolar system and denying that position to China or any other contender. Yet to succeed in achieving its geopolitical goals, the United States must navigate between two rocky shores. It should neither strive to be a hegemon nor an inactive arbiter, which, as it did twice in the twentieth century, only appears in Eurasia to fight great power wars; rather, it should endeavor to be the strongest pole in a multipolar environment, constantly active but never so overweening as to ultimately undermine its own position. This is a tall order, but the prize is worth the effort, as doing so will allow the United States to remain the strongest power in the world.

Conclusion

Surely, American leaders will struggle mightily over the question of what their country's role will be in the twenty-first century. Given its distance from the theater of geopolitical decision, Washington has a great deal of flexibility, and the role that it will endeavor to play is far from certain at this point. There are many factors that may tempt the United States to shy away from pursuing a vigorous policy in Eastern Eurasia; under the best of circumstances, acting as the outside arbiter in the region would be a difficult task for a modern democracy. Moreover, at present, even many American leaders who are, in principle, willing to engage wholeheartedly in Eastern Eurasia do not yet recognize that the multipolar geopolitics of the twenty-first century will be radically different from the geopolitics of the Cold War. The United States must, however, play a nuanced role in Eastern Eurasia if it is to shape the international security environment to suit its preferences; there is no other plausible way that it can remain the most influential power in the world.

Americans might find neoisolationist withdrawal from Eurasian politics satisfying in the short term, but this would doom Washington to near-irrelevance. In turn, this ultimately might prove disastrous. Similarly, if Washington were to adopt the European tactic of attempting to achieve goals through transnational institutions, it would be de facto choosing to remove itself from great power politics – a US military that would only be used with the permission of the international community (including the consent of both China and Russia, which of course are both permanent members of the UN Security Council) would not participate in great geopolitical struggles. The opposite tack is, however, also impractical: the United States cannot realistically hope to replicate the Cold War experience with NATO; that tightly bound alliance was a marvelous innovation, perfectly suitable to the bipolar and intensely ideological Cold War, but irrelevant to the Eastern Eurasia of tomorrow. Instead, the United States is faced with the daunting task of managing its own "soft landing" from the heights of unipolarity. However, if it does this well, it will be able to continue to shape in a fashion that will serve its interests and minimize the probability of a critical breakdown in the multipolar system resulting in great power war and/or the emergence of a Eurasian hegemon.

5 Strategizing without a license

The non-state challenge to world order

Heretofore in this assessment of the future of international politics, the discussion devoted to actors below the great power level has been very limited, as the sheer number of political entities active in Eastern Eurasia is so large that addressing even a substantial percentage of them would overwhelm the analysis. However, in order to assess the future of the great power system, one must consider the broad events shaping the international political environment, and one of the most important features of today's political landscape is the ongoing struggle against Islamist extremism that Washington refers to as the Global War on Terrorism or, more recently, the Long War.[133] Beyond its obvious significance for the near- and medium-term future, the GWOT also foreshadows one of the more difficult challenges that the United States and other great powers likely will face in the future: the continuing development of a variety of military and civilian technologies and the dispersal of those technologies will make it increasingly likely that sub-state actors will be able to both attract followers and inflict grave damage even on militarily very powerful countries.

Fortunately, there presently are no Islamist great powers, and there is no prospect that any will emerge in the foreseeable future (although one can contrive distressingly plausible scenarios in which the Pakistani state and its nuclear arsenal fall into Islamist hands), and thus the issue at hand is only indirectly related to great power politics. Islamist terrorism does, however, present an alarmingly violent challenge to international order and it presently is *the* strategic obsession of the United States – and likely will remain so at least for several more years, thus distracting Washington from the great power struggles described herein – and thus is clearly relevant to the this work. In addition, Islamists are a massive, and apparently increasing, menace to Russia's domestic tranquility,[134] and also present a not-inconsiderable threat to EU countries and the PRC.

It would, however, be shortsighted to assume that Islamist terrorist groups will be the *only* significant terror organizations of the twenty-first century. Terrorism is a tactic that can be adopted by the adherents of almost any ideology, and for reasons discussed below there is every reason to believe that global Islamist organizations such as al Qaeda represent the vanguard of a powerful development driven by mass-communications technology and other factors: the emergence of international groups, controlled by strategic entrepreneurs who will be able to present a substantial threat to world order and the security of individual states.[135] Some discussion of international terrorism and the danger that it may present even to great powers, thus, is warranted, as "strategic entrepreneurs" likely will play a significant role in the international political system, and how the great powers choose to address the challenges presented by substate actors will shape relationships within the great power "club."

The Islamist threat in context

Islamist terrorism is precisely the sort of transnational phenomenon that convinces some commentators that geopolitics is no longer a relevant field of intellectual inquiry. Islamist terrorist networks are international in character, terrorists move easily from one country to another and frequently communicate among themselves and to outsiders through the internet, and there is no readily identifiable geographical center of gravity that would, if conquered, remove the terrorist threat to the West.[136] Islamist terror is not, however, truly a post-geographic problem, and when three critical points are considered, it becomes very clear that it is indeed a problem with a strong geographic component.

First, it is clear that state sponsorship remains an important factor in international terrorism. While some terrorist groups survive without state backing of any kind, this, generally, has not been the case with the most significant terrorist groups originating in the Muslim world. Islamist groups of various kinds – Hezbollah, Hamas, Palestinian Islamic Jihad, the al Qaeda network, and others, as well as, essentially secular organizations such as the Palestine Liberation Organization, all have relied on direct and/or indirect state assistance of various kinds.[137] Al Qaeda, for example, in the past relied greatly on states such as Sudan for safe haven, and, later, was very closely linked to Afghanistan's Taliban regime. (Indeed, the loss of its Afghan sanctuary and the subsequent scattering of the al Qaeda leadership likely had a very significant effect on the organization's ability to launch terrorist attacks against the United States.) Islamist groups are used as instruments of state power, a fact that provides the United States and its allies with leverage against both the terrorists and their sponsors. Terrorists may be elusive, but their state supporters have immobile financial, military, and political assets that can be destroyed in retaliation for the acts of their minions. At the extreme, a government can be overthrown and its territory occupied, as occurred in Afghanistan and Iraq – a precedent that should give even a reckless terrorist sponsor pause.

Second, if human geography is considered – as it most definitely should be – there is clearly a geographical aspect to the problem of Islamist terrorism. Islamism is, obviously, a phenomenon with both a political-ideological and religious character, and it is not spread evenly throughout the world (or even the Islamic-majority portions thereof). Indeed, there is not even a single "Islamism" any more than there is a single "Fascism" – there is the obvious cleavage between Sunni and Shia radicals, but beyond that there are subtler differences associated with particular groups and their political environment.[138] Some Islamist organizations, including a variety of Chechen, Pakistani/Kashmiri, and Palestinian groups, have a nationalist character, and most of the terrorists associated with those groups presumably are chiefly interested in striking their own local nemesis; the "Great Satan" may be loathed, but he is far away, while hated Russians, Indians, or Israelis are near at hand. Only a small proportion of individuals who are radicalized intellectually go on to become *jihadis*, much less the sort of transnational terrorists who threaten the United States. (The Gulf states obviously are a key recruiting ground for the latter, particularly al Qaeda terrorists.[139]) It was obvious after the September 11 attacks that Islamists worldwide (as well as a distressingly large number of non-Islamist Muslims) derived psychological satisfaction from the strike against the United States, but those who actually carried it out were members of an elite transnational "Murder, Inc.," and apparently regarded seriously the very ambitious goals publicly stated by bin Laden, including the humbling of the United States and the establishment of a caliphate.[140] Given the character of their ideology, all Islamists in some sense are a threat to the United States, but they are not all equally threatening.

It is obvious that some Muslim societies produce a far greater number of *jihadis* on a per capita basis than do others. Many observers have attempted to link terrorism to economic deprivation, but the connection between the two, on the whole, is weak. Some terrorists clearly do feel a high degree of socio-economic frustration – Arab *jihadis*, for example, are drawn disproportionately from the middle class of their societies, and many are young males who have had difficulty finding work appropriate to their high level of education. Yet, if there were a simple correlation whereby greater poverty equals more terrorism, the overwhelming majority of transnational Islamist terrorists would come from tragically impoverished countries such as Nigeria and Bangladesh rather than richer lands like Saudi Arabia and the United Arab Emirates. Clearly, Islamist terrorism is not just the twenty-first-century equivalent of a bread riot, but a complex phenomenon resulting from a mixture of religious-ideological indoctrination and both broad cultural and personal psychological factors. It is far from certain, however, that Islamist terrorism presents such a grave and persistent challenge to world order that it will play a truly major role in shaping the geopolitical environment over the long term. As a rule of thumb, it requires powerful polities to change the international scene significantly, for either better or worse, and – bin Laden's fantastical caliphate aside – not only is there, as previously noted, very little prospect that an Islamist great power will appear, but there is even some indication that the citizens of the only Islamist major regional power, Iran, are growing very impatient with their repressive and economically incompetent theocrats.

Third, there is the all-too-obvious point that Islamist terrorism is an acute problem in the Persian Gulf region and therefore threatens the ability of states worldwide to obtain oil at reasonable prices. Indeed, insofar as Islamist extremism has an international center, it is the Persian Gulf, as the one existing Islamist medium power is located there, as is the Saudi peninsula, a hothouse of Islamist radicalism and a piece of territory which al Qaeda is obsessed with placing in "pious" hands. Also, Iraq of course is in the Gulf region, and at present Islamists are struggling mightily to ensure that the latter country does not develop into a stable ally of the United States and model for the development of other democratic and intellectually progressive Arab states.

Although Iran, eventually, may reject Islamist radicalism, this does not necessarily mean that the Islamist threat to world order is waning – it is all too easy to devise scenarios in which, for instance, the Saudi royal family is compelled to take a one-way trip to friendlier shores and the world's largest proven oil reserves fall into the hands of Islamists. However, it should be understood that even an event of this magnitude would not ensure the triumph of Islamism in the Muslim world. Indeed, a truly significant geopolitical event such as the fall of the Saudi regime might instead inspire the great powers to impose their own order in the Persian Gulf. In recent years, the American "sheriff" has been attempting to reshape the face of Middle Eastern politics with a rump posse and a decidedly unhelpful group of European and other townsfolk, confident in their own belief that they can cut side deals with the outlaws, constantly criticizing and undermining the lawman's efforts. The appearance of a Saudi counterpart to Mullah Omar – and the related prospect of outrageous oil prices as far as the eye could see – might convince most of the townsfolk that the time had come to join the posse, or at least stay out of the way while the sheriff and his deputies mete out rough justice. With the exception of Russia, a major oil exporter, the great powers have every incentive to ensure that oil remains within a reasonable price band, and stratospherically high petroleum prices could cause a major worldwide recession, or even a Second Great Depression; the latter outcome of course would do grievous harm to all of the world's major economies, including Russia. When truly vital national interests are at stake, sentimental attachments to international law and organizations tend to be pushed to the side, and if governments must be overthrown and control over oil supplies established, statesmen can be enormously inventive at providing tactful justifications for the brutal exercise of power.

Islamism casts a menacing shadow, but it is not an ideology whose adherents presently are capable of threatening world order as acutely as National Socialists and Communists once did. The latter two groups had the machinery of mighty states at their disposal, with all that implies – armies of millions, enormous industrial production, and a resulting ability to threaten to extinguish democratic governance in the twentieth century's central region of geopolitical struggle. The Islamists, by contrast, are in every respect quite poor compared to their foes.

This very weakness, however, is a strength in at least one respect: lacking a single clear state center of gravity, it is very difficult for the United States and its allies in the GWOT to actually crush Islamism definitively and thus eliminate its intellectual appeal. By May 1945 it was clear to all but the most deluded Nazis that the Allies' application of massive violence was putting an end to the National Socialist dystopia. Similarly, when the Soviet flag came down from the Kremlin, it confirmed what many had already come to suspect – that far from being the future, Marxism–Leninism soon would be endorsed only by aging despots and tiresome cranks. No such obvious defeat awaits the Islamists – Afghanistan has already fallen, and it did little, if anything, to dissuade *jihadis* from carrying on with their cause. Moreover, while the Islamist movement has well-known international leaders, it would be unreasonable to suppose that their elimination would significantly damage Islamism as a movement. Even the confirmed demise of Osama bin Laden probably would do little to shake the loyalty of al Qaeda supporters; indeed, violent death would place him among the ranks of the "martyrs." Even the overthrow of the Iranian government would not strike Islamism itself a mortal blow, though it might shake deeply the confidence of Shia extremists.

These challenges are further sharpened by the fact that Islamism is a religiously based ideology – if the policy recommendations of a Hitler or Lenin prove catastrophic, that serves as proof to all but the most fanatical believers that their ideas are flawed. The Islamists, however, purport to be Allah's instruments; their failures do not necessarily falsify their theological statements, but could merely demonstrate that, being mere humans, they simply failed in their efforts to implement the divine will. Such supernatural appeals do have certain disadvantages – a long series of failures would likely cause many observers who were previously inclined to be sympathetic to wonder why, if the terrorists indeed enjoyed divine favor, there had been no celestial intervention on their behalf – but these do not carry quite the same emotional impact as Soviet T-34 tanks rolling down the streets of Berlin.[141]

Overall, it would be judicious to regard Islamism as a significant threat to US, Russian, and European national security and, to a limited degree, to world order. It is not, however, so acute a threat to the United States as would be presented by a revisionist great power bent on overturning the international status quo. Islamist terrorist groups are merely the largest current faction in a very old category of international actor: non-state organizations seeking to achieve their political goals through violent means. There is, however, a clear risk that terrorist groups in general will prove increasingly dangerous as technology continues to advance, placing potentially dangerous tools in the hands of an increasing number of radical organizations. Worryingly, many groups may soon enjoy the ability to inflict massive casualties and/or greatly disrupt the orderly working of the international economic system. Moreover, it should be expected that Islamism will cease to be the only intellectual movement spawning substantial numbers of transnational terrorist groups. Thus, it should be expected that the number and ideological variety of terrorist groups will grow significantly in the coming years.

Edward Luttwak compellingly argues that successful strategies contain the seeds of their eventual obsolescence because, over time, foes adapt to those strategies. Strategic actors are not inert; they modify their own behavior in response to the behavior of others, and when a foe develops a powerful new strategy, they seek to neutralize that new strategy, or even, if possible, find some way in which it may be turned against its inventor.[142] Moreover, strategic actors who are not involved directly in the quarrel nonetheless observe the activities of their peers, learning from their innovations and errors. This, no doubt, is how Islamists and others came to adopt suicide bombing; having seen the use of suicide bombing by the (non-Muslim) Tamil Tigers of Sri Lanka,[143] they comprehended how they could use this technique to further their own strategic goals. Given Islam's strong taboo against suicide, one might think this knowledge would have been useless to them. However, they solved this problem just as Lenin did when he wanted to bring revolution to industrially backward Russia: by turning theory (or, in this case, theology) on its head. They argued, in effect, that in certain circumstances, Islam not only permitted killing oneself, but endorsed the act in the strongest terms and promised suicide murderers heavenly delights.

Since suicide bombing, gruesome videotaped murders, and mass-casualty terrorism are not the exclusive intellectual property of Islamists, it is should be expected that adherents of other ideologies will adopt these methods, as well as create new ones. Indeed, the Islamists themselves have poured fuel on ethnic and religious fires burning in many parts of the world, and it is all-too-possible that many innocent Muslims will suffer at the hands of anti-Muslim terrorists (or "militias" which use terror) intent on avenging wrongs committed against their own communities by Islamists.[144] Islamists may be at the cutting edge of "postmodern terrorism," but its techniques are open to all who care to adopt them.[145] It should be remembered that the emergence of postmodern transnational terrorism has been observed by millions who personally may be uninterested in the struggle between Islamism and its foes, but do have other obsessions: environmental degradation, the mistreatment of animals, the desire to operationalize the teachings of a cult leader, ethnic bitterness, a wish to overthrow their government, hatred for globalization, or whatnot. By observation, they, too, are learning which terrorist techniques might be effective in furthering their goals and how counterterrorists seek to defeat those methods.

It is likely that, when future historians look back on this "post-9/11 era," they will see Islamism as having been in the vanguard of an important shift in the threat that terrorist groups posed to international order and the domestic security of great powers. Al Qaeda demonstrated conclusively that it had become possible for a relatively small group to inflict grievous damage even to a superpower, and pointed the way forward for any group inclined to use terrorist techniques to obtain its own goals. While the current GWOT is focused on protecting the West from Islamists, all of the great powers potentially are vulnerable to large-scale terrorist attacks that may inflict enormous human and economic damage.

Rise of the Lilliputians

The notion that strategy may be properly practiced only by the duly authorized representatives of states is a relatively new one. Even a casual student of history can name all manner of individuals who have practiced "statecraft" regardless of whether they headed formal states: among others, nomadic barbarian chieftains, heads of military religious orders such as the Teutonic Knights,[146] popes and other clerics, warlords, and revolutionaries all have practiced strategy. The modern state is a recent innovation but strategy is not, and one of the great successes of the former was in pushing non-state actors ever more to the margins of international political life.[147]

Even in the twentieth century, perhaps the historical zenith for state power, non-state actors did not disappear; rather, the most notable of them focused on winning control over states – Mao Zedong, for example, took a revolutionary party with military resources and used it to take command of the most populous state on earth. The first half of that century was a heyday for conspiratorial political parties willing to use violence to threaten an established political order – the Russian Bolsheviks, the Italian Fascists, and the German National Socialists all were eminent practitioners of this brutal art[148] – because the political conditions of that period offered unusually rich opportunities for clever thugs who aspired to command a great power. The danger over the next few decades, however, is not so much that a Lenin or Hitler will come to control a major state – although that possibility should never be dismissed casually – but that terrorists with minimal material and human resources nonetheless will be able to inflict immense damage to such polities. Many observers have warned of the possible use of WMDs by terrorists,[149] and continuing proliferation will cause this threat to become progressively more acute. This is made all the more disturbing by the fact that *the number of non-state actors practicing violence may grow exponentially in the coming decades.*

Francis Fukuyama has written insightfully about how social order can evolve from the chaos of human interaction, and the fact that individuals with common goals can self-organize to achieve those goals is an important one to bear in mind when discussing terrorism and similar phenomena.[150] While many terrorist groups indeed are used (and sometimes even created) by states, many of the most dangerous recent practitioners of political violence began their careers as talented amateurs who surrounded themselves with a circle of associates and from this foundation created a great movement. Some had mentors, like Stalin and Trotsky, who surely learned much from observing Lenin's machinations, but many (including, most famously, Hitler) basically were autodidacts who learned strategy as they practiced it.[151] Few of the most notorious leaders of the twentieth century spent much of their lives in formal military or governmental institutions that teach the art of strategy over long decades, giving promising individuals incrementally greater responsibility while imbuing them with the culture of the institution. Rather, from Mussolini to bin Laden, most were strategic entrepreneurs who created their own opportunities.[152]

Given the ongoing revolution in communications, this entrepreneurial trend is likely to accelerate. It, of course, now is possible for millions to voice their theories via the internet, but isolated individuals present a negligible threat to international order – they are the descendants of oddballs with mimeograph machines and, like their forbears, are harmless when they attract no wider support. However, the occasional bin Laden is mixed in among these eccentrics, and such individuals – intelligent, charismatic, and thoroughly unreasonable but *not* instrumentally irrational[153] – truly are dangerous.

Bin Laden himself is especially notable because he may be the prototype for a new kind of strategic entrepreneur. Most of the twentieth century's particularly notorious strategists were Horatio Algers of a sinister kind: starting as political malcontents with few or no followers, they, nonetheless, were able to build powerful national political movements because they possessed formidable military, oratorical, organizational, and/or other skills. However, these individuals were also exceptionally fortunate. Budding tyrants are not unlike sea turtle hatchlings – for every lucky one who survives fate's whims and goes on to control a state, hundreds or thousands of his or her fellows meet an early and disastrous end. Most of them are executed by intraparty rivals or the governments which they sought to overthrow, die in a cell, or otherwise are neutralized well before they reach power. And, of course, even those few who do seize a crown often suffer later reverses and fail to die content in the knowledge that they have lived up to their full despotic potential – as Saddam Hussein no doubt could have attested.

By contrast, Osama bin Laden became a substantial international danger despite the fact that he never took over his home country of Saudi Arabia. Thanks to his partnership with Mullah Omar he enjoyed considerable influence in Afghanistan for a time, but the latter was a backward, disordered, and impoverished polity. Yet bin Laden was able to leverage his personal fortune, charisma, and considerable organizational talent to make himself a feared figure who successfully struck the continental United States. He is seen by many millions as an embodiment of *jihad*, and thus commands their affection; in short, he has made himself a sort of outlaw international leader.[154] Bin Laden never will be invited to address the UN General Assembly, but al Qaeda is a force in international politics greater than the majority of countries who sit in that body.

What is perhaps most interesting about bin Laden's rise is the fact that he simply attached himself to a powerful preexisting social, religious, intellectual, and political trend: the rise of Islamist radicalism in the twentieth century.[155] There is, in principle, no reason why other religions, ideologies, and social movements could not give rise to their own bin Ladens. There are millions of people seething with rage for one reason or another and awaiting a charismatic leader who will organize them and channel their anger toward a hated foe.[156] Indeed, it should be noted that even minor entities may prove to be quite dangerous. Aum Shinrikyo, an apocalyptically-minded Japanese cult,[157] provides a worrying example, as it had sufficient human and material resources to develop chemical weapons.[158] The most important terrorist attack undertaken by Aum Shinrikyo – a sarin gas attack on the Tokyo subway system – essentially failed, but the fact that the group was able to organize a large-scale assault that used self-produced chemical weapons is quite disturbing. This was, after all, merely one fringe entity – a minor blip on the global socio-intellectual radar, one of thousands of cults, terrorist groups, ultranationalist organizations, and other entities that exist worldwide. The "democratization" of mass destruction, as WMDs progressively are proliferated to ever more actors, state or otherwise, presents grave dangers.[159]

What is particularly disturbing as one contemplates coming decades is how the proliferation of weaponry may intersect with a parallel global phenomenon: the blooming of a thousand deadly flowers, as modern communications and computer technology make it simple for those interested in mischief to organize and spread their message. The fact that would-be terrorists and other dangerous elements can easily use the Internet to find individuals who share their goals and come together is undesirable but unavoidable in a free (or even partially free) society.

One of the consequences of the information age is that the sheer *quantity* of information traveling through what David J. Lonsdale calls the "infosphere"[160] makes it very easy for malefactors to carry on recruiting and planning while evading the notice of authorities. Moreover, and perhaps even more importantly, the anonymity of modern communications makes the "buy-in" risk for would-be recruits very low, and this is a notable change from the past. Formerly, it generally was rather difficult for an individual with radical political beliefs actually to join an organization dedicated to criminal political activity. Few individuals were sufficiently radicalized that they were willing to seek out groups that committed criminal acts; in most countries, the decision to join an illegal political group, even a non-violent one, was a life-altering choice that carried substantial risks. Thus, recruitment generally would occur on an individual basis, with both sides of the equation accepting danger – recruiters and those they recruited had to accept the possibility that they might be dealing with police informants or provocateurs. Recruitment issues surely did much to limit the size of radical political organizations, even those which were not illegal. It is notable that throughout much of the late nineteenth and early twentieth centuries radical political philosophies such as anarchism and Communism had millions of sympathizers in the United States. Yet, even in the Great Depression, and despite the fact that membership was legal, the Communist Party of the United States (CPUSA) never enjoyed a membership remotely approaching the number of individuals who were sympathetic to its cause, despite the USSR's continuing financial and other support for this nominally independent creature.[161]

Lowering the initial "buy-in" costs that individuals must pay if they are to become involved with a radical movement allows them to slowly become involved in political extremism while running few risks. At first, an interested individual may confine him- or herself to posting on message boards and similar anonymous activity – actions that, at least in a Western democracy, carry virtually no risk, even if the posted messages are illegal (such as a call to murder specific public officials or incitement to riot might be in the United States). This period of consequence-free integration into a "culture of violence" can allow a relatively smooth transition from legal to illegal political activities, which is quite different, for example, from the jarring chasm that a would-be anarchist terrorist had to cross.

The relative ease with which a disgruntled citizen can become a malefactor should be a matter of serious concern. The ability of a tiny percentage of the population to organize itself into a dangerous political movement is obvious to anyone who contemplates the recent history of the anti-globalization movement. Most anti-globalization protesters are non-violent, but small numbers of violent anarchists and other troublemakers have created enormous security problems for the organizers of any major IMF, World Bank, or G-8 meeting – and anti-globalization militants generally confine their illegal activities to vandalism and assault. (If the hooded anarchists lurking outside G-8 meetings carried Glocks instead of sticks and intended to kill rather than wound those whom they were confronting, they would present an exponentially larger security threat. As a result, high-profile international economic meetings surely would no longer be held in city centers, but would be conducted at very secure locations, such as military bases.) In a small but noticeable way, violent anti-globalization protesters have degraded world order, as they have made a previously mundane activity, the conduct of international economic summits, hazardous.[162]

While terrorism today, generally, is associated with national and religious movements, nationalist and religious militants do not possess a natural monopoly on terrorist violence. The proponents of virtually any set of ideas can choose to act violently if they care deeply enough about their cause and come to believe that bloodshed is necessary if their goals are to be achieved in a timely fashion. Environmental extremists, for example, have a clear potential reason to practice violence: many of them believe that global warming and environmental degradation may soon render the earth virtually uninhabitable, a condition that would result in the deaths of billions of humans and untold trillions of other creatures. If the deaths of a relatively small number of people – and in these terms, even several million victims of WMD terrorism would be *comparatively* few – resulted in the adoption of a worldwide rollback of industrialization and a (supposedly) sustainable lifestyle on the part of all people, a radical might see the use of terrorism as morally justified.

Utopian dreams often precede horrific violence (as the history of the twentieth century all-too-clearly attests), and surely many new violent groups will arise in the coming decades. One can expect that a bewildering variety of "boutique" terrorist groups will form as small numbers of like-minded obsessives form extreme subcultures in which political violence is considered acceptable, or even laudable. Most Western countries have had to deal with such groups in the past – the Symbionese Liberation Army (SLA), for instance, was a tiny group with virtually no support in the wider society (indeed, the majority of Americans never had the slightest knowledge of the SLA's very peculiar ideology and probably wondered where the homeland of the "Symbionese" was located), that nonetheless garnered worldwide attention. Also, it is notable that Timothy McVeigh was intellectually nurtured in a political subculture (the American militia movement) that contains a not-insignificant percentage of individuals who ideologically support, but do not actively undertake, violent revolution against the US government, and McVeigh himself is a disquieting example of how much damage even one disturbed individual with very limited resources can inflict. A hundred McVeighs springing from various parts of the political spectrum would damage enormously the civil order of the United States or any other democratic state.

When all of these factors are considered, it is clear that terrorism should be expected to increase mightily in this century. However, heretofore the discussion essentially has extrapolated only from existing trends. As well as providing terrorists with new weapons, massive technological change will be a potent force encouraging considerable – perhaps enormous – numbers of individuals to resort to terrorism. Genetic, biotechnological, artificial intelligence, and other scientific research will promise not only mammoth changes in human lives, but even in what they are – their lifespan, intelligence, and so forth. There is already much intellectual opposition to the possibility that humans and their society will change radically, and the broad mass of humanity has not yet become engaged in debates over – indeed, is not aware of the potential for – massive, technologically-driven change to the species *homo sapiens sapiens*. Yet they will, *because such issues will engage profoundly their religio-political passions*. With such enormous perceived stakes, the rise of terrorist groups dedicated to fighting a desperate rear-guard action "against the future" is certain. The only questions are those of detail – which specific issues will excite the most terrorist violence, how many individuals will rally to the "anti-future" banner and what level of support they will enjoy in broader societies, and so forth.

The great powers and the terrorists

At least in the near-term, Islamist extremism, a worldwide movement that has been gaining momentum for decades and which has produced many of the world's most dangerous terrorist groups, presents the most significant threat to global order. Islamism is the focus of the GWOT but, regardless of the outcome of the ongoing conflicts in Iraq and Afghanistan, it should be expected that the GWOT will not be concluded definitively because Islamism lacks a state center of gravity and, given its theological character, many of its adherents are unlikely to be shaken by worldly setbacks such as those that caused many followers to lose faith in ideologies such as National Socialism and Communism. While effective prosecution of the GWOT should inflict grave damage on international terror networks and at least to some degree reduce the threat presented by existing Islamist terror groups, there is no solid reason to believe that the United States and its allies will "win" the GWOT and that Islamist terrorism therefore will cease to be a substantial threat to world order at any point in the near future.

Indeed, the very use of the word "war" in reference to the struggle against Islamist extremists is unfortunate in one important respect: at least in Western countries, the public tends to associate that term with legally declared conflicts among states that have a formal conclusion. The GWOT, in contrast, is more accurately understood to be a struggle by the United States and those states that would, for whatever reasons, wish to assist it, to maintain international order in the face of opposition by religious-ideological extremists who wish to sow violence and disorder so that they may advance their own agendas. The fact that a not-insubstantial (and probably growing) number of Islamist extremists exist is not, by all appearances, a problem that the United States can solve. Rather, American leaders must accept the existence of tens of millions of potentially violent Islamists as a fact and operate on the assumption that Islamism will not disappear as a major ideology at any time in the foreseeable future. Moreover, Islamism's character as a movement is such that armed forces cannot *decisively* defeat this global menace militarily.

The GWOT, thus, is a struggle in which success is relative rather than absolute. If Washington can so damage international Islamist terror groups that they are unable to undertake successful mass casualty terrorist attacks on US soil, it is fulfilling, tolerably, its obligation to protect its citizens. Moreover, if the United States is able to successfully cooperate with others to prevent mass casualty attacks on their homelands it is doing a commendable job of serving as a bulwark of world order. Eventually, perhaps, Islamism will lose force as an ideology and "burn out," just as anarchism did in the United States and Europe. What was once a potent political movement lost its momentum and its followers quietly drifted away, taking on other causes or even becoming disengaged from politics altogether. *Even if that occurs, however,* when *it would occur cannot be predicted accurately – Islamism could be a potent force for many decades.* Moreover, as this work argues, the downfall of Islamism would not end the danger of catastrophic terrorist attacks; regardless of Islamism's fate, new and malevolent political movements will continue to appear.[163] Indeed, Islamism itself may, instead of "burning out," transform, changing its focus from its current obsessions – remaking Muslim societies and conducting war against Christian, Jewish, Hindu, and other "infidels" – to fighting a *jihad* against the technological forces mentioned above.

Even very competitive states may have a common interest in fighting terrorism, and it of course is possible for a terrorist group to be antagonistic toward many states simultaneously, even if it focuses its activities on only one or two of them. Although the United States and Israel are the overriding obsessions of the "Islamist International" at the moment, the PRC, the EU states, Japan, Russia, India, Saudi Arabia, and a host of other powers also are loathed. The Islamists do not lack ambition; they essentially are at war with the world, a fact that has encouraged several powers that often are confrontational toward Washington, such as Russia and the PRC, to assist it in conducting the GWOT.[164] Moreover, even when a polity does not feel that it is directly threatened by a particular terrorist group, it may fear the consequences of international turmoil and violence – of particular importance is the fact that disorder is bad for international business, a fact illustrated by the global economic repercussions of the September 11 attacks. Even against Islamism, however, one cannot assume that the great powers will lock arms and present a strong and consistent united front. Certainly, they, thus far, have found themselves incapable of agreeing on a common strategy, with most of them vehemently disagreeing with the US decision to invade Iraq, an action which the Bush Administration (wisely or unwisely) considered central to the GWOT.

The most significant question for the purposes at hand is how terrorism will impact relations between the great powers. It seems unlikely that terrorists will actually draw these states together in ways that will change radically how global power politics are conducted overall. It is, however, possible that the great powers will grow increasingly reluctant to support violent non-state groups who act against their peers. The chief reason for this is the increasingly high "stakes" accompanying support for terrorists. *As the potential potency of terrorist attacks increases, making it possible for non-state actors to inflict devastating damage on great power homelands, it is in the common interest of all great powers to strengthen disapproval for such actors and discourage support for them.* Thus, there is even a good case for arguing that the great powers will find it in there interest to share intelligence and otherwise cooperate in the elimination of troublesome groups.

This is not, however, to argue that great powers never will support violent non-state actors. It is easy to imagine that most of the great powers will support such groups at various times, just as they have in the past. However, it is, perhaps, unlikely that the major states will promiscuously support such groups in the fashion that, for example, the Soviet Union did during the Cold War. That state supported terrorist groups, rebels, and other violent non-state actors focused on a bewildering variety of causes; virtually any group that promised to create difficulties for one or more of the USSR's foes could find a friendly ear in Moscow. Soviet leaders could be so promiscuous in their support, frankly, because they could be confident that their clients were either incapable or uninclined to do so much damage to Western interests that a third world war might result. Similarly, the United States supported actors such as the Nicaraguan Contras and the Afghan *Mujahadeen*, even though the latter were in combat with Soviet troops, with little fear that such activities would provoke a superpower war. Support for violent non-state actors, in essence, was seen by the Cold War superpowers as a means of conducting proxy conflict on a limited scale.

Supporting Islamist or similarly apocalyptic-minded groups, however, presents great dangers. Indeed, the Americans almost certainly would not have supported the *Mujahadeen* if they had known that so many of them eventually would morph into extremely dangerous anti-Western terrorists, and the dangers of "blowback" now are well-appreciated. Beyond this, however, is the even more appalling possibility that one might support an actor who "goes too far." The USSR likely spent little time worrying whether the Irish Republican Army (IRA) would plant a radiological device in London; regardless of whether such an attack was within the IRA's capabilities, the IRA leadership could be assumed to understand that an assault of this kind would not be in its interests. Given the events of September 11, 2001, prudent states are unlikely to be so sanguine in the future. To support terrorists who occasionally detonate car bombs on a foe's streets is one thing, but to be indirectly responsible for an extraordinarily devastating attack is quite another.

The latter event can be expected either to lead directly to war or a very dangerous tit-for-tat, as the aggrieved enemy undertakes to respond in kind, perhaps,
for example, by providing WMDs for a non-state actor to use against one's own
homeland.

The emerging environment is, in short, one in which restraint by great powers
would be universally beneficial, and this is the sort of situation which can give
rise to informal or formal constraints on the behavior of those states. The alleged
creation of a taboo against nuclear use is perhaps the best example of this; none
of the great powers have used nuclear weapons in warfare since 1945.[165] Most
likely, however, constraints on the support of violent non-state actors would not
be nearly as sweeping as the nuclear taboo, which restricts the use of nuclear
weapons of all descriptions, including relatively small and "clean" weapons.
Instead, self-imposed limitations on support for non-state actors likely would be
narrow, perhaps only restricting support for groups which endeavor to commit
violent acts on a great power homeland. Thus, it would still be possible for a
major state to support groups which "make trouble" in various ways, but threatening the security of a foe's homeland might be regarded as unacceptable. This
would enhance the security of all the great powers because all of these polities
are vulnerable to WMD-armed terrorists or rebels. Of course, great powers
would also be surrendering possible gains which they would derive from the
support of apocalyptic terrorists, but there is at least a weak precedent for this: it
appears that for more than sixty years, the great powers generally have been
quite reluctant to support violent proxy operations on the territory of their
peers.[166]

This price, however, may appear eminently reasonable – after all, it is
unlikely that any of the great powers would be able to use non-state actors to
secure critical goals, but all could suffer grievous harm at their hands.[167] It thus
would be sensible for all the great powers to refrain from supporting non-state
actors that threaten the soil of their peers. There is, however, no guarantee that
all these states will choose to be reasonable; they may find that the temptation to
support terrorists sufficiently strong that it overcomes their more cautious
instincts. Indeed, it might only be necessary that one great power be willing to
support terrorist actions against a foe's homeland to destroy mutual restraint, as
it is unlikely that its peers would be willing to grant the troublemaking state an
enormous asymmetrical advantage.

Conclusion

The early twenty-first century will most likely see the proliferation of political
movements that use terrorism. Most of the terrorist groups active in Western
countries no doubt will present only a small threat to domestic and international
order, becoming heirs to the tradition of incompetent terrorism pioneered by
organizations such as the Weathermen and the Baader-Meinhof Gang, but it is
quite probable that one or more terrorist groups will emerge that are as dangerous as al Qaeda but have no ideological association with Islamism. At this point,

it is unknowable which, if any, political movements will eventually spawn significant terrorist activity; while anti-globalization, environmentalism, and animal rights movements all are noteworthy contenders, they merely are today's obvious candidates. No one can know what new ideologies will be created by technological and social change, but a violent "neo-Luddite" response to genetic engineering, artificial computer intelligence, and other advances is utterly predictable.

In any event, it is probable that terrorism will continue to be a significant threat to the world's major states. It is, however, unlikely that terrorism will be a critical factor, much less *the* factor, shaping great power politics in this century. One should not, however, dismiss terrorists and other non-state actors inevitably as being minor players whose activities ultimately will matter little to the major states. Rather, their future importance will be largely determined by the *interaction* of such states and entrepreneurial non-state users of violence. If the former shy away from using the latter as cat's paws against their peers, then non-state violent actors probably will not shape profoundly the century's politics. This would not mean that they would never again succeed in attacks similar in scale to 9/11; indeed, non-state actors may even succeed in constructing (or obtaining from a roguish less-than-great power) and using WMDs. However, a limited number of terrorist attacks – no matter how horrible – will not determine the destinies of mighty states to any substantial degree. Although the destruction of downtown New York or Washington is a monstrous prospect, such an act would not permanently undermine US military or economic power, though it certainly would inflict very substantial temporary damage on the American economy. The same can be said of the destruction of downtown New Delhi, Beijing, Moscow, or Tokyo; any observer who does not believe this would do well to consider the stunning damage on Russia/the Soviet Union from 1914 to 1945, and the fact it was enormously more powerful at the end of that period than it was at its dawn.

If, however, the great powers do choose to freely make use of non-state actors to inflict damage on their peers, they will be opening a Pandora's Box. In that case, violent non-state actors may be very important indeed, and their actions would likely have a key impact on global politics. In that case, the overall damage inflicted by terrorist attacks would likely be far greater than would otherwise be the case, as great power patrons could supply weapons (perhaps including WMD), intelligence, and other resources in abundance. Also, great powers which, by proxy, attacked the homeland of their peers would be courting outright war, with ever-greater escalation quite possibly leading to a major conflict.[168] It should be recalled that the catalyst for World War I was a Bosnian Serb assassin whom a great power believed to be sponsored by a state, even though Serbia was a minor polity and the murder of the Archduke Franz Ferdinand was more significant as a potential blow to Austrian prestige (insofar as to not take action would make Vienna appear weak) than in terms of *direct* damage to its vital interests. A world in which all the great powers had reason to fear that one or more of their peers might be plotting to use a proxy to inflict a devastating attack on them would be all the more unstable. Such conditions would likely make the international environment one in which paranoia would be all-too-likely to trump sweet reason when great powers made decisions relating to war and peace.

In short, the great powers have a practical choice to make – whether to show restraint in the support of violent non-state actors who may act against their peers or take their chances "riding the tiger," hoping to gain by the actions of their proxies while themselves avoiding critical damage. It is impossible at this point to know which course they will choose.

6   Strategy 2.0

Great power competition in an era of technological revolution

Discussions of technology and the future of world politics all too often degenerate into meaningless utopian assertions about creating the conditions for permanent global peace. Worthy as this goal is, there is no sound basis for believing that it will be attained in this century for the quite simple reason that this would require a revolution in human nature that is likely not forthcoming. The impact of technology on global politics is, however, an issue of great importance because it is probable that in the near future the *grammar* of international politics and war will change dramatically even if its essential *character* does not. Polities will continue to compete, and will threaten, and sometimes use, organized violence against each other; however, how they make war will change radically.

Faster, cheaper, better: the technological explosion

In *The Age of Spiritual Machines*, inventor Ray Kurzwell argues that there is a "Law of Accelerating Returns" which states that, "As order exponentially increases, time exponentially speeds up (i.e., the time interval between salient events grows shorter as time passes)."[169] The counterpart of this Law is the Law of Increasing Chaos, which states that, "As chaos exponentially increases, time exponentially slows down (i.e., the time interval between salient events grows longer as time passes)." Kurzweil contends, however, that the evolution of machine intelligence is essentially governed solely by the former Law – that "order," expressed by ever more powerful computer processing, is exponentially increasing and will continue to increase, thus making the development of truly intelligent machines not only possible, but inevitable. Indeed, Kurzweil contends that the exponential increase in computer processing will result in personal computers "able to simulate the brain power of a small village by the year 2030, the entire population of the United States by 2048, and a trillion human brains by 2060."[170]

Although this prediction may sound bizarre, it is notable that Kurzweil's calculations simply assume the continuation of longstanding trends that began *c*.1900 with mechanical computing devices and continued with electromechanical, vaccum-tube, discrete transistor, and integrated circuit computers.[171]

Kurzweil assumes that these trends will persist even though he presumes that sometime in the early twentieth century (*c*.2020) the integrated circuit chip will reach a technological dead end and that it will be physically impossible to further improve these devices. However, there are promising technologies in development – including optical and DNA computing,[172] crystal computers, nanotubes, and even quantum computing – that Kurzweil and others believe will allow calculating power to continue to increase exponentially.[173] A rough analogy to his argument could be made in the field of transportation: humans can travel within the earth's atmosphere at a rate faster than the speed of sound, but they cannot use horse-drawn carriages, conventional automobiles, or even propeller-driven aircraft to do so. In order to make the leap to such speed, it was necessary to develop a new technology – the jet engine.

Whether Kurzweil's predictions will come to pass, of course, is uncertain at this time.[174] However, it should be noted that – bold though his arguments are – he is far from alone in his belief that the technological landscape will change radically in the twenty-first century. Great progress is underway in many scientific fields, and several areas of inquiry stand out as having potentially enormous long-term influence on international politics. Computer science is only one of these fields; others include robotics, biotechnology, genetics, and nanotechnology.[175] Moreover, these research areas are not altogether distinct – they overlap, and in the future will interact in, heretofore, unimagined ways that will yield powerful technological advances.

Despite the large number of reputable scientists and other authorities writing on the subject of imminent, large-scale change, political and other social scientists generally appear reluctant to address the issues raised by their hard science counterparts.[176] Yet proper strategic analysis demands a long-term perspective – indeed, one of the attributes shared by the most-admired strategic practitioners is their ability to craft policies that will create a salubrious international atmosphere in which their polity can thrive over the long term.[177] Moreover, as the topic of this work is the geopolitics of the twentieth-first century, it is necessary to address a key question: Will technology render geopolitics obsolete as an area of study?

For the purposes at hand, it is not necessary to determine precisely how various technologies will develop in the coming decades (a task for which the author, in any case, is not qualified). It is, however, crucial to explore how massive technological change will influence the character of the international political system and create the conditions for an RSP. To undertake this analysis, it is perhaps useful to group technological change into several different groupings that highlight particular issues relevant to grand strategy – economic, military, and socio-cultural – and then to examine how they relate to global politics and strategy.

The RSP and the next revolution in military affairs

The Second American RMA is not over, but it is not too soon to, at least in a very broad fashion, discuss the characteristics of the *next* RMA and its relevance to the RSP. An RSP is a much more Epoch-shaping event than is a single RMA, but this RMA will be intimately connected to, indeed, will be the offshoot of, the technological forces driving the RSP.

It is not the purpose, herein, to describe the next RMA in detail; indeed, even attempting this would most likely be a pointless task, because it would require such extrapolation as to be no more reliable than science fiction. The purpose here is not to say that a specific technology will be the trump card that changes how war is fought. What is important, however, is that there is a wave of technological innovation so great, and so widely dispersed among a variety of fields, that it can be reasonably projected that how advanced states fight wars will change dramatically.

While the Second American RMA essentially was a repudiation of the Nuclear American RMA, the coming RMA will likely contain aspects of *both* these predecessors. For decades, most observers have, rather casually, placed nuclear arms alongside chemical, biological, and radiological devices in the category of "weapons of mass destruction," treating them as something other than "conventional" weapons. The catch-all WMD categorization always was dubious – after all, it is difficult to argue convincingly that a canister of mustard gas is more a weapon of mass destruction than is a 15,000-pound BLU-82 "daisy cutter" bomb – but it will grow ever more questionable as time passes and new weapons are developed that do not necessarily cause wide-scale indiscriminate devastation but are hardly conventional in any usual sense of the term.

Biotechnology, computer science, robotics, and other fields all promise to provide a cornucopia of militarily applicable technologies in the near future. In this regard, it should be noted that all of these fields – with the arguable exception of computer science – are at a very early stage of development; their greatest discoveries still lie ahead. It is not necessary to "pick winners," knowing which specific technological development will have the greatest impact on warfare, but we must understand that these, and other, fields will have an enormous effect.

The situation now, perhaps, is comparable to that in the early twentieth century; close observers of the American Civil and Franco-Prussian Wars knew that the grammar of warfare had changed greatly from days of Napoleon, and these insights, in turn, fed into planning and operational strategy. However, it seems that very few of even the most knowledgeable observers considered the possibility that these changes, *when taken together*, would cause the Western Front to become a maze of trench lines that would be almost impossible to break until an intrawar military revolution, the most critical aspect of which related to the use of artillery, took shape.[178] This lack of foresight was no minor problem, especially for the Central Powers. Indeed, had Germany understood just how improbable a rapid victory on the Western Front was, it almost certainly would not have gone to war in 1914.

Given the rapidity and significance of technological change, an RMA can be anticipated even if its exact nature cannot. While this work offers no specific vision of how battlefields will look in a few decades, one should be confident that they will be extraordinarily different from those of today, and not merely in the essentially evolutionary manner assumed in documents such as the US military's *Joint Vision 2020*. Future battlefields will include a panoply of new weapons that, in turn, will alter tactics and operations in decidedly non-trivial ways. Just as the Iraqi military, which would have stood a fair chance against the pre-RMA conventional US military of 1970, was hopelessly outmatched by the 2004 US military, the latter would be unable to cope with a great power force shaped by the forthcoming RMA.

In recent centuries, RMAs, as they generally are defined, have only emerged from countries that were part of the great power system – European states or, in the two most recent cases, the United States. *This is a relic of the Columbian Epoch, and should not be expected to continue.* It certainly is possible that the first state to piece together emerging technologies into a coherent revolution will be the United States (the result being a Third American RMA), but that result is by no means guaranteed.

Much of the research relevant to the next RMA is taking place outside of the United States. Cutting-edge science is being practiced in, among many other places, South Korea, India, Japan, China, and Taiwan. The fact that such countries are doing much of the research that will go into the RMA itself is notable; the technologies relevant to recent technologically-driven RMAs (interchangeable parts and factory assembly, breech-loading rifles, modern artillery, nuclear weapons, and so forth) were developed chiefly in Europe (including Russia) or the United States. (This has not always been the case – for example, Europeans did not invent gunpowder or artillery, but the Gunpowder Revolution nonetheless was European.) Potentially even more significant, however, *is the fact that great powers other than the United States have a very strong incentive to initiate an RMA that would overthrow the military status quo.* Under current conditions, it would be extraordinarily expensive and difficult to develop a force that can match the US military. The most expeditious solution to this problem is to "overturn the chess board" and, insofar as possible, neutralize the advantages which Washington holds.

This does not, however, mean that the budding RMA is a "repudiation" of the Second American RMA; it is, in this respect, quite unlike the latter's attempted "end run" around the Nuclear RMA. The early designers of the weapons systems and operational art that became the Second American RMA were endeavoring to insure that the United States could win wars against a numerically superior Soviet opponent without the use of nuclear weapons. Those who craft the forthcoming RMA, however, would be perfectly happy to incorporate aspects of the Second American RMA insofar as this furthers their own purposes. For this reason, it may be somewhat difficult to ascertain the point at which the Second American RMA ends and the next one begins, particularly if the United States makes a serious effort to stay at the forefront of military research and development.

Some might contend that such ambiguity makes it more sensible to speak of one long, "evolutionary revolutionary" RMA that began in response to the

Nuclear Revolution but will continue for several more decades. However, this would understate the magnitude of the difference between the character of cutting-edge military practices today and those of twenty or thirty years in the future, which will likely be comparable to that between the warfare of Charles XII of Sweden and Napoleon Bonaparte, if not greater.

While the most notable characteristics of the Second American RMA were the improvement of munitions accuracy and the strengthening of the command, control, and communications (C^3) networks linking soldiers to each other and their distant superiors, the next RMA will change the character of the battlefield even more fundamentally. The aforementioned rapid technological process that is occurring in a number of fields can be expected to yield all manner of militarily useful advances ranging from largely independent (i.e., not human-controlled) battlefield robots that can perform reconnaissance and combat tasks to terrifying arms such as biological weapons tailored to cause fatal, difficult-to-cure, and easily transmitted illnesses.

The following broad conditions are likely to prevail over the next two or three decades: nuclear weapons will continue to be strategically relevant and will continue to proliferate horizontally; during the early decades of the Post-Columbian Epoch, the United States will continue to enjoy a lead in most areas of military technology at any given time, but as time passes the military technology "tree" will continue to branch out, offering opportunities for polities to acquire strategically new and potent capabilities that would allow them to inflict damage on stronger opponents; and one or more great powers will acquire potentially potent military technologies that Washington is unwilling, for ethical reasons, to obtain.

It is not claimed, herein, that any single technology is *the* "key to the next RMA." It should be emphasized that the next RMA will likely involve a number of overlapping technologies that together will make warfare – and society in general – quite different. Thus, this RMA is inextricably bound to the budding Revolution in Strategic Perspective, but the RMA will not cause the RSP. Both the RMA and RSP will be the result of the technological, economic, and social change that is occurring, but the RSP is, strategically speaking, the more fundamental of the two phenomena. The next RMA will, like its predecessors, be a transient phenomenon, giving the state(s) which are its leading edge a very substantial, but temporary, military advantage. At most, a state may be able to leverage this RMA to secure temporary global hegemony. This would be no mean feat – and such an accomplishment most likely would require at least one world war – but, by itself, it would not insure *permanent* strategic dominance; hegemony built on shaky foundations can be expected to collapse quickly. Over the long term, the more significant factor for the success of a great power will be in how it adapts overall – socially, economically, militarily, and so forth – to the profoundly different strategic conditions of the twenty-first century.

A thought experiment: the military application of artificial intelligence to airpower

The artificial intelligence (AI) field should mature substantially over the next two decades. At the least, this should make it feasible to develop weapons systems that operate with very little human oversight. One of the most important such weapons likely will be "smart" unmanned combat aerial vehicles (UCAVs). Today's unmanned aircraft are remotely piloted by humans, with all the disadvantages that implies: the human pilot must remain in contact with the distant aircraft, interpret complex data and make decisions based on it, and so forth. Moreover, although UCAVs have been used to deliver missiles in combat – perhaps, most notably in Yemen, where a high-level al Queda operative and his traveling party was blown up by a Hellfire missile delivered by a Predator drone in 2002 – there has yet been no "true UCAVs" similar to a modern fighter aircraft in combat capabilities. However, in principle there is no reason why such a device could not be built, and, indeed, it would offer truly enormous financial and combat advantages over even the most advanced manned aircraft.

Unlike human pilots, computers do not demand a salary, and their logistical needs are, comparatively speaking, minimal as they do not require barracks facilities, food, and so forth. Nor do they undergo a program of training and ongoing pilot certification or decide to leave the service to pursue careers in the private sector. These costs and logistical inconveniences are far from trivial: over the course of a twenty-year career, it costs the US military several million dollars to train, maintain, and pay wages and benefits to a pilot and his/her family, and after retirement hundreds of thousands more is typically paid in retirement benefits. Most important of all, however, is the fact that the death of a human pilot in training or combat is a tragedy, while the destruction of a computer is merely an inconvenience. The US military rightly places enormous emphasis on the minimization of casualties, and piloting combat aircraft is one of the most hazardous of all military activities.

In addition to the aforementioned benefits, UCAVs could prove to be vastly superior to, but far less expensive than, manned aircraft. The human anatomy places very significant limitations on the design of aircraft. Even the most talented human is very vulnerable to the effects of gravitational forces; a metal airframe can tolerate without damage far more extreme "g-forces" than could any human pilot. Moreover, a pilot must interact with his or her aircraft – the cockpit is devised to allow the pilot to receive information about its status and to use this data to guide the vehicle. Removing the pilot – indeed, the entire cockpit in its present form – potentially allows for the creation of a combat aircraft far more maneuverable than any previously built.

Human brains are very complex devices with impressive capabilities. Humans (or at least some humans) excel at tasks for which computers heretofore have displayed little or no talent – writing art criticism, lecturing on theology, and marketing soft drinks are all quite different activities, but, at present, computers do none of these well. (Indeed, the arguments between believers in "hard-AI" such as Kurzweil and their more skeptical counterparts largely revolves around the question of whether a computer can have the capacity to "think humanly.") [179] However, chip-based processing has its own advantages and computers are excellent at sorting and manipulating certain types of information very rapidly. The most obvious example of this is the performance of mathematical calculation – if an average human is given a list of a thousand twenty-digit numbers and asked to add them together, he or she can do so, but it will require many hours of effort and the answer arrived at almost certainly will be incorrect. A typical desktop computer running the appropriate software of course can provide a correct answer almost instantaneously.

Although no software program as yet has been developed that would allow a computer to pilot a combat mission without human assistance or interaction, it is almost certain that one will be developed in the not-very-distant future. Making the decisions required to fly an aircraft on a combat sortie would require a fairly modest level of AI; a computer would have to be capable of assessing threats, deciding on an appropriate response to a given hazard, constantly monitoring data on the speed and performance of the aircraft, and so forth. (One need only consider how much "piloting" the software guiding a cruise missile to its target does to see that many of its functions formerly associated with human pilots can already be performed by computers.) Unlike writing a good novel, which requires "emotional intelligence" (or a least a very impressive simulation thereof), as well as an ear for dialogue, a talent for description, and other literary skills, a typical air combat mission is well-suited to the strengths of a sufficiently powerful computer. Indeed, computer programs already often "pilot" aircraft during their landing for the very good reason that they can more reliably execute this dangerous maneuver than a well-trained and talented human can. Given that AI already has developed to this level, it is hardly unreasonable to postulate that computers will soon fly combat missions without any need for direct human assistance. Regardless of whether one agrees with Kurzweil that the development of "hard" AI will allow computers to surpass human intelligence, removing humans from the cockpit requires only very "soft" AI and thus appears very likely indeed.

Far from being wild-eyed speculation, even if one has very conservative expectations, the replacement of human pilots with essentially autonomous computer pilots is something that should occur relatively soon, given the logic of current technological development. This will not, however, be a simple and seamless process. Besides the obvious technological hurdles, an even more important factor in the development of *truly* unmanned (as opposed to remotely piloted) combat aerial vehicles will be the willingness of humans to "take themselves out of the loop." Even once computers can make air-combat-related judgments reliably (or at least as reliably as humans do), many politicians and military officers nonetheless will resist surrendering decisionmaking authority to machines. Most leaders value their authority and are reluctant to surrender it, while the notion that machines could make tactical decisions without human input is unsettling to many people. Thus, there will be institutional resistance in every country to allowing fully autonomous UCAVs, and humans will likely act as UCAV "pilots" even after their presence is, by any rational technical standard, counterproductive.

The first state to enjoy the dividends – which perhaps will be very large indeed – of fully automated UCAVs will not necessarily be the first that is technologically capable of developing such devices. Indeed, they possibly already could exist, if in the 1990s and early 2000s the United States had cared to devote the resources necessary to developing them. The fact that the United States was willing to spend many billions developing and deploying the F-22 (which, given its fly-away cost, might as well literally be made of gold), but has been comparatively miserly in spending money on crude unmanned aerial vehicles used for surveillance (although, increasingly, adapted to deliver munitions) and almost totally ignored the obvious and *truly* transformative possibility of removing humans entirely from direct participation in aerial combat illustrates not so much the limits of human imagination as of human nature.[180]

There literally are thousands of people throughout the US government who are aware, to one degree or another, of how quickly AI is developing in the private sector. This is not secret knowledge in any sense. Indeed, discussions of developments in this field are a regular feature of technology magazines and other popular outlets. More than a few, no doubt, have speculated on how AI could transform US military capabilities (and, to be fair, the Defense Department has devoted some "seed money" to the development of AI).[181] However, there has been no sense of real urgency in this, largely because of overall US military supremacy.

As any astute observer of international affairs could warn, "victory disease" is a potent foe of the preeminent. There is an understandable tendency to continue policies which led to past triumphs. A sense of strategic inferiority and resulting acute fear of future defeat, in contrast, tends to create an institutional culture friendly to creativity. (If the Soviet Union were still alive and intimidating, the United States, in an effort to gain a critical edge over the USSR, would likely already have devoted significant resources to the development of AI UCAVs.) *Its own past successes are perhaps the most significant handicap that the United States has coming into the RSP period.* In contrast, certain rising polities are likely to exhibit the combination of aggressiveness and fear that will incline them toward cleverness and risk-taking. Such were the characteristics of the Western European seapowers of the early Columbian Epoch, and in an RSP environment they are invaluable.

Despite the all-too-likely resistance to them, the fielding of AI UCAVs is one of the most feasible and least shocking changes in military affairs likely to occur in the next few decades. It is for this reason that it is discussed herein. As one of the *less* controversial military developments to occur in the RSP environment, it provides a good yardstick for imagining the level of resistance that truly divisive technologies would encounter. The thought of deploying AI UCAVs would make most of today's leaders vaguely uncomfortable, as they would be ceding decisionmaking power to a machine in politically sensitive situations, but would not threaten their core moral notions.

UCAVs possessed of very rudimentary AI do not raise difficult questions about what the limits of AI research should be (i.e., whether fully self-aware machines, if they can be built, should be created), and certainly do not bring the future character of humanity itself into question. Certain research related to biotechnology, however, may do exactly that. If the adoption of AI UCAVs is difficult, one can only imagine the resistance that efforts to, say, genetically manipulate human beings would encounter. (Already, overblown, and in some cases altogether groundless, fears are proliferating about many different technologies, including genetic engineering, nanotechnology, and AI.[182])

From the moral or ethical perspective of many, resistance to the "Brave New World" of the RSP may be laudable. However, the purpose of this work is not to judge the rights or wrongs of various applications of technology to achieve specific outcomes. Rather, it is to underline a cold strategic point that what can be done to gain military-political advantage, will be done, eventually. The "strategic economy" does not long tolerate market failures – a particular power may choose to refuse to adopt an obviously profitable course, but all powers will not do so forever. Absent world government or an airtight, universal agreement controlling the development of new technologies – an utterly improbable and unattractive vision of a world in which humanity has halted progress – certain governments will choose to leverage "RSP technologies" for strategic advantage. Some of the latter may fail catastrophically in their attempt to do so – wasting billions on technological dead ends, "overreaching" and undertaking projects so unacceptable to their populations as to result in their downfall, or whatnot. Others, however, will succeed, and will be in a position to become the commanding actors on the world stage.

The case for technological exuberance

Given the difficulties in predicting how technology will develop in the future and which technologies will have the largest impact, either positive or negative, on societies, this work does not presume to argue that policymakers should favor certain technologies over others, much less attempt to organize their military around a particular budding technology. This "fog of technology" does not, however, render it impossible to make certain general observations regarding which strategies are most likely to be successful in twenty-first century conditions.

Efforts to very closely "guide" and discipline technological development so that it does not move beyond certain arbitrary parameters – for example, endeavoring to insure that bioengineering technologies do not "improve humans too much" by greatly enhancing their intelligence and/or physical attributes – quite possibly could backfire catastrophically on states that impose such rules.[183] Such restrictions could be expected to have the same impact as Ming China's naval conservatism, hobbling states that abide by them, while permitting less hidebound challengers to best the "Neo-Luddites" over the long term. In recent years, we have seen many states that tried to control access to information technology, and virtually all observers would agree that they paid a steep price for doing so. (The Soviet decision to carefully restrict access to personal computers and photocopiers even while these items were becoming ubiquitous in Western offices is a classic example.)

Attempting to place limits on research into and dissemination of what one might call the "RSP technologies" would likely have an exponentially greater impact, as, taken together, these technologies will have a far more transformative impact on society. It should be emphasized that for this to be true, it is not required that "techno-optimists" such as Ray Kurzweil be correct in detail; rather, it is only necessary that current trends in the RSP technologies do not cease abruptly. In short, if we assume that advances in computer science, robotics, biotechnology, and so forth are not soon going to halt altogether, then these fields will have a radical impact on how humans live – and thus in how they compete for international political preeminence. Given the balance of evidence at present, it is actually more conservative strategically to assume that an RSP will occur than that it will not. One can draw a parallel to global warming – while it is possible that global temperatures will stay the same in the future, or even that the planet will cool, the prudent strategist must account for the possibility that significant warming will occur and that this will have an impact on global politics. Similarly, while it is possible that the march of technology will stop, there, at present, is no compelling evidence that it will do so; therefore, prudence demands preparing for an RSP. Indeed, it is far more vital that the great power strategist plans for the impact of RSP technologies, than for global warming, as the former almost certainly will be overwhelmingly more important to rich and dominant countries than will the latter, as many of the direct effects that global warming might have on such states (agricultural difficulties, problems related to rising tides, and so forth) can be mitigated or eliminated through the application of technology.

In light of the dangers of ignoring the possibility of an RSP and of refusing to embrace its technologies, one might ask how a state could best position itself to benefit from the RSP. In this regard, three "steps" useful in leveraging the RSP should be highlighted: understanding, acceptance, and encouragement. First, leaders who comprehend that an RSP is in the offing have an enormous advantage over those who are unaware of this development or refuse to accept its reality. The basic reason for this is obvious: policymakers who understand that enormous and rapid change is occurring can, if they choose to, plan accordingly, implementing those policies that are seen as most likely to allow successful adaptation to the changing international environment. Acceptance and encouragement of RSP-related technologies, in turn, are necessary in order to create and implement such policies. Acceptance implies that a leader understands that no polity has the ability to prevent the RSP and that policy must reflect the fact that seeking to constrain research into and implementation of RSP-related technologies will handicap a state over the long term. Encouragement means that leaders seek to "speed up" change and its related social, economic, military, and other changes. This, of course, is the opposite of seeking to prevent the RSP.

It is not at all difficult to imagine why acceptance may be such a very difficult step for many leaders, particularly in democratic states. As RSP-related technologies develop, they will raise great controversy, and it is beyond doubt that many individuals will oppose development of particular technologies for moral and/or ethical reasons. Public debates surely will be highly charged, and thus will bear some resemblance to the debate over abortion in the United States. Indeed, some of the "values debates" of tomorrow will tread similar ground, raising fundamental questions of what it means to be human, what limits society may place on an individual's control of his or her own body, and so forth. Moreover, class issues will play a role of many of these controversies, as many RSP technologies can be expected, at least when they are first available, to be very expensive. For example, the manipulation of fetuses to control for physical or mental traits would present a "perfect storm" of controversy, offering practices that would make many individuals uncomfortable for religious or other reasons, inviting alarmists to warn of a "Brave New World," and exciting resentment among those who could not afford to take advantage of such technology.

Given that the early decades of the RSP are ripe for highly emotional debate, policymakers in many democratic societies will find it difficult to support a largely unregulated regulatory environment in which researchers are free to develop RSP technologies. Such technologies would offer enormous potential benefits to individuals, providing, over the long term, longer, healthier, and more prosperous lives, but such prospective benefits would not insure public willingness to offer latitude to researchers. Such powerful technologies would, after all, have potential downsides, and critics would emphasize these; indeed, some critics surely would demand that some variant of the precautionary principle be applied to certain technologies – that is, that development of these technologies should only be allowed if researchers can prove that no harm would result from their work. Such a high standard essentially would choke off research and development whenever it was applied. We already have an early example of efforts to apply the precautionary principle to an RSP-related field – many environmentalists and others have called for limits on the planting and consumption of genetically modified crops.[184] Thus far, such critics have enjoyed limited success in Europe,[185] but very little in the United States. In any case, however, the fact that genetically modified food has become a major public issue in many democratic countries despite a dearth of evidence indicating that consumption of such products is harmful to humans, may foreshadow far more contentious debates over other technologies.

At least in democratic societies, controversy over maturing technologies cannot simply be wished away. Even if the policymaking elite strongly favors unfettered research and development of RSP-related technologies, staunch public opposition to particular technologies will impact regulatory and other policies. In short, even a leader who accepts that technological progress is necessary to strategic competitiveness cannot "wish away" public opposition to certain kinds of research. This places potentially very great demands on policymakers in democratic countries who have made the intellectual leap to "acceptance" – they will have to act with circumspection so as not to push research beyond the limits which public opinion will accept, as it will be incumbent upon them to prevent a disastrous luddite backlash that would be truly damaging to their nation's long-term strategic prospects. By contrast, their authoritarian counterparts will enjoy more freedom to do as they wish, as they are comparatively insulated from public opinion. *This asymmetry could be one of the most significant handicaps that democratic great powers will face in this century, and it is possible (though by no means certain) that it will undermine radically their ability to compete successfully in the struggle to take advantage of the RSP.*

Encouragement is the third area relevant to policymakers who wish to remain competitive in RSP-related technologies. Obviously, given the factors noted above, policymakers in democracies who wish to encourage research into certain fields will find it difficult or impossible to do. However, in other cases it will be possible to use a variety of incentives – government grants and other research support, advantageous tax treatment, and so forth – to encourage technological development. All of the RSP-related technologies mentioned in this work already receive support from various states, and one would not be surprised to see this increase, as the economic and military potential of various developing technologies becomes clearer. Also, the fact that much scientific research takes place in the private sector and that many businesspeople therefore have an incentive to lobby governments for financial aid is significant – there is what one might call a built-in lobby for RSP technologies in all of the great powers.[186] In addition, as noted above, many budding technologies also have relevance to defense and, therefore, defense ministries put a considerable amount of money into relevant research. This is particularly notable in relation to the United States, which maintains a very large and well-funded defense research and development establishment.[187]

Conclusion

One should emphasize that there is no "magic formula" which would allow a state to take advantage of the RSP – in every country, local political and socio-economic conditions determine the constraints which policymakers face, and it will be necessary for farsighted leaders to adapt accordingly. However, it is logical to expect that those states which prove to be open to technological and consequent social transformation will have a critical advantage over those which are highly resistant to such change. For the reasons noted above, however, it may be very difficult or impossible for leaders to overcome such resistance. The short- and medium-term risks that accompany boldness almost always are more obvious than are the long-term risks of a reactionary stance. Thus, a policy elite may be seduced by the temptation to defy potentially disruptive change, as were the mandarins of the Ming dynasty who decided to turn their backs on oceanic exploration were leaving more forward-thinking leaders isolated and ignored. Yet, even if a critical mass of policymakers are willing to leap into the unknown, it is not assured that those they lead will be, and in a democracy this fact can undermine even the wisest policy.

It is, therefore, entirely likely, if not probable, that democratic states will suffer important disadvantages relative to their authoritarian brethren. Strategically speaking, the ability of authoritarian governments to undertake mighty enterprises that more timid democratic rulers (who must concern themselves with maintaining the support of their electorate over the span of years – for the benefit of their party, if not always necessarily for themselves) are apt to be cautious of is both one of their notable virtues and greatest vices. Focusing on the history of the twentieth century, some might be inclined to regard this trait as entirely negative; Nazi Germany, Fascist Italy, and Imperial Japan certainly did not profit from their readiness to leap into great power wars, and both the Soviet Union and its people would likely have done much better over the long term if Moscow had allocated more of it resources to fulfilling the desires of domestic consumers and less to efforts to defeat capitalism globally. There is, however, also much historical evidence that one could cite to illustrate the virtues of "nimble authoritarianism." For example, acting as a revolutionary committee of one, Julius Caesar crossed the Rubicon and brought low the mightiest republic (albeit admittedly an oligarchic one) in, at the time, the history of the world; the leaders of Muscovy and their successors managed to convert their small and poor polity into the world's largest country, and along the way defeated, among many others, Novgorod, which maintained a relatively republican form of government; and the United States demonstrated in Vietnam that a democratic republic can enjoy almost every imaginable advantage over an authoritarian foe, yet lose if the latter is disciplined and smart while the former is feckless and indecisive. There are a myriad of other examples that one could cite, but the main point is simple: although consensual government may well be superior to authoritarianism in many respects, this provides no guarantee that democracies will outperform their undemocratic competitors in this century.

This harsh fact, along with the relative freedom that authoritarians enjoy in being able to implement schemes that are opposed by most of their subjects, will offer immense opportunities to some very thuggish great power rulers. This is not to counsel despair to democrats – their defeat in the most important political struggles of this century certainly is not foreordained. However, if they are too timid to risk embracing the technologies associated with the RSP, it is all-too-likely that they will be eclipsed by less cautious authoritarian great powers. In short, democratic leaders, most certainly including those in the United States, have some very difficult strategic challenges with which to grapple, and these are intertwined with (often unpleasant) ethical debates, but at the root, all these relate to which risks leaders are willing to accept. Certainly, they may choose to resist "unnatural" or "dehumanizing" change that may spring from advances in biotechnology, AI, and other fields, but if they do so, it behooves them to honestly confront the fact that they will be granting strategic advantages to competitors that may prove to be decisive over the long term. In short, the United States and its ideological compatriots could, potentially, be tomorrow's Ming China and Ottoman Empire.

Conclusion

In recent years, many of those skeptical about the future importance of geography in war and statecraft have been inclined to argue, not unreasonably, that technological trends will make geographical factors nearly irrelevant.[188] This is in some respects a very compelling point; technology progressively has placed humans less and less at the mercy of physical geography and climate.[189] Among other things, mastery over geography has allowed humans to redirect rivers, strip-mine mountains, and cut canals physically separating previously-connected continents. The human ability to use tools to manipulate the environment will continue to increase in the coming decades – indeed, advances in nanotechnology and robotics might exponentially improve human control over matter – but because humans are physical beings who occupy space and have physical needs geography cannot be dethroned from its central position in the international sphere.[190]

It is easy to assume that technological improvements inevitably will decrease the importance of geography. Yet recent decades are hardly the first time that a technological gap has been critical to the fortunes of great powers: indeed, the very concept of a revolution in military affairs is built on the presumption that technologies – whether they are stirrups or nuclear warheads – can have a critical impact on the outcome of conflicts if they are leveraged properly. The current era is hardly the first in which disadvantaged forces have suffered at the hands of those wielding superior technology – even if American B-2 pilots appeared to inflict more "shock and awe" in Afghanistan than did conquistadors wielding steel and crude firearms in Mexico, the ultimate result was similar. A nuanced reading of history indicates that, in reference to international politics, geography and technology have a relationship that is far more complex than a simple inverse one in which increases in the latter diminishes the importance of the former.

During the Columbian Epoch one of the keys to international political power was harnessing technology so as to better exploit geography – the most prominent example of this of course being the ability to use the sea to create and sustain world-spanning empires. A geopolitical skeptic might protest that this was an example of technology conquering geography, but this perspective is flawed. The world's oceans did not become irrelevant – quite the opposite, as the distinction between polities that could leverage technology to use the oceans effectively and thereby achieve political ends and those that could not was one of the defining political facts of that era.[191] Geography is not rendered irrelevant, much less conquered, by technology – rather, the gap between those polities that are more or less capable of coping efficiently with geographic challenges is often what separates military winners from losers, and there is no sound reason to believe that this rule will be overthrown in the twenty-first century.

The connection between geography and politics will not be severed in this century, but those societies that pursue scientific advancement wholeheartedly will likely enjoy a critical advantage over those that do not. Just as the development of technologies relevant to oceangoing provided a critical strategic advantage to Western European powers during the early Colombian Epoch, technologies applicable to ground, sea, air, and space power will reward the powers that perfect them. The key issue is relevance – much of the confusion over the emerging strategic era results from a failure to perceive that a technology that may have no direct relation to geography may nonetheless enhance military systems that operate in a given geographical environment. The software that makes the US Navy's Aegis system possible enhances sea power, the wireless networking of US ground forces enhances land power, and so forth.[192] Surely, robotics, nanotechnology, biotechnology, and other research areas will yield technologies that will be of enormous benefit to their possessors when applied to military purposes.

Geopolitics and the revolution in strategic perspective

The combination of the birth of the Post-Columbian Epoch, and the resulting return to multipolarity, and the ongoing and multifaceted technological revolution has created profound instability in the international system. The quasi-unipolar system already is greatly decayed – indeed, future historians will likely consider the international debate before the 2003 Iraq invasion as the "beginning of the end" for unipolarity – and the strengthening of China, India, and other great states continues apace.

This strategic instability and enhanced great power competition will create very considerable risks – most importantly, the pause in major war, that began in 1945, will most likely come to an end. One certainly can see why certain well-intentioned leaders will surely attempt to create mechanisms that will control great power behavior and prevent the outbreak of armed conflict. Yet, such efforts are doomed to fail, and, most likely will, like the creation of the League of Nations, do more harm than good. Ambitious great powers can only be stymied by their peers. While it is imaginable, though unlikely, that those peers will act through an international body such as the United Nations, that institution merely would provide a "flag of convenience." Far more than any other political entities, it is the great powers which will determine the course of humanity in this century.

In this environment, the value for strategic adaptability is enormous. The "rules" that governed the geopolitics of the late Columbian Epoch are being overthrown, although not in the ways that many assume – in the developed world, the state is not surrendering its central role to a colorful "neo-medieval" collection of terrorists, multinational corporations, and other actors. (The poorest and most disordered parts of the world are, of course, another matter.) Rather, the "ice is cracking."

The collapse of the old Europe-centered multipolar system and the resulting bipolar period created a period of high stability in which global politics revolved around the Cold War struggle. No great powers emerged that were both inclined to, and capable of, fundamentally altering the character of the Cold War international system. From the 1960s onward, Japan and Germany arguably had the combination of resources needed to act as fully independent great powers, but they were constrained by overwhelming Soviet military power, and thus the perceived need for US protection, and their own history. India tried to place itself at the center of a global Non-Aligned Movement and leverage that role to make itself a "diplomatic superpower." However, this effort was stillborn because New Delhi lacked both financial resources and a compelling ideological "story" that could create a cohesive global movement placing the very different post-colonial states under one umbrella (which India of course would hold). After the Sino-Soviet break, only China managed to function as an independent great power, but it was too weak relative to the superpowers to form a third pole in global politics – though it did try, unsuccessfully, to leverage Maoist ideology so as to become the recognized leader of the global Communist movement. Thus, it was reduced to maneuvering between the two superpowers.

The overthrow of today's quasi-unipolarity is inevitable, because that system is fully satisfactory only to the United States. An Americentric global political system restrains the ambitions of every state but the United States, and this simply is not acceptable to the strong-minded leaders of a diverse group of great powers. Of course, one could argue that the current system is the best one overall, as America is a benign quasi-hegemon that presides over a system encouraging free markets and increasing prosperity while discouraging military aggression and making great power war almost unimaginable. True though this may be, it is insufficient to maintain unipolarity. As Thucydides reminds us, human nature does play a critical role in affairs of state, and considerations of national honor and greatness can and do drive decisionmaking.[193]

A number of states have the resources necessary to act as highly independent great powers. The EU may succeed in harnessing the assets of the states that comprise it and conducting a *truly* united foreign policy, thus making Brussels into a great power. India and, especially, China are undergoing spectacular economic transformations that finally are providing those countries with the assets necessary to further their very considerable ambitions. For differing reasons, Russia and Japan may be doomed to decline over the very long term, but at least for several more decades both states will continue to be capable of acting as major powers.

Still towering above all of these polities, however, is the United States, and, if it acts wisely, Washington will remain the greatest of the world's powers. It should be emphasized that the argument, herein, for the inevitable decline of the United States from its present quasi-unipolar position is not intended as an indictment of any specific American leaders, nor of US policy generally. Like any country, the United States makes more than a few blunders in the conduct of its foreign policy, but these are not the ultimate cause for the ongoing crumbling of unipolarity (though such errors certainly hasten the coming of unipolarity). Simply stated, the fact is that the United States, struggle though it might, cannot hold off the development of multipolarity indefinitely – the geopolitical environment and the *zeitgeist* both are extremely unfavorable to permanent unipolarity. As American leaders must understand if they are to navigate successfully in the global political environment of the twenty-first century, some things simply are beyond Washington's control.

Managing relative decline always is a painful task, and, given human nature, it is unsurprising that relatively few powers promptly face the facts of long-term decline and take effective action to contain their losses and create the conditions for a "soft landing." Yet, the current situation in which the United States finds itself should not be regarded as an especially grim one. Its ongoing decline does not reflect critical flaws in the structure of the American system that doom the United States to the status of a second-tier power. Rather, it is the inevitable outcome of the artificially inflated position that the United States enjoyed as a result of the collapse of the previous bipolar system (which itself resulted from the collapse of the multipolar system that preceded it). The end of the Columbian Epoch created unique conditions that allowed the United States to, briefly, enjoy a status unique in human history: it was the quasi-hegemon of the world. If American leaders act prudently, no competing power will replace the United States in that position, much less take on the role of true hegemon.

Washington should have two central foreign policy goals in the next two decades. First, it must strive to bring about the development of a healthy multipolar system in which it remains the world's greatest single power. Second, it must seek to ensure that it does not become a victim of the Revolution in Strategic Perspective, failing to adapt to the changing character of the international order.

The first task is the easier of the two, as a healthy multipolar system appears to be developing even without significant American guidance. China presently is the most muscular of the Old World powers, but, unlike the USSR in 1945, it does not possess overwhelming superiority over all of the other states of Eurasia. The United States must remain vigilant against any other major state gaining too much power, or building a potentially dangerous partnership with a peer – and it must be ready to act vigorously, and even go to war, if there is a serious danger that a new Eastern Eurasian hegemon will emerge. Absent such an extreme circumstance, however, the main task of the United States will be to build on its existing alliances with states such as Japan, South Korea, and Australia, and, when possible and desirable, enter into close relationships with new partners of all types while not gratuitously antagonizing China or any other great power.

In principle, there is nothing particularly difficult about this course – it is the sort of workaday diplomacy that the United States already engages in with countries throughout the world. The difficulty for US policymakers will be in making the transition from the imperial present, in which Washington is the center of global politics and diplomacy is artificially simplified by that fact. Because of its quasi-hegemonic role, the United States is deeply involved in almost all key international questions of the day, even when it has no direct interest in the matter at hand.

Being relieved of these burdens would offer some distinct advantages to the United States; freed of the illusion that it is the world's policeman (a thankless task if ever there was one), it could focus on issues that truly matter to its security. However, this may prove to be a very difficult transition. American policymakers have become used to unipolarity, and for many of them the movement away from hegemony will seem like an unnecessary surrender of power. It will be difficult to convince them that the current system is untenable, and thus that the United States must accommodate itself to the growing power of other major states and that it will better guard its interests by guiding the transition to a multipolar world system than by attempting, futilely, to maintain unipolarity. Yet, even though a healthy multipolar system could well develop despite even stubborn American resistance, it is important to US interests that Washington accepts the reality of multipolarity, as only by doing so that the adoption of a truly coherent grand strategy is possible. This, in turn, is needed if the United States is to ensure that it remains the greatest single power.

The second task is far more difficult because of the stunningly complex conditions of the RSP environment. There are no simple guidelines for success in the Post-Columbian Epoch, much less a single, obvious answer to all the quandaries created by the technological explosion, but there are general strategic rules of thumb that should be kept in mind.

First, the demise of the Columbian Epoch and the birth of the current, Post-Columbian Epoch has shifted the world's geopolitical center from Europe to Eastern Eurasia. For a very long period of time (quite likely centuries) the latter can be expected to be the area in which most of the great powers are located physically, and the outcome of the struggles for power in this meta-region will be the main factor determining the position of the various major states. Therefore, if any single state or coalition should successfully establish itself as the hegemon of Eastern Eurasia, it will become *inter alia* the most powerful state/coalition in the world.

Second, the ongoing and interrelated revolutions in biotechnology, nanotechnology, robotics, computer science, and other areas are laying the groundwork for an RSP. Technological change will alter fundamentally the social, economic, and political conditions which shape strategy. The only successful polities will be those whose leaders revise fundamentally their strategic perspective, thus enabling their states to profit from the radically changed conditions which will result from a technological "super-revolution."

Resistance to advancing technology can only result in strategic disaster. Of course, it is highly unlikely that any major polities will have a reactionary stance toward technology per se; rather, it will be the socio-economic and ethical/religious implications of technological developments that will frighten leaders. However, polities controlled by technological reactionaries are certain to suffer enormously. Like the worldview of the Mandarins who chose to turn China inward, away from ocean-going exploration, technological reactionaries will doom their states to long-term decline. This does not mean that policymakers must abandon all regulation of scientific experimentation. Indeed, it is unlikely that any society will choose to adopt an entirely *laissez-faire* policy toward science and technology. Democratic polities, in particular, will be under very great pressure to tightly constrain certain forms of experimentation. Doing so would all-too-likely grant a critical strategic advantage to their authoritarian competitors.[194]

Third, the technological "super-revolution" will result in extraordinarily potent war-fighting innovations. Given the pace of technological change, it should be expected that within two decades a new RMA, the successor to the increasingly-mature Second American RMA, will be in evidence. The specifics of this RMA are not readily predictable, but for the purposes at hand, it is most important to understand that in order for a state to be at the forefront of this RMA, its leaders will have to have decisively revised their strategic perspective so as to account for the "RSP environment." Again, resistance to the social and other changes that will result from technological innovation will disadvantage fundamentally a state in the highly competitive great power environment of the Post-Columbian Epoch.

Fourth, the use of state violence on a massive scale remains a distinct possibility. The peculiar international political circumstances that have prevailed since 1945 – the dominance of two cautious superpowers until 1991 and one benevolent quasi-hegemon thereafter – have been friendly to international peace. This period is now ending, and its likeliest replacement is a multipolarity with a decidedly "Wild East" aspect. An Epochal shift is occurring in the geographic center of world politics, rising polities such as China and India are scrambling for position, and the great powers have not established anything remotely approaching a Concert of Europe system which would guide their interactions and create a mechanism for peaceful dispute resolution.[195] Such conditions are extraordinarily dangerous.

Fifth, great powers will remain the most significant actors in global politics, although, it is to be expected that terrorist groups, multinational corporations, global religious organizations, and other non-state actors will play important roles in the international politics of this century. Nonetheless, the sheer weight of military and other resources that the great powers possess will have far more influence over the character of international politics than do these other entities. It is probable, given the factors discussed herein, that terrorism will present a growing global problem, and it is probable that one or more major powers will suffer a truly devastating terrorist strike on its soil. However, it is the great powers themselves which will largely determine the degree to which terrorist "strategic entrepreneurs" threaten international order. If the great powers demonstrate very little tolerance for transnational terrorism and cooperate against groups that threaten to attack the soil of any of them, terrorism will be a limited menace. If, however, they choose to freely use apocalyptic-minded terrorists against each other, perhaps even supplying them with weapons of mass destruction, terrorists will be a substantial threat to the great powers. Even more importantly, such reckless behavior would create excellent conditions for international crisis and great power war.

Sixth, given the speed of technological and other change in the Post-Columbian Epoch, it will not require many years of unwise policy decisions to create irreversible great power decline – perhaps as little as one or two decades of policy poorly adapted to the prevailing strategic conditions may grievously erode a state's global position, making full recovery very difficult. This would be quite unlikely in the early part of the previous age, in which, as we have seen, entities such as Ming China and the Ottoman Empire enjoyed a long period in which they *could* have corrected their policy course.

These observations should be sobering to US leaders, as current American preeminence does not provide the very generous margin of error that they might have assumed to exist. Today, the United States is, overall, the best-positioned of the great powers, but it does not enjoy any guarantee, whatsoever, that it will long remain the greatest of the powers. If Washington proves unwilling, or unable, to transform its strategic prospective, the power of the United States could dissipate with astonishing rapidity. Thus, it cannot afford to adopt the conservative strategic view that is typical of dominant states, because this inevitably would result in strategic disaster over the long term. In short, the United States does not dare risk cautiousness. If it is to thrive in the Post-Columbian Epoch, it must adopt a position of "judicious radicalism," boldly throwing itself into the maelstrom of social, economic, military, and political change that will define the early decades of this era. This of course is a terrifying prospect for most policymakers; the potential profits that accompany dangerous options rarely sway them from a course that will pay modest but certain dividends. However, the profits that accompany fearlessness will be so overwhelming in the coming decades that a cautious state would soon find itself to be hopelessly inferior to its less risk-averse competitors.

The global security environment is at the cusp of the most extraordinary period of systemic change since the time, five centuries ago, when it was first created. The shifts from unipolarity to multipolarity and of the center of international political struggle from Europe to Eastern Eurasia both are of enormous geopolitical significance. However, the combination of these changes with the technological ones discussed, herein, creates a trend that exponentially is more powerful. The ancient rules of strategy remain operative, because they are rooted in human nature rather than specific circumstance, but its grammar is undergoing a fundamental transformation. Some great states will adopt a strategic perspective appropriate to this Post-Columbian Epoch; others will not, and they will suffer accordingly.

Notes

1 This all-too-appropriate phrase was the title of a much-noted article: Charles Krauthammer, "The Unipolar Moment," *Foreign Affairs*, 70:1 (Winter 1990/1991), pp. 23–33.
2 Halford J. Mackinder, "The Geographical Pivot of History," *Geographical Journal* 23, 421–37; reprinted in *Democratic Ideals and Reality: A Study in the Politics of Reconstruction*, NDU Press Defense Classics (Washington, DC: National Defense University Press, n.d.), pp. 175–6. *Democratic Ideals and Reality* was originally published in 1919; the NDU edition includes that work as well as "The Geographical Pivot of History" and two other articles by Mackinder. For a full discussion of the "Pivot" paper see Brian W. Blouet, *Halford Mackinder: A Biography* (College Station, TX: Texas A&M University Press, 1987), pp. 108–22.
3 See Jonathan Brent and Vladimir P. Naumov, *Stalin's Last Crime: The Plot Against the Jewish Doctors* (New York: HarperCollins, 2003).
4 See A. James Gregor, *The Faces of Janus: Marxism and Fascism in the Twentieth Century* (New Haven, CT: Yale University Press, 2000).
5 In a passage that is admirably predictive of the danger that National Socialism soon would present, Mackinder, writing shortly after the end of World War I, warns: "Even with revolution in Germany let us not be too sure in regard to its ultimate effect.... The end of the present disorder may only be a new ruthless organization, and ruthless organizers do not stop when they have attained the objects which they at first set before them." *Democratic Ideals and Reality*, p. 110.
6 See, for example, Mackinder, *Democratic Ideals and Reality*, 99.
7 See Hew Strachan, *The First World War* (New York: Viking, 2003), esp. pp. 3–31 and 99–127. Indeed, one of Austria's goals even before the crisis of July 1914 was to acquire either Romania or Bulgaria as an ally. As Strachan notes, Romania was not a negligible military power: "Vienna needed an ally in the [Balkan] region and the obvious candidate seemed to be Romania. It had a wartime army of up to 600,000 men, a powerful consideration when Austria-Hungary's own peacetime military strength was only 415,000." (p. 7)
8 Whether an author chooses to pin the "great power" label on a given state ultimately requires a subjective decision on his or her part. For the purposes of this work, five states are considered to have the combination of wealth, population, diplomatic influence, and other assets necessary to be considered great powers. In approximate order of current overall power, these are: the United States, China, Russia, Japan, and India. A sixth entity, the EU, is regarded as a likely future great power. The EU states certainly have the assets necessary to make a great power, but, heretofore, there is little compelling evidence that the EU itself can act as a single unit in military/strategic affairs. However, the EU bureaucracy is striving mightily to create a more-than-declaratory Common Foreign and Security Policy, and eventual success in this endeavor appears entirely possible. The author freely admits that his choices

are arbitrary, and that there is a very wide "spread" between the present overall power of the United States and that of, say, Japan or India.

9 It should, however, be noted that it would be unfair to both Mackinder and Spykman to claim that the geopolitical perspective of one is "correct" while that of the other is "incorrect"; both thinkers contributed mightily to the development of geopolitical theory, and the differences in their perspectives are themselves illuminating. Also, even the most talented geopolitician realistically cannot aspire to create a theory that is applicable for all time – even leaving aside the dynamic character of international political life, technological change would preclude the possibility of an "eternal geopolitics."

10 Nicholas J. Spykman, *The Geography of the Peace* (New York: Harcourt, Brace, 1944), p. 43. Interestingly, although both Mackinder and Spykman agree on the centrality of Eurasia in political affairs they diverge on many related issues. For instance, Spykman regards Africa as an "off-shore" continent (idem, p. 38), while Mackinder considers it part of the "World-Island." Mackinder argues that, "The joint continent of Europe, Asia, and Africa, is now effectively, and not merely theoretically, an island ... [T]he three so-called new continents are in point of area merely satellites of the old continent. There is one ocean covering nine-twelfths of the globe; there is one continent – the World Island – covering two-twelfths of the globe; and there are many smaller islands, whereof North America and South America are, for effective purposes, two, which together cover the remaining one-twelfth." *Democratic Ideals and Reality*, pp. 45, 46–7.

11 Great power wars of hegemony may of course begin in strategically marginal regions and their immediate cause may be a minor issue, for example, the assassination of an Austrian archduke. However, the marginal region, generally, will not be the center of military activity in the contest, and obtaining control of the marginal area will not result in overall victory for the would-be hegemon. In the case of World War I, the ultimate question was whether the German bid for hegemony in Europe would succeed – a far larger matter than the subject of political arrangements in the Balkans – and it was decided on the Western Front.

12 Some observers would differ with this assessment. For example, William Odom argues that, "Russia is no longer a great power and is unlikely again to become one over the next several decades." William Odom, "Realism About Russia," *The National Interest*, 65 (Fall 1991), pp. 56–66.

13 For an interesting analysis of China's future energy and food requirements and the possible political significance of these needs see Thomas M. Kane and Lawrence W. Serewicz, "China's Hunger: The Consequences of a Rising Demand for Food and Energy," *Parameters*, 31:3 (Autumn 2001), pp. 63–75.

14 A very different view on the likelihood of such wars occurring in the future is offered in Martin Van Creveld, *The Rise and Decline of the State* (Cambridge, UK: Cambridge University Press, 1999), pp. 337–54.

15 For critiques of Haushofer's work see Holger H. Herwig, "Geopolitik: Haushofer, Hitler and Lebensraum," in Colin S. Gray and Geoffrey Sloan, *Geopolitics, Geography, and Strategy* (London: Frank Cass, 1999); Hans W. Weigert, *Generals and Geographers: The Twilight of Geopolitics* (New York: Oxford University Press, 1942); Derwent Whittlesey, *German Strategy of World Conquest* (New York: Farrar and Rinehart, 1942); and Idem, "Haushofer: The Geopoliticians," in Edward Mead Earle, ed., *Makers of Modern Strategy: Military Thought from Machiavelli to Hitler* (Princeton, NJ: Princeton University Press, 1973; originally published 1943), pp. 388–411.

16 As Gray states, "Geopolitics must be distinguished from *Geopolitik*. Studies in the former category constitute what today tends to be termed policy science – that is, they seek to explore the structure of policy problems, without necessarily prescribing (let alone rationalizing) particular courses of policy action. *Geopolitik*, by

contrast, refers to the vast body of German geopolitical writing and 'magic' cartography which flourished from the early 1920s until the demise of the Third Reich. It drew, very freely, upon the scholarly research and speculation of the respectable, and respected, geopolitical thinkers outside of Germany, but its motive force was propagandistic." Colin S. Gray, *The Geopolitics of the Nuclear Era: Heartlands, Rimlands, and the Technological Revolution*, Strategy Paper No. 30 (New York: National Strategy Information Center/Crane, Russak & Company, 1977), p. 19.

17 See Geoffrey Parker, *Geopolitics: Past, Present, and Future* (London: Pinter, 1998), pp. 37–9.

18 One edited collection even organizes works by Karl Haushofer, Adolf Hitler, Theodore Roosevelt, and Halford Mackinder into a section entitled "Imperial Geopolitics." Gearóid Ó Tuathail, Simon Dalby, and Paul Routledge, eds, *The Geopolitics Reader* (New York: Routledge, 1998).

19 For example, "Even if one recognizes, weighing the possible and the impossible in space and time, the danger which is connected with it, but which can be reduced, precisely through scientific geopolitical work, the striving for what appears impossible becomes understandable. Thus, one may comprehend now, how one may feel the duty to further keep alive and carry the burning wish to contemplate the greatest view on earth, the ancient longing of the Germanic peoples for the wide, warm seas, until its solution, somehow, through a more favorable world fate. . . . Should it only be the attraction of the *Nitimur in vetitum cupimusque semper negata* (we always strive for the forbidden and crave for what is denied us) that leads the German to the warm sea, which are supposed to be prohibited to him alone, and which he so ardently is craving for throughout his entire history?" Karl Haushofer, ed. and updated Lewis A. Tambs, trans. Ernst J. Brehm, *An English Translation and Analysis of Major General Karl Ernst Haushofer's Geopolitics of the Pacific Ocean: Studies on the Relationships between Geography and History*, Mellen Studies in Geography series (Lewiston, NY: The Edwin Mellon Press, 2002; first German edn published 1924), pp. xxviii–xxix.

20 Geoffrey Sloan, "Sir Halford J. Mackinder: The Heartland Theory Then and Now" in Colin S. Gray and Geoffrey Sloan, *Geopolitics, Geography, and Strategy* (London: Frank Cass, 1999), p. 1.

21 Mackinder unquestionably was imperialist (although not crudely jingoistic), but relatively few Britons of his time and station were actively anti-imperial – particularly in the early twentieth century, there was broad support across the British political spectrum for the preservation of the empire. The health of the empire was widely considered inseparable from the health of Britain itself and it was thought, not unreasonably, that a Britain shorn of its empire would no longer be a great power of the first rank. Mahan presents a somewhat more complex case. As Jon Sumida compellingly argues, while he "has often been caricatured as little more than a prophet of national aggrandisement through command of the sea, remembered for the influence rather than the substance of his thought, and relegated to a side corridor in the pantheon of discredited thinkers," the truth is far more complex. ("Alfred Thayer Mahan, Geopolitician," in Gray and Sloan, *Geopolitics, Geography, and Strategy*, p. 59.) Mahan's strategic views did develop over time as he moved from staunch anti-imperialism to supporting limited territorial acquisition, but he was never a "place in the sun" imperialist who simply argued for the acquisition of virtually any available acreage anywhere on the globe. He sought to obtain territories of perceived strategic value, not to maximize the number of people and the amount of land under the control of the United States government. Nicholas Spykman, by contrast, was not an imperialist in the sense that Mackinder or even Mahan were. By the 1940s, the American policymaking establishment had definitively turned against formal imperialism (in America, the public and elite popularity of overseas empire had been at its height at the same time as Mahan enjoyed his

greatest influence – the last years of the nineteenth century and the early years of the twentieth century). Spykman clearly did not endorse the United States' acquisition and administration of imperial territory, although, given their strong flavor of *Realpolitik*, his policy recommendations make him vulnerable to accusations of "imperialism" in the imprecise and polemical sense in which the word is often used.

22 "In international society all forms of coercion are permissible, including wars of destruction. This means that the struggle for power is identical with the struggle for survival, and the improvement of the relative power position becomes the primary objective of the internal and external policy of states. . . . Power means survival, the ability to impose one's will on others, the capacity to dictate to those who are without power, and the possibility of forcing concessions from those with less power." Nicholas J. Spykman, *America's Strategy in World Politics: The United States and the Balance of Power* (New York: Harcourt, Brace, 1942), p. 18.

23 Gearóid Ó Tuathail, "Understanding Critical Gepolitics: Geopolitics and Risk Security," in Gray and Sloan, *Geopolitics, Geography, and Strategy*, p. 108.

24 Ibid., p. 108.

25 Mahan most likely had the greatest influence of any geopolitician, Anglo-American, or otherwise. For an excellent examination of his role in shaping US policy, see Warren Zimmermann, *The First Great Triumph: How Five Americans Made Their Country a World Power* (New York: Farrar, Straus, and Giroux, 2002).

26 For a brief discussion of the various schools of realist thought see John Mearsheimer, *The Tragedy of Great Power Politics* (New York: Norton, 2001), pp. 17–22.

27 Hans J. Morgenthau, *Politics Among Nations: The Struggle for Power and Peace*, 5th edn (New York: Alfred A. Knopf, 1978; first edn published 1948), pp. 164–5 and 165–6.

28 "The Geographical Pivot of History" in *Democratic Ideals and Reality*, p. 176. Fairgrieve makes a similar point when he provides a context for his assertion that "the history of the world has been controlled by those conditions and phenomena which we class together under the title Geography." James Fairgrieve, *Geography and World Power* (New York: E.P. Dutton, 1941), p. 1. "We must know what is meant by 'control.' Perhaps it may be a help if we say what it does not mean and if we take some examples. It does not mean 'make' or 'cause': that is something higher. . . . [M]en can control a stream coming down a hillside to the extent that they can dig a channel for it, line its banks with stone prevent it coming beyond the channel; they can lay pipes to take a portion or all of it where they desire, but they cannot make the stream, in the sense of bringing the water into existence. Man can control his use of coal; he can determine whether he may use its energy to warm himself by its aid, or to cause a locomotive to draw him, or to make an engine drive a mill to make clothes for him, but he cannot make the coal. The idea of choice is fundamental in the conception of the control of man's actions by geography. A stream flows downhill under the action of gravity, always taking the line of greatest slope at any one point. Here the control is direct, simple and predictable. The actions of men, and specially of individual men are not predictable; men can choose what they can do, and herein lies the difference. Because man's body is composed of matter he is subject to the laws of matter; he tends to go downhill, to take the easiest path, but he may choose to go uphill – if there is a hill to ascend. Geography supplies the hills, and the plains." (p. 8)

29 Fairgrieve perhaps comes closer than Mackinder to geographical determinism: "Is there no short way in which we say what history *is*? Many answers may be given, and to the one given here there may be objections and there certainly are qualifications, but *it may be said that in its widest sense on its material side history is the story of man's increasing ability to control energy*." Ibid., p. 4; emphasis in original. However, even Fairgrieve's arguments do not rely on geographic determinism; as

the quotation cited above indicates, human choice remains a critical element in the international political equation. In Fairgrieve's view, a society must know how to use wisely the gifts that geography bestows if it is to obtain and keep international power.

30 In his last article on geopolitics Mackinder even notes that, "I make no pretense to forecasting the future of humanity." "The Round World and the Winning of the Peace" in *Democratic Ideals and Reality*, p. 195; originally published in *Foreign Affairs* (July 1943).

31 See Carl von Clausewitz, *On War*, ed. and trans. Michael Howard and Peter Paret (Princeton, NJ: Princeton University Press, 1984), *passim*.

32 See Sun Tzu, *Sun Tzu: The New Translation*, trans. J.H. Huang (New York: Quill, 1993) and Niccolò Machiavelli, *The Prince*, trans. and ed. Angelo M. Codevilla (New Haven: Yale University Press, 1997).

33 The United States faced numerous geographic obstacles in its effort to effect regime change in Afghanistan and Iraq. While both campaigns were successful, this speaks more to the low quality of the opposition that the Americans faced than to the relevance of geography. Most Taliban fighters essentially were ill-trained militia grossly outclassed by the US military, while the bulk of Iraqi soldiers, including even the "elite" Republican Guard, had little will to sacrifice their lives to preserve the Saddam regime. Indeed, more than a few Iraqi soldiers, surely, were silently cheering on their nominal foes. For various perspectives on the invasion of Iraq, see Anthony H. Cordesman, *The Iraq War: Strategy, Tactics, and Military Lessons* (Washington, DC: Center for Strategic and International Studies, 2003); Michael R. Gordon and Bernard B. Trainer, *Cobra II: The Inside Story of the Invasion and Occupation of Iraq* (New York: Pantheon, 2006); John Keegan, *The Iraq War* (New York: Knopf, 2004); Williamson Murray and Robert H. Scales, Jr, *The Iraq War: A Military History*, new edn (Cambridge, MA: Harvard/Belknap Press, 2005); Bing West and Ray L. Smith, *The March Up: Taking Baghdad with the First Marine Division* (New York: Bantam, 2003).

34 For instance, Admiral Bill Owens (USN, ret.) likely exaggerates grossly the degree to which technology will soon allow US military leaders to control any battlefield: "I believe the technology is available to the U.S. military today and now in development can revolutionize the way we conduct military operations. That technology can give us the ability to see a 'battlefield' as large as Iraq or Korea – an area 200 miles on a side – with unprecedented fidelity, comprehension, and timeliness; by night or day, in any kind of weather, all the time. In a future conflict, that means an Army corps commander in his field headquarters will have instant access to a live three-dimensional image of the entire battlefield displayed on a computer screen." William A. Owens, *Lifting the Fog of War* (New York: Farrar, Straus and Giroux, 2000), p. 13.

35 See, for example, Spykman, *America's Strategy in World Politics*, pp. 265–341.

36 A geopolitical theory that simply treated geography as the sole significant factor shaping human history would not only be inherently flawed, but whatever explanatory value it may have previously possessed would be rapidly diminishing because the link connecting climate, topography, and natural resources to national wealth is weakening overall. There are of course exceptions to this trend – Kuwait and Bahrain, for example – but few states today are rich chiefly because they possess valuable resources.

37 If not for an accident of geography – the fact that Iraq is located in the world's greatest petroleum-producing region and itself is possessed of great quantities of oil – Saddam Hussein's regime certainly would not have sustained the interest of the United States government for well over a decade. Oil wealth allowed Saddam to build a military large enough to overwhelm his small, but very oil-rich, neighbor Kuwait, while the possibility that Iraq would become a regional hegemon with the

ability to manipulate world petroleum prices mandated American intervention to lib-
erate the conquered country. Later, the sale of oil (illegally diverted in defiance of
UN sanctions) and kickbacks arranged through the UN-run Oil-for-Food program
allowed Saddam to maintain his internal security network and his hold on power,
until Washington finally decided to eliminate a longstanding nuisance, invading Iraq
and overthrowing the Ba'ath Party.

38 As Mackinder argued in 1904, "A generation ago steam and the Suez canal
appeared to have increased mobility of sea-power relative to land-power. Railways
acted chiefly as feeders to ocean-going commerce. But trans-continental railways
are now transmuting the conditions of land-power, and nowhere can they have such
an effect as in the closed heart-land of Euro-Asia, in vast areas of which neither
timber nor accessible stone was available for road-making." "The Geographical
Pivot of History," reprinted in *Democratic Ideal and Reality*, p. 259.

39 "On the subject of railroads, Mackinder was clearly impressed by the Russian
potential, and the impact that such a development would have on the balance of
power, strengthening land-power while weakening sea-power. He could see that a
network of railroads would lead to economic development, and make troop movements faster on land, all at the expense of the sea powers, particularly at the expense
of their elaborate base structures.... Mackinder was afraid that the railroads would
restore the advantage of the central position to the land powers. James Trapier Love,
Geopolitics and War: Mackinder's Philosophy of Power (Washington, DC: University Press of America, 1981), p. 23.

40 Samuel Huntington argues persuasively that the Orthodox and Western civilizations
are distinct, although it should be noted that the French- and German-speaking
Russian aristocracy of the nineteenth century was, unlike the Russian peasantry that
composed the vast majority of the population, culturally Westernized to a very great
degree. Given that Russia was ruled by an autocratic tsar and its upper bureaucracy
staffed by this aristocratic elite, it is hardly surprising that Moscow generally acted
in a fashion quite similar to other European great powers. Indeed, it is probable that
today's Russian elite is more "non-Western" than were its nineteenth century predecessors – today's Russian rulers came of age during the Soviet Union's failed experiment in creating a distinctive Soviet Civilization and now operate in an
environment in which robber barons, Mafiosi, present and former agents of the intelligence apparatus, and other rogues all cheerfully scheme to outmaneuver (and
sometimes jail or murder) each other, a political milieu decidedly unlike that prevailing in Western Europe. On the interaction between Western and Orthodox civilization, see Samuel Huntington, *The Clash of Civilizations and the Remaking of
World Order* (New York: Simon and Schuster, 1996), pp. 139–44.

41 Some thinkers speculate that humanity may be surprisingly close to abandoning the
shackles of physicality and effectively merging with computers to create an essentially new species in which "people" are largely indistinguishable from "computers." This obviously would be a change of the most fundamental sort for
humankind. For the purposes at hand, fundamental changes of this kind might be
considered as among the developments that may occur during this century, but eval-
uating the likelihood of an evolution of this kind is far outside the scope of this
work.

42 Another possible fundamental change that may occur in this century is the use of
advanced pharmacology and/or genetic manipulation to shape human nature.
Francis Fukuyama expresses great concern and disapproval of this possibility in
Francis Fukuyama, *Our Posthuman Future: Consequences of the Biotechnological
Revolution* (New York: Picador, 2003).

43 As Mackinder notes, "Each century has its own geographical perspective. Men still
living, though past the age of military service, were taught from a map of the world
on which nearly all the interior of Africa was a blank.... The geographical

perspective of the twentieth century differs, however, from that of all the previous centuries in more than mere extension. In outline our geographical knowledge is now complete." *Democratic Ideals and Reality*, pp. 21–2.

44 Mackinder, "The Geographical Pivot of History," *Democratic Ideals and Reality*, 175–6.

45 The great advantages of the Pivot/Heartland, Mackinder surmised, were its enormous resources and inaccessibility to seapower. As Brian W. Blouet explains, "Mackinder argued that in the heartland of Eurasia there was a pivotal region that lay beyond the reach of sea power.... When the railways were built this vast interior region would produce increased quantities of wheat, cotton, fuels, and metals while remaining apart from oceanic commerce." Brian W. Blouet, *Geopolitics and Globalization* (London: Reaktion, 2001), p. 27. Mackinder's notion of the parameters of the Pivot/Heartland changed over roughly four decades from when he first proposed the idea to when he last wrote on it, but he always argued that the Pivot/Heartland's character and military potential made it a critical region of the world.

46 Nevertheless, German near-success in World War II and the Soviet Union's imperial gains during and after that conflict demonstrated convincingly that a powerful Heartland polity *could* provide a potent challenge to the political autonomy of the Western Europe states.

47 On this episode see J.F.C. Fuller, *The Generalship of Alexander the Great* (New York: Da Capo Press, n.d.; originally published 1960), p. 130; Mary Renault, *The Nature of Alexander* (New York: Pantheon, 1975), pp. 172 and 181; Ulrich Wilcken, *Alexander the Great* (New York: Norton, 1967), p. 186.

48 For an excellent discussion of Philip II of Spain's global politics see Geoffrey Parker, *The Grand Strategy of Philip II* (New Haven, CT: Yale University Press, 1998).

49 For a brief summary of the importance of the empire to Portugal's economy and the crown's efforts to secure a monopoly of lucrative businesses such as the spice trade, see Rondo Cameron and Larry Neal, *A Concise Economic History of the World: From Paleolithic Times to the Present* (New York: Oxford University Press, 2003), pp. 139–41. Also see Bailey W. Diffie and George D. Winius, *Foundations of the Portuguese Empire, 1415–1580*, Europe and the World in the Age of Expansion series, vol. 1 (Minneapolis, MN: University of Minnesota Press, 1977), esp. pp. 407–15.

50 One arguably could include other regional centers of power, such as India/South Asia. In any case, India's substantial population and economic vitality during much of the Columbian Epoch should be noted.

51 This is illustrated by the fact that one author is bold enough to argue for the existence of a single "Islamo-Christian" civilization, an entity that would spill over both of the other major regional power centers. See Richard W. Bulliet, *The Case for Islamo-Christian Civilization*, new edn (New York: Columbia University Press, 2006).

52 It is, for example, very difficult to explain the British and American bombing campaign in World War II without reference to this fact. There was nothing in the broad Anglo-American culture, which made a very clear distinction between combatants and civilians, to justify the mass death of non-combatant civilians in the notoriously imprecise and quite ruthless bombing campaigns conducted against Germany and Japan. However, given the military benefits that, it was believed, would flow from a comprehensive bombing campaign, both London and Washington chose to conduct massive bombing campaigns against their enemies.

53 For example, the United States today certainly has an interest in the world price of oil, and if plausibly threatened with a huge and apparently permanent increase in the world price band, Washington would take action, probably including military action

if necessary, to prevent it. However, no American administration would consider simply seizing the Saudi and Kuwaiti oilfields, declaring the area US territory, and leveraging control of the fields to manipulate the world price downward. Such a course would probably have the desired strategic effect (although it would likely also have other, very undesirable, consequences), but would be unthinkable to a twenty-first-century American policymaker. Militarily speaking, it would be eminently plausible, but American strategic culture simply would not permit it. However, sixteenth-century European policymakers, faced with a similar problem, would not consider such a course of action at all outrageous and, so long as they believed military success to be likely, an aggressive colonial endeavor would likely be the course of action that they would choose.

54 A history of these fascinating voyages is offered in Louise Levathes, *When China Ruled the Seas: The Treasure Fleet of the Dragon Throne, 1405–33* (New York: Simon and Schuster, 1994). For short accounts see Bailey and Winius, *Foundations of the Portuguese Empire*, pp. 66–7; Jacques Gernet, *A History of Chinese Civilization*, 2nd edn (New York: Cambridge University Press, 1996), pp. 398–402; and F.W. Mote, *Imperial China, 900–1800* (Cambridge, MA: Harvard University Press, 1999), pp. 613–17.

55 Thomas M. Kane succinctly discusses some of the factors influencing China's decision to reject sea power: "In the mid-1400s ... China's bid for seapower fell victim to court politics. The Confucian scholars who ran China's bureaucracy were traditionally hostile to seafaring, both because Confucius himself had depicted merchants as social parasites and because the court eunuchs who controlled the fleet were their political rivals.... Maritime trade declined in economic importance as well. China's currency collapsed during the mid-1400s, forcing Chinese merchants to pay for their goods in gold and silver. Officials who might once have seen trade as a valuable source of revenue began to perceive it as a dangerous drain on China's reserves of precious metals. The Ming Dynasty constructed a series of canals which made inland water transport cheaper and safer than coastal shipping. Meanwhile, invasions from Central Asia distracted officials from maritime affairs." *Chinese Grand Strategy and Maritime Power* (London and Portland, OR: Frank Cass, 2002), p. 28.

56 As Steven Mosher notes, "For more than two thousand years the Chinese considered themselves the geographical, and geopolitical, center of the world. From their earlier incarnation as an empire they spoke of China as *Zhong Guo*, 'The Middle Kingdom,' or even more revealingly, as *Tian Xia*, 'Everything Under Heaven.' They believed their emperor to be the only legitimate political authority in their known world and viewed themselves as the highest expression of civilized humanity." *Hegemon: China's Plan to Dominate Asia and the World* (San Francisco, CA: Encounter, 2000), p. 2.

57 Given its cosmopolitan perspective, it is unsurprising that the most powerful Western religious institution, the Roman Catholic Church, took an active interest over centuries in the worldwide spread of Catholicism. Moreover, the major West European Catholic powers were generally friendly to the Church's missionary activity in their empires and, at least formally, considered the propagation of the Faith to be an important state activity. The effects speak for themselves: today there are far more active Catholics in the former colonies of France, Spain, and Portugal than there are in Europe itself.

58 At least terms of political theory, this obligation perhaps weighed especially heavily on Muslim leaders, as the notion of a secular state was alien to classical Islamic thought. Although Western thinkers generally endorsed the division of secular and religious authority, Islamic thought inextricably intertwined state and religious authority. As Roger Scruton argues, even today "Islamic jurisprudence does not recognize secular, still less territorial, jurisdiction as a genuine source of law. It

proposes a universal law that is the single path (*shariʻ*) to salvation. And the *shariʻa* is not understood as setting limits to what can be commanded, but rather as a fully comprehensive system of commands – which can serve a military just as well as a civilian function. Nor does Islam recognize the state as an independent object of loyalty. . . . Nor is there any trace in Islamic law of the secular conception of government that Christianity inherited (via St. Paul) from Roman law." *The West and the Rest: Globalization the Terrorist Threat* (Wilmington, DE: Intercollegiate Studies Institute, 2002), p. 66. It should be noted, however, that there are examples of Western European states blurring the distinction between secular and church institutions; most notably, King Henry VIII took on an unusual role that mixed secular and religious authority by breaking with Rome and making himself the head of a separate Church of England.

59 Philip II was a particularly striking figure in this respect. Noting several statements by Philip, Geoffrey Parker argues that they contained multiple layers of "messianic vision." "First, Philip believed that God had chosen him to rule expressly to achieve His purpose for the world. Second, he was equally convinced that God held him under special protection, to enable him to achieve these goals (although the process might prove neither obvious nor easy). Third, he felt certain that, if necessary, God would intervene directly in order to help him succeed." *Success is Never Final: Empire, War, and Faith in Early Modern Europe* (New York: Basic Books, 2002), p. 30.

60 Moreover, this was despite the fact that in the early sixteenth century Ottoman sultans also began to use the title of caliph, thus at least theoretically accepting the duty to see to the spiritual health of Islam and its further propagation over the earth.

61 Bernard Lewis, *What Went Wrong? The Clash Between Islam and Modernity in the Middle East* (New York: Perennial, 2003), p. 11.

62 See Warren Treadgold, *A History of the Byzantine State and Society* (Stanford, CA: Stanford University Press, 1997), pp. 301–22.

63 For a brief history of this critical engagement, see J.F.C. Fuller, *A Military History of the Western World, Vol. I: From the Earliest Times to the Battle of Lepanto* (New York: Da Capo, n.d.; originally published 1954), pp. 559–78.

64 See Parker, *The Military Revolution*, pp. 105–6.

65 Bernard Lewis makes the interesting point that the Ottoman elite remained quite uninterested in the New World for centuries: "A Turkish version of Columbus's own (now lost) map, prepared in 1513, survives in the Topkapi Palace in Istanbul, where it remained, unconsulted and unknown, until it was discovered by a German scholar in 1929. A Turkish book on the New World was written in the late sixteenth century, and was translated from a variety of European sources – oral rather than written. It describes the flora, fauna, and inhabitants of the New World, and, of course, expresses the hope that this blessed land would in due course be illuminated by the light of Islam and added to the sultan's realms. This too remained unknown until it was printed in Istanbul in 1729." *What Went Wrong?*, pp. 37 and 39.

66 On Spanish imperial overextension, see Anthony Pagden, "Heeding Heraclides: Empire and Its Discontents, 1619–1812," in Richard L. Kagan and Geoffrey Parker, eds, *Spain, Europe, and the Atlantic World: Essays in Honor of John H. Elliott* (Cambridge: Cambridge University Press, 1995), pp. 316–33.

67 Perceptive analyses of the death of the Ottoman Empire and how it set the course for the later political history of the Middle East are offered in Efraim Karsh and Inari Karsh, *Empires in the Sand: The Struggle for Mastery in the Middle East, 1789–1923* (Cambridge, MA: Harvard, 1999) and David Fromkin, *A Peace to End All Peace: The Fall of the Ottoman Empire and the Creation of the Modern Middle East* (New York: Avon, 1990).

68 Niall Ferguson observes that, "[W]hat is very striking about the history of the Empire is that whenever the British were behaving despotically, there was almost

always a liberal critique of that behavior from within British society. Indeed, so powerful and consistent was this tendency to judge Britain's imperial conduct by the yardstick of liberty that it gave the British Empire something of a self-liquidating character. Once a colonized society had sufficiently adopted the other institutions the British brought with them, it became very hard for the British to prohibit that political liberty to which they attached so much significance for themselves." *Empire: The Rise and Demise of the British World Order and the Lessons for Global Power* (New York: Basic Books, 2003), p. xxii.

69 A powerful defense of Mackinder's theories, and his continuing relevance to international politics, is offered in Colin S. Gray, "In Defence of the Heartland: Sir Halford Mackinder and his Critics a Hundred Years On," *Comparative Strategy*, 23:1 (January–March 2004): pp. 9–25.

70 Notably, this tentativeness very much is on display in the work of Leon Kass, formerly the chair of the President's Council on Bioethics (2002–2005), and therefore a key policymaker in this area. For example, in a highly influential essay originally published in *The New Republic* (2 June 1997), he makes explicitly emotional arguments against human cloning: "We are repelled by the prospect of cloning human beings not because of the strangeness or novelty of the undertaking, but because we intuit and feel, immediately and without argument, the violation of things that we rightfully hold dear. Repugnance, here as elsewhere, revolts against the excesses of human willfulness, warning us not to transgress what is unspeakably profound. Indeed, in this age in which everything is held to permissible so long as it is freely done, in which our given human nature no longer commands respect, in which our bodies are regarded as mere instruments of our autonomous rational wills, repugnance may be the only voice left that speaks up to defend the central core of our humanity." "The Wisdom of Repugnance" in Leon R. Kass and James Q. Wilson, eds, *The Ethics of Human Cloning* (Washington: The AEI Press, 1998), p. 19.

71 Notably, today's PRC is ideologically a *very* young country indeed – the rejection of Maoism and creation of today's essentially "post-Marxist" Chinese Communist Party (CCP) is a very recent development that more-or-less began with the death of Mao Zedong in 1976.

72 For an enlightening discussion of long-term continuities in the governance of Russia, see Steven Rosefielde, *Russia in the Twenty-First Century: The Prodigal Superpower* (Cambridge, UK and New York: Cambridge University Press, 2004), *passim*.

73 See Kane, *Chinese Grand Strategy and Maritime Power, passim*.

74 This is in stark contrast to some would-be superpowers, such as the Third Reich. It is difficult to ascertain definitively what the limits were of Hitler's territorial and military ambitions, but Norman J.W. Goda persuasively argues that in 1940–1942 Hitler was attempting to obtain military bases that were intended for eventual use in an invasion of the Western Hemisphere. *Tomorrow the World: Hitler, Northwest Africa, and the Path Toward America* (College Station, TX: Texas A&M University Press, 1998).

75 As Zbigniew Brzezinski notes, "China's continued economic success remains heavily dependent on the inflow of Western capital and technology and on access to foreign markets, and that severely limits China's options." *The Grand Chessboard: American Primacy and Its Geostrategic Imperatives* (New York: BasicBooks, 1997), p. 186.

76 As Georg Schwarzenberger elegantly states, "In any balance of power system, the jealousies of other greater powers tend to raise obstacles to unlimited expansion by any one power. There usually comes a point when any of them can expand further only the risk of a major war." *Power Politics: A Study of International Society*, 2nd edn (London: Stevens and Sons, 1951), p. 49.

77 For an illustration of the continuing Vietnamese suspicion of China see Henry

Kamm, *Dragon Ascending: Vietnam and the Vietnamese* (New York: Arcade Publishing, 1996), pp. 125–33.

78 Harry Harding contends that the United States "should increasingly treat India on a par with China as a major regional power with global aspirations, rather than as regarding it simply as Pakistan's counterpart in a South Asian balance of power." "The Evolution of the Strategic Triangle: China, India, and the United States," in Francine R. Frankel and Harry Harding, eds, *The India–China Relationship: What the United States Needs to Know* (New York: Columbia University Press/Woodrow Wilson Center Press, 2004), p. 343. Harding raises an important issue. When considering Indian strategic interests, American leaders often have tended to focus on the India–Pakistan competition. This was never an entirely satisfactory perspective – India always has had global diplomatic ambitions – but it becomes ever more outdated as India grows increasingly wealthy and powerful.

79 Philip C. Saunders has a somewhat different view, believing that the United States may be able to weld together a "virtual alliance" in the Asia-Pacific that would be institutionally unlike NATO but would offer significant benefits in the containment of China. "A Virtual Alliance for Asian Security," *Orbis*, 43:2 (Spring 1999), pp. 237–56. Also, Bradley A. Thayer considers the possibility of establishing an "Asian Treaty Organization" in "Confronting China: An Evaluation of Options for the United States, *Comparative Strategy*, 24:1 (January–March 2005), pp. 71–98.

80 See C. Dale Walton, "The Decline of the Third Rome: Russia's Prospects as a Great power," *Journal of Slavic Military Studies*, 12:1 (March 1999), pp. 51–63.

81 At present, the SCO has four members aside from China and Russia: Kazakhstan, Kyrgyzstan, Tajikistan, and Uzbekistan. India, Iran, Mongolia, and Pakistan all enjoy observer status, and all of them, other than India, clearly have indicated a desire to join the SCO.

82 See Jim Yardley, "Russia Denies War Games with China are a Signal to Taiwan," *New York Times* online edn, 19 March 2005; Jane McCarthy, "Old Enemies' Wargames Send a Powerful Message to the US," *Times* (London) online edn, 3 August 2005; and Chris Buckley, "China and Russia are set to Begin Joint Military Exercises Today," *New York Times* online edn, 18 August 2005.

83 Notably, Colin S. Gray argues that a Russo-Chinese alliance is likely. *Another Bloody Century: Future Warfare* (London: Weidenfeld & Nicolson, 2005), pp. 382–3.

84 See Colin S. Gray, *The Sheriff: America's Defense of the New World Order* (Lexington, KY: The University Press of Kentucky, 2004).

85 An intriguing analysis of Soviet strategic errors during the Cold War is offered in Thomas M. Nichols, *Winning the World: Lessons for America's Future from the Cold War* (New York: Praeger, 2002).

86 "The dawn of the Cold War can only be seen as a tragedy or a mistake if it is assumed that the Soviet Union could somehow have been accommodated within the structure of the international system and swayed from its aggressive aims. To believe that this was possible is to believe that Soviet goals were almost entirely opportunistic, little more than a territorial imperative devoid of any other objective but to satisfy a lust for ever larger chunks of real estate. But the desire to spread the reach of the Soviet Union was inherent in the very nature of the Soviet state. This desire may have found a special virulence in the way it was expressed by Stalin, but it was nonetheless a defining characteristic of the Soviet system that both predated and outlived him." Nichols, *Winning the World*, p. 60.

87 When discussing German aggression in particular, the peculiar personal psychology of Adolf Hitler surely was of critical importance in shaping his regime's behavior. Hitler's neuroses and worldview are addressed in detail in Jay Y. Gonen, *The Roots of Nazi Psychology: Hitler's Utopian Barbarism* (Lexington, KY: University Press of Kentucky, 2000); Fritz Redlich, *Hitler: Diagnosis of a Destructive Prophet* (New

York: Oxford University Press, 1998); Ron Rosenbaum, *Explaining Hitler: The Search for the Origins of His Evil* (New York: HarperPerennial, 1999); Robert G.L. Waite, *The Psychopathic God: Adolf Hitler* (New York: Da Capo Press, 1993; originally published 1977); and Idem, *Kaiser and Führer: A Comparative Study of Personality and Politics* (Toronto: University of Toronto Press, 1998).

88 See Colin S. Gray, *The Sheriff: America's Defense of the New World Order* (Lexington, KY: University Press of Kentucky, 2004), pp. ix, 35.

89 Donald Rumsfeld, "Secretary Rumsfeld Speaks on '21st Century Tranformation' of US Armed Forces (transcript of remarks and question and answer period)," Speech delivered at National Defense University, Fort McNair, Washington, DC, 31 January 2002, accessed at www.defenselink.mil.

90 A particularly strong examination of the American RMA debate is Colin S. Gray, *Strategy for Chaos: Revolutions in Military Affairs and the Evidence of History*, Strategy and History series (London: Frank Cass, 2002). A now-classic "RMA enthusiast" argument is offered Martin Libiki, *The Mesh and the Net: Speculations on Armed Conflict in an Age of Free Silicon*, McNair Paper #28 (Washington, DC: Institute for National Strategic Studies/National Defense University, 1994). Some of the many other influential works related to the RMA debate include Lawrence Freedman, *The Revolution in Strategic Affairs*, Adelphi Paper 318 (London: International Institute for Strategic Studies, 1998); William A. Owens, *Lifting the Fog of War* (New York: Farrar, Straus and Giroux, 2000); Alvin and Heidi Toffler, *War and Anti-War: Survival at the Dawn of the 21st Century* (Boston: Little, Brown, 1993); and Barry D. Watts, *Clausewitzian Friction and Future War*, rev. edn, McNair Paper #68 (Washington, DC: Institute for National Strategic Studies/National Defense University, 2004).

91 On the Nuclear RMA, see Gray, *Strategy for Chaos*, pp. 222–69.

92 In words grimly applicable to central nuclear war, Mackinder states, "Let anyone try to realize what would happen to himself if all those on whom he depends – the postmen, railwaymen, butchers, bakers, printers, and very many others – were suddenly to vary their settled routines; he will then begin to appreciate in how great a degree the power of modern man over nature is due to the fact that society is a Going Concern, or, in the language of the engineer, has momentum. Stop the running long enough to throw men's habits of gear with one another, and society would quickly run down to the simple reality of control by nature. Vast numbers would die in consequence." *Democratic Ideals and Reality*, p. 8.

93 See Gray, *Strategy for Chaos*, p. 249.

94 As William E. Odom explains, "Air-Land Battle … was not based on tactical nuclear weapons but rather the so-called 'emerging technologies' and 'smart weapons' made possible by microcircuitry technology and lasers. They permitted the production of highly accurate, longer range, artillery and rocketry for NATO's FOFA, i.e., 'follow-on forces attacks.' They also made possible the huge increase in tactical speed and agility provided by M-1 tanks, Bradley Fighting Vehicles, and a number of other new systems allowing fairly deep ground counterattacks and spoiling attacks. Thus the Soviet general staff faced the prospect of a series of NATO deep attacks that might unhinge Soviet offensive operations." "Comment on the 1964 Warsaw Pact Plan," Parallel History Project on NATO and the Warsaw Pact, n.d., accessed at www.isn.ethz.ch. On the development of AirLand Battle, see John J. Romjue, "The Evolution of the AirLand Battle Concept," *Air University Review*, 35:4 (May–June 1984), pp. 4–15, accessed online at www.airpower.maxwell.af.mil/airchronicles/aureview. A strong contemporary criticism of the doctrine is offered by Jon S. Powell, "AirLand Battle: The Wrong Concept for the Wrong Reason," *Air University Review*, 36:4 (May/June 1985), pp. 15–22.

95 However, it should be noted that during the early stage of the Second American

RMA, the United States had not yet clearly rejected nuclear usage; indeed, it was actively developing several technologies intended to make more discriminate nuclear warfare possible but also were applicable to conventional warfare. "[M]ilitary planners borrowed concepts developed in the course of the vain attempt to generate decisive and discriminating nuclear strikes and began to apply them to conventional operations, along with many of the technologies that supported them. The technologies developed in an effort to refine nuclear strategy had obvious applications from the start in conventional operations. Satellites were in use for reconnaissance purposes by 1961 and for communications (in Vietnam) in 1965. The first tactical computers were used in 1966. The Internet can be traced back to a Pentagon-backed project to link together computers in the 1960s.... Most of the core technologies now associated with the RMA could be listed by the early 1970s: precision guidance; remote guidance and control; munitions improvements; target identification and acquisition; command, control, and communications; and electronic warfare." Freedman, *The Revolution in Strategic Affairs*, p. 21.

96 This is hardly surprising when one considers broad American culture and, specifically, US military subculture. Napoleon's famous insult that Britain was a "nation of shopkeepers" was worn as badge of honor by his British contemporaries. American culture is a postmodern version of Napoleon's Britain, and it has a commercial, legal, and technological orientation. A twenty-first-century Napoleon could nicely summarize the United States as a nation of businesspeople, lawyers, and engineers. The broad American culture is technophilic and many individuals who populate the military – pilots, communications and radar specialists, and many others – have jobs that require considerable comfort with high technology equipment, and the US military thus is even more technologically oriented. This has many advantages – it is a good thing that today's Pentagon is not populated by hidebound senior officers similar to Civil War logisticians obsessed with the concern that the repeating rifle would cause soldiers to fire their ammunition too quickly – but it also has a notable downside. US strategic culture (on both the military and civilian sides) tends to be resistant to the notion that there are some strategic goals, such as eliminating insurgent opposition to the new government of Iraq, that cannot be achieved quickly, and that some strategic problems are in fact conditions that perhaps can be mitigated but cannot be eliminated. The international dislike, particularly in the Islamic world, of the United States is one such condition; the simple fact that America is so very rich and powerful, that its media products are beamed to homes worldwide, and that the latter present a lifestyle repugnant to a continuum of individuals ranging from European radical environmentalists to Pakistani Islamists ensures that there will be a very substantial number of people in the world who passionately hate the United States and a non-negligible number who want to kill Americans simply because they are Americans.

97 See Douglas C. Lovelace, Jr, *The Evolution in Military Affairs: Shaping the Future U.S. Armed Forces* (Carlisle Barracks, PA: Strategic Studies Institute/U.S. Army War College, 1997).

98 For an "anti-blitzkrieg" view, see John Mosier, *The Blitzkrieg Myth: How Hitler and the Allies Misread the Strategic Realities of World War II* (New York: HarperCollins, 2003).

99 On the Napoleonic and World War II German RMAs, see MacGregor Knox, "Mass Politics and Nationalism as Military Revolution: The French Revolution and After" and Williamson Murray, "May 1940: Contingency and Fragility of the German RMA," in MacGregor Knox and Williamson Murray, eds, *The Dynamics of Military Revolution, 1300–2050* (Cambridge, UK: Cambridge University Press, 2001), pp. 57–73 and 154–74.

100 This of course was not always the case. From the War of Independence until at least World War II, some of the most colorful characters in military history, including

Generals "Mad" Anthony Wayne, William Tecumseh Sherman, U.S. Grant, Thomas "Stonewall" Jackson, Douglas MacArthur, and George S. Patton, held high rank in the American or Confederate armies. However, recent decades have been far less kind to officers of questionable sanity or sobriety, or who simply do not fit in well in a managerial culture. Although somewhat flamboyant figures such as Generals Norman Schwarzkopf occasionally still attain high rank, the prevailing military culture clearly is more salubrious for "managerial personalities" such as Colin Powell and Wesley Clark.

101 "Text of the Strategic Offensive Reductions Treaty," 24 May 2002, accessed at http://www.whitehouse.gov/news/releases/2002/05/20020524-3.html.

102 On horizontal proliferation and related issues, see C. Dale Walton, "Navigating the Second Nuclear Age: Proliferation and Deterrence in this Century," *Global Dialogue*, 8:1 (Winter/Spring 2006), pp. 22–31.

103 The "usual non-proliferation suspects" argue that sufficiently intensive and thoughtful engagement will convince Iran to see the error of its ways. As with North Korea, there is every reason to believe that such optimism is based on fantasy. A brief argument for why this is the case is offered in C. Dale Walton, "Get Used to It: Iran Will Have Nukes," *St. Louis Post-Dispatch*, 13 April 2006, 9(B).

104 On the latter case, see Victor Davis Hanson, *Carnage and Culture: Landmark Battles in the Rise of Western Power* (New York: Doubleday, 2001), pp. 170–232.

105 This view still is rejected by many American observers, and was a decidedly minority viewpoint in the 1990s. As Andrew Bacevich argues, during that decade, American military thinkers intended to rely on the advantages flowing from the RMA to ensure awe-inspiring dominance over the long term: "At root, the expectation that the United States could sustain broad-gauged military preeminence rested on a specific understanding of the role that technology – in particular information technology – has come to play in modern warfare. That role was purported to be a decisive one.... [H]aving assessed the security implications of globalization – a process ostensibly making the world more complicated and dangerous than ever before – the United States after the Cold War committed itself to establishing a level of military mastery without historical precedent.... Swift, unerring, implacable, and invincible, U.S. forces aimed to achieve something approaching omnipotence: 'Full Spectrum Dominance.'" *American Empire: The Realities and Consequences of U.S. Diplomacy* (Cambridge, MA: Harvard University Press, 2002), pp. 131 and 133.

106 Robert Baer's damning and compelling memoir argues that the CIA, and the American government more broadly, ignored clear evidence that an Islamist terrorist threat to the United States was developing in the 1980s and 1990s, and that the events of 11 September 2001 resulted from the American unwillingness to take the actions necessary to address that danger. *See No Evil: The True Story of a Ground Soldier in the CIA's War on Terrorism* (New York: Three Rivers Press, 2002).

107 It should be noted that defeating the United States in conventional war would not necessarily require the development of a comprehensibly strong military force. It may be possible for America's opponents to develop niche military capabilities that would allow them temporarily to exploit key vulnerabilities in the US force structure in a small, but critical, geographical area and thus win a limited conflict. Thus, for example, it might not be necessary for China to defeat the United States Navy outright in order to outmaneuver the United States in a conflict over Taiwan. If the PRC could merely blind the United States by temporarily damaging its satellite network and use submarines, cruise missiles, and other hazards to make the waters surrounding the ROC very dangerous, a US president might lack the will to place tens of thousands of American lives at grave risk, especially if the Chinese invasion was well-executed and the PRC very quickly established a strong beachhead. For a thoughtful exploration of how Beijing might endeavor to prevent American

intervention in a PRC–ROC conflict, see Paul Dodge, "Circumventing Sea Power: Chinese Strategies to Deter U.S. Intervention in Taiwan," *Comparative Strategy*, 23/4–5 (October–December 2004), pp. 391–409.

108 American leaders obviously are not ignorant of the fact that their enemies may cooperate and, at least to a limited degree, this has driven US force planning in the post-Cold War period. The long-running debate in the 1990s over whether it was necessary that the United States have a military force of such size and quality that it could win two simultaneous major theater wars ("win-win") or if it is sufficient to have a military prepared to win one in one theater while holding in another and then transfer forces to the remaining theater to secure a second victory ("win-hold-win") clearly was shaped by the possibility of enemy cooperation – in that case, collaboration between medium power rogues. The possibility of great power cooperation obviously presents much more daunting challenges than does roguish camaraderie.

109 See, for example, Robert Wright, "They Hate Us, They Really Hate US," *New York Times* online edn, 14 May 2006; James Dao, "One Nation Plays the Great Game Alone," *New York Times* online edn, 6 July 2002; and Nicholas D. Kristof, "Why Do They Hate Us?" *New York Times* online edn, 15 January 2002.

110 Huntington, *The Clash of Civilizations and the Remaking of World Order*, p. 59.

111 Richard Nixon and Henry Kissinger attempted to apply this insight in their Vietnam War negotiations through what has become known as the "Madman Theory," an attempt to convince Hanoi that Nixon was so psychologically unstable and prone to violence that settling the war on US terms would be preferable to running the risk that the American president would lash out at his enemy with extreme violence. See Jeffrey Kimball, *Nixon's Vietnam War* (Lawrence, KS: University Press of Kansas, 1998), pp. 63–86.

112 An excellent analysis of Napoleonic diplomacy is offered in Paul W. Schroeder, *The Transformation of European Politics, 1763–1848*, The Oxford History of Modern Europe series (New York: Oxford University Press, 1994).

113 For a decidedly different view, see Eric Hobsbawm, "America's Imperial Delusion," *Guardian* (London) online edn, 14 June 2003; Margaret Drabble, "I Loathe America, and What It has Done to the Rest of the World," *Daily Telegraph* online edn, 8 May 2003; and Stephen Chan, *Out of Evil: New International Politics and Old Doctrines of War* (Ann Arbor, MI: University of Michigan Press, 2005).

114 Adam B. Siegel, "Base Access Constraints and Response," *Airpower Journal*, Spring 1996, accessed online at www.airpower.maxwell.af.mil.

115 It of course is entirely appropriate, indeed helpful, for less powerful allies to question decisions by a superpower comrade that appear unwise. Moreover, a superpower must acknowledge the reality that domestic politics in allied countries will occasionally require *pro forma* declaratory opposition to its policies – every French president must "ruffle the eagle's feathers" a bit, and every American president knows that. However, the opposition to Operation Iraqi Freedom went far beyond the normal boundaries of friendly disagreement. As soon as the United States decided on its course in Iraq, regardless of whether that course was prudent or feckless, its interests were deeply engaged in the overthrow of the Saddam regime and the successful reconstruction of that country. Nevertheless, several formal allies of the United States actively conspired to sabotage the policy of the United States and, thus, to harm its national interests.

116 For a defense of EU action related to Iraq by two key European policymakers, see Romano Prodi and Chris Patten, "Europe's Commitment to Iraq," *Washington Post* online edn, 26 June 2004.

117 Michael Lind bluntly describes the Cold War relationship between the United States and NATO-Europe: "America's Cold War strategy of dual containment required the United States to act as a hegemon, rather than as the leader of a traditional alliance of equals or near equals ... America's hegemonic alliance was based on the unilat-

eral extension of a U.S. security guarantee to clients, of which the most important were West Germany and Japan." *The American Way of Strategy: U.S. Foreign Policy and the American Way of Life* (New York: Oxford University Press, 2006), p. 115.

118 At its most extreme, the United States could have chosen to withdraw its troops from Europe or even remove the nuclear umbrella from over its NATO allies. This of course would have been immensely foolish strategically, but it was not impossible – after all, Senator George McGovern, the 1972 Democratic nominee for president, proposed a US troop withdrawal from Europe during his campaign – and the possibility of a future resurgence of American isolationism always concerned European leaders.

119 Indeed, this belief even plays a role in US domestic politics. One of the main themes of the 2004 US presidential election was John Kerry's reasonable contention that the Bush Administration had gravely damaged Washington's relationship with its allies, but his criticisms tended to carry the unspoken assumption that continuing unipolar leadership is possible so long as American diplomacy is competent. See, for example, Robin Toner, "Kerry Says He Would Clear the Air with U.S. Allies," *New York Times* online edn, 26 May 2004.

120 It is, however, necessary to note that most such cases are imperfect in their unipolarity. For instance, the Roman Empire was long confronted by a strong Parthian Empire that was capable of placing Rome's Eastern provinces in peril; in the east, Rome did not possess consistently overwhelming power relative to its Parthian rival, although it did eventually deal the latter a series of blows that critically weakened it. One even could argue that, long before the formal division of the Roman Empire, most of the Empire was part of a unipolar regional system but that its Easternmost portions were part of a bipolar regional system.

121 A classic work on the crimes related to Soviet collectivization is Robert Conquest, *The Harvest of Sorrow: Soviet Collectivization and the Terror-Famine* (New York: Oxford University Press, 1986). As Richard Pipes notes, "Collectivization degraded the peasant even more than did pre-1861 serfdom, since as a serf he had owned (in practice, if not in theory) his crops and livestock. His new status was that of a slave laborer who received the bare minimum of subsistence: for backbreaking work in 1935 a peasant household earned from the kolkhoz 247 rubles a year, just enough to purchase one pair of shoes." *Communism: A History*, Modern Library Chronicles (New York: Modern Library, 2003), p. 61.

122 It is notable that among the strategically ineducable was onetime Vice President Henry Wallace, an individual who was removed from the 1944 Democratic presidential ticket and replaced by Harry Truman only at the demand of tough-minded elements in his party. Since Roosevelt himself preferred to keep Wallace on the 1944 ticket, it is clear that the presidency very nearly fell into the hands of a man whose view of the Soviet Union was staggeringly unguarded and positive – a fact that was very much on display in his unsuccessful presidential run as the candidate of the Progressive Party in 1948. The period from Roosevelt's death to January 1949 of course was an absolutely critical one in the Cold War, and it is quite probable the history of that conflict – and perhaps its ultimate outcome – would have been very different indeed if President Wallace had been deciding whether to lay the groundwork for containment of the Soviet Union.

123 To the degree possible, the author has avoided references to "balancing," as the American debate between "primacists" and advocates of "offshore balancing" is not the focus herein, although it would be broadly accurate to describe this work as falling in the latter camp, as the author does not consider American unipolarity to be sustainable. An introduction to the two contrasting schools of thought is offered in Christopher Layne and Bradley A. Thayer, *American Empire: A Debate* (New York: Routledge, 2006). In regard to American policy in this century, the author

prefers to speak of "arbitration" rather than "balancing." The goal of the policy recommendations, herein, is to preserve Washington's position as being clearly the
greatest of the world's powers and that it can leverage that position to maintain a
dominant (though not a hegemonic) role in the international system, not simply to
ensure that no single continental power becomes too powerful and overthrows the
multipolar system. The latter is merely subsidiary, a prerequisite for achieving the
former goal.

124 See "The Treaty of Westphalia," 24 October 1648, translation posted by The Avalon
Project at Yale Law School, accessed at www.yale.edu/lawweb/avalon.

125 Indeed, it should remembered that the characteristic of Bonapartism that most
unsettled European contemporaries was not that the new imperial order had arisen
from the ashes of the French Revolution and thus replaced the Bourbons, who had
been accepted as the legitimate dynastic rulers of France. Rather, it was that the
militaristic French emperor was entirely unwilling to be reasonable and accept a
peace that would allow France to enjoy territorial gains and other benefits but
permit the other European great powers to also survive as fully independent actors.
See Paul W. Schroeder, *The Transformation of European Politics, 1763–1848,
passim.*

126 A common international rulebook does not, of course, invariably prevent war – it
merely assists policymakers who mutually wish to avoid military conflict. When one
or more great powers *actively desire* war, they can have it. A good example of this
is the prelude to World War I. Although for decades most observers accepted what
one might call the "Tuchman interpretation" of the conflict – that European leaders
stumbled into war as a result of the crisis of August 1914 – Donald Kagan and
others have argued convincingly that Germany in fact manipulated the circumstances following the assassination of Archduke Ferdinand to goad Europe into a
general war. See Donald Kagan, *On the Origins of War and the Preservation of
Peace* (New York: Anchor Books, 1996). The perspective of Germany's leaders is
notable: they apparently were convinced that a general great power war was
inevitable, sooner or later. Given the socio-economic transformation occurring in
Russia that would allow that most populous of European powers to support an
enormous army of ever-higher quality, Berlin would be increasingly militarily disadvantaged relative to its foes. This reasoning was not spurious; Russia was developing rapidly, and another decade or two of peaceful rule under the tsar might well
have made a conflict between Germany/Austria and France/Russia a losing proposi-
tion for Berlin and Vienna even if Britain had remained aloof from the conflict.
Similarly, in Eastern Eurasia a relatively strong power such as China might – especially if it concludes that it has systemic economic problems that will undermine its
growth over the long term – eventually decide that its position is endangered by an
economically vibrant strategic competitor such as India and conclude that preventa-
tive war is in its interest.

127 See Huntington, *The Clash of Civilizations*, pp. 26–7

128 As Jeremy Black notes, "Despite the well-prepared nature of the navy when war
broke out in 1793, there was nothing inevitable about British victory in the naval
and trans-oceanic struggles.... The combination of revolutionary zeal and mobil-
ization was less beneficial to the French navy than to the army, and was indeed
counter-productive given the effects of the Revolution on the officer corps. Never-
thess, victory on land brought France the support of other naval powers. Thus the
situation during the American War of Independence was repeated: Britain was
opposed by the other leading European naval powers." *Britain as a Military Power,
1688–1815* (London: UCL Press, 1999), p. 222.

129 For a classic example of the American media's tendency toward "strategic panic"
see R.W. Apple, "A Military Quagmire Remembered: Afghanistan as Vietnam,"
New York Times online edn, 31 October 2001. Three weeks after the article, which

warned that "signs of progress [in Afghanistan] are sparse," was published, Kabul fell to US and Northern Alliance forces.

130   The now-common attachment of the label neoconservative to such individuals as Dick Cheney, Donald Rumsfeld, Paul Wolfowitz, and Douglas Feith is an example of an intellectual inaccuracy that has become conventional wisdom through repetition in the media. While there once was a discernable neoconservative movement in the United States, its was led by figures such as Irving Kristol and Norman Podhoretz and the aforementioned current and former policymakers in the George W. Bush Administration had no significant connection to it. For a more accurate appraisal of the current "neoconservatives," see Max Boot, "The Myth of an American Neoconservative Cabal," Council on Foreign Relations, accessed at www.cfr.org, originally published in the *Daily Star* (Lebanon), 14 January 2004.

131   See Kagan, *Of Paradise and Power*, pp. 27–42.

132   Max Boot makes a useful distinction between "hard" and "soft" Wilsonians: "The Wilsonian label has become affixed to those who believe that US foreign policy should be guided by ideals, not just, as advocates of realpolitik believe, the protection of narrowly defined strategic and economic interests ... 'Soft Wilsonians' share with former Presidents Woodrow Wilson and Jimmy Carter a faith that multilateral organizations like the League of Nations or the United Nations should be the main venues in which the United States should promote its ideals, and that international law should be its main policy tool. They are willing to use force, but preferably only when (as in Haiti or Kosovo) the intervention is untainted by any hint of national interests ... 'Hard Wilsonians' place their faith not in pieces of paper, but in power, specifically the power of the United States. They believe that the US should use force if necessary to champion its ideals as well as its interests not only out of sheer humanitarianism, but also because the spread of liberal democracy improves American security, while crimes against humanity (such as the mass murders perpetrated by former Iraqi President Saddam Hussein or former Yugoslav President Slobodan Milosevic) inevitably make the world a more dangerous place." Boot, "The Myth of an American Neoconservative Cabal."

133   It, of course, is necessary to make a distinction between Islam as a faith and Islamism, a totalitarian religio-political movement that has emerged out of that faith. On the characteristics of Islamism, see Jean Beth Elshtain, *Just War Against Terror: The Burden of American Power in a Violent World* (New York: Basic, 2003), p. 3.

134   See Steven Lee Myers, "Putin Says Russia Faces Full 'War' to Divide Nation," *New York Times* online edn, 5 September 2004 and the translated transcript of Putin's 4 September 2004 address to the Russian people, reprinted as "Putin Tells the Russians: 'We Shall be Stronger,'" idem.

135   This chapter does not address criminal gangs, "narco-terrrorists," local militias, and similar petty villains. All of these categories overlap to some degree, but groups in any of them tend to lack either the motivation or ability to present a major challenge to international order. Such actors might be a very dangerous force in specific countries, such as Columbia, Sierra Leone, or even Russia, but they generally lack the motivation and/or ability to threaten deeply international economic prosperity and political order.

136   On the "globalized" character of al Qaeda, see Rajan Menon, "Terrorism, Inc.," *Los Angeles Times* online edn, 22 August 2004.

137   See Michael Ledeen, *The War Against the Terror Masters: Why It Happened, Where We are Now, How We'll Win*, rev. edn (New York: Truman Talley Books, 2003), *passim*.

138   There are, for instance, substantial religious differences between Salafists and other Sunni "fundamentalists"; moreover, there are various schools of Salafi thought. See

Robert A. Pape, *Dying to Win: The Strategic Logic of Suicide Terrorism* (New York: Random House, 2006), pp. 105–7.

139 As many observers have noted, the great majority of the September 11 terrorists were of Saudi nationality. See the chart accompanying George J. Tenet, "Unclassified Version of the Director of Central Intelligence George J. Tenet's Testimony Before the Joint Inquiry into the Terrorist Attacks Against the United States," 18 June 2002, accessed at www.cia.gov.

140 See Bruce Lawrence, ed., *Messages to the World: The Statements of Osama Bin Laden* (New York: Verso, 2005), *passim*.

141 On the problems related to delegitimization of Islamist terrorists, see C. Dale Walton, "Preserving a Culture of Liberty: American Homeland Defense and the Effective Prosecution of the War on Terrorism," *Journal of the Institute of Justice and International Studies*, 3 (2003), pp. 243–51, published online at www.cmsu.edu/cjinst/issue3.pdf.

142 Edward N. Luttwak, *Strategy: The Logic of War and Peace*, rev. and enlarged edn (Cambridge, MA: Belknap Press/Harvard University Press, 2002), *passim*.

143 On the use of suicide bombing by the Tamil Tigers, see Pape, *Dying to Win, passim*.

144 Indeed, Islamist radicals are largely responsible for creating conditions in which a cycle of interfaith violence can be expected to occur in some of the most populous areas of the world. There is, for example, a very real possibility that violence between Christians and Muslims in Africa, South Asia, and elsewhere will greatly worsen, and that there will be awful terrorism and other violence in countries such as Nigeria, a state split between Christians and Muslims that already has seen substantial interfaith bloodshed. Indeed, given the level of violence that Islamists have committed against Christians in Egypt, Iraq, Sudan, Pakistan, and elsewhere, it would hardly be surprising if international terrorist groups purporting to defend the lives and property of Christians eventually emerged. Such violence, and the possibility of a Christian "backlash," is discussed in Philip Jenkins, *The Next Christiandom: The Coming of Global Christianity* (New York: Oxford University Press, 2002), pp. 163–90.

145 The degree to which terrorist techniques have developed in recent years is illustrated in a 1994 article that popularized the term "postmodern terrorism." One passage in particular today makes grim reading: "Airline hijackings have become rare, since hijacked planes cannot stay in the air forever and few countries today are willing to let them land, thereby incurring the stigma of openly supporting terrorism. Terrorists, too, saw diminishing returns on hijackings. The trend now seems to be away from attacking specific targets like the other side's officials and toward more indiscriminate killing." Walter Laqueur, "Postmodern Terrorism," *Foreign Affairs*, 75:5 (September/October 1996), p. 25. Obviously, the al Qaeda 9/11 plot not only avoided the "diminishing returns" that previously had discouraged hijacking, but maximized publicity returns while committing mass murder *and* attacking "specific targets": the civilian and uniformed US military high command and, with United Flight 93, presumably either members of the US Congress or Executive branch.

146 The Teutonic Knights, of course, practiced a form of statecraft that mixed political considerations with holy war. Given the rise of Islamist states such as Sudan, this seems oddly contemporary. On the Teutonic Knights' crusading, see Eric Christiansen, *The Northern Crusades*, 2nd edn (New York: Penguin, 1997). Various perspectives on Christian holy war are offered in Karen Armstrong, *Holy War: The Crusaders and Their Impact on Today's World*, 2nd edn (New York: Anchor Books, 2001); Geoffrey Regan, *First Crusader: Byzantium's Holy Wars* (New York: Palgrave Macmillan, 2001); and Peter Partner, *God of Battles: Holy Wars of Christianity and Islam* (Princeton, NJ: Princeton University Press, 1997).

147 It is, however, worth noting that the United States was itself formed by a revolutionary committee of individuals whose right to sign a Declaration of Independence on

behalf of the various colonies which they supposedly represented was vigorously, if unsuccessfully, disputed by the state that had previously controlled those colonies.

148 An interesting exploration of the similarities and contrasts in how the Italian Fascists and German Nazis came to power is offered in Robert Paxton, *The Anatomy of Fascism* (New York: Vintage, 2005), *passim.*

149 See, for example, Graham Allison, *Nuclear Terrorism: The Ultimate Preventable Catastrophe* (New York: Times Books, 2004).

150 *Trust: The Social Virtues and the Creation of Prosperity* (New York: The Free Press, 1995).

151 The mental prowess of Hitler and other notorious characters often, and unwisely, is slighted because of the mistaken perception that acknowledging their intelligence somehow forgives their character. However, it is fair to say that at least the more villainous of strategic entrepreneurs do tend to have notable "blind spots" in their critical reasoning skills. In a passage that could apply equally well to Osama bin Laden, Alan Bullock writes, "[I]t is a mistake to underestimate the power of Hitler's mind, and of the mental system that he put together from the material he picked up from his reading and experience. But everything he ever said or wrote reveals that his mind lacked not only humanity, but the capacity for critical appreciation, for objectivity and reason in the assimilation of knowledge, which have traditionally been seen as the hallmarks of an educated mind, and which Hitler openly despised." *Hitler and Stalin: Parallel Lives* (New York: Alfred A. Knopf, 1992), p. 22.

152 Lee Harris makes an excellent point in this regard: "Our hindsight is unavoidably distorted. When we think of Hitler or Mussolini or Lenin, we think of them strutting grandiloquently across the stage of history, magnified many times their original size in order to fit the huge dimensions suggested by their gigantic effect on the human race. From such great effects one is tempted to deduce a great cause. But such is not the case.... What gave them power – aside from sheer dumb luck – was their deliberate deployment of ruthlessness. They stopped at nothing, and nothing held them back. Both agents and victims of a fantasy ideology, they transformed themselves through the power of group hypnosis into men who were able to overcome all the inhibitions of their own middle-class and often prosperous and cultured backgrounds." *Civilization and Its Enemies: The Next Stage of History* (New York: Free Press, 2004), p. 108.

153 The distinction between irrationality and unreasonableness is explained in Keith B. Payne, *Deterrence in the Second Nuclear Age* (Lexington, KY: University Press of Kentucky, 1996), pp. 53–4.

154 Al Qaeda has a symbiotic relationship with Islamism: because the latter exists as a major international intellectual force, the former has many potential recruits; the successes of the former, in turn, surely convinces many observers to believe that Islamism is impressively powerful, and inclines some "fence-sitters" to support the Islamists intellectually and/or materially. Because Islamists are a radicalized subset of a much larger group, Muslims in general, even miniscule percentage gains in support for the former can translate into many thousands of recruits and millions of dollars in financial support. However, this process can also operate in reverse: some Muslims who might otherwise be sympathetic to Islamist teachings no doubt are appalled by al Qaeda's tactics and thereby become disenchanted with Islamism in general.

155 There of course always have been religious extremists of every description, but Islamism is the product of a specific history – most importantly, it is difficult to imagine the emergence of Islamism as a major force if not for the relative economic, military, and political decline of the Islamic world in recent centuries – and is very much a twentieth-century intellectual movement. (Indeed, it clearly owes a considerable intellectual debt to secular movements such as National Socialism and

Marxist-Leninism, an ironic fact given the attitudes of these ideologies toward monotheism.)

156　For a classic discussion of how mass frustration and anger give rise to fanatical movements, see Eric Hoffer, *The True Believer: Thoughts on the Nature of Mass Movements* (New York: Perennial Classics, 2002; first published 1951).

157　On the motivation for the attack, see Robert Jay Lifton, *Destroying the World to Save It: Aum Shinrikyô, Apocalyptic Violence, and the New Global Terrorism* (New York: Metropolitan Books, 1999), *passim.*

158　The possibility that terrorist groups may be able to develop relatively simple but extremely dangerous biological weapons is even more threatening. For instance, the 1918 influenza virus conceivably could be used as a weapon of mass destruction, and the full genome of the virus was made available on an internet database in 2005. Ray Kurzweil and Bill Joy, "Recipe for Destruction," *New York Times* online edn, 17 October 2005.

159　Lawrence Freedman argues that, "Non-state actors are unlikely to obtain nuclear weapons, given the technical and financial requirements of doing so, but may find chemical or biological weapons more accessible." *The Revolution in Strategic Affairs*, Adelphi Paper 318 (New York: Oxford University Press, 1998), p. 46. This is a prudent perspective, although it is important that the possibility that a finished weapon will fall into terrorist hands not be ignored. In regard to the threat presented by "bio-terrorism" in particular, see William Butler, "Germ Wars: The Biological Threat from Abroad," in James F. Hoge, Jr and Gideon Rose, eds, *How Did this Happen? Terrorism and the New War* (New York: PublicAffairs, 2001), pp. 211–15 and Judith Miller, Stephen Engelberg, and William Broad, *Germs: Biological Weapons and America's Secret War* (New York: Simon and Schuster, 2001).

160　See David J. Lonsdale, "Information Power: Strategy, Geopolitics and the Fifth Dimension," in Colin S. Gray and Geoffrey Sloan, eds, *Geopolitics, Geography, and Strategy* (London: Frank Cass, 1999), pp. 137–57.

161　Two fascinating collections of documents illustrating the relationship between the Soviet Union and the CPUSA are: Harvey Klehr, John Earl Haynes, and Fridrich Igorevich Firsov, *The Secret World of American Communism* (New Haven, CT: Yale University Press, 1995) and Harvey Klehr, John Earl Haynes, and Kyrill M. Anderson, *The Soviet World of American Communism* (New Haven, CT: Yale University Press, 1998).

162　The radicalization of the fringe of the animal rights and environmental movements provides another worrying precedent. As with anti-globalization protestors, the majority of environmental and animal rights activists are non-violent; some, however, have adopted tactics such as harassing and physically threatening employees of institutions that conduct research on animals, destroying property through various means, including arson, and spiking trees, thereby placing loggers in great danger. See Doug Bandow, "American Terrorism, Environment-Style," *Human Events*, 59:3 (29 September 2003), p. 27; Catherine Bennett, "Animal Rights 'Activists'? No, Terrorists," *Guardian* (London) online edn, 9 September 2004; and Timothy Garton Ash, "We Must Stand Up to the Creeping Tyranny of the Group Veto," *Guardian* (London), 2 March 2006. While violence, heretofore, has been limited, with very few environmental or animal rights activists willing to commit acts likely to result in fatalities, it of course is possible that the more extreme elements within these movements will become more violent over time.

163　Hoffer intriguingly argues that, "When people are ripe for a mass movement, they are usually ripe for any effective movement, and not solely one with a particular doctrine or program.... Since all mass movements draw their adherent from the same types of humanity and appeal to the same types of mind, it follows: (a) all mass movements are competitive, and the gain of one in adherents is the loss of all the others; (b) all mass movements are interchangeable. One mass movement readily transforms itself into another. A religious movement may develop into a social revolution or a nationalist movement; a social revolution, into militant nationalism or a religious movement; a nationalist movement into a social revolution or a religious movement." *The True Believer*, pp. 16 and 17.

164 In the case of these two powers, it is easy to see why they are motivated to help. Moscow has struggled with the Chechen ulcer for over a decade now, and Islamism has been an important motivating factor in the rebellion; foreign Islamist fighters continuously pour into Chechnya and, at the very least, the Americans divert the attention of some of the Islamists who would otherwise beleaguer Russia and damage the international terrorist networks that maintain the "pipeline" which allows guerrillas and weapons to flow into Russia. Given that it has a restive Uygur Muslim minority, China also has good reason to fear Islamism.

165 The author intentionally has avoided arguing that an anti-terrorism "taboo" may be developing, as this very strong word arguably is misused in reference to the non-use (since 1945) of nuclear weapons. It is difficult to gauge how strong the reluctance of great powers to use nuclear weapons actually is because there has been occasion since World War II in which any nuclear-armed states have faced *truly* severe pressure to use them. For example, most American leaders believed that the military and diplomatic risks accompanying nuclear use in Korea and Vietnam outweighed the benefits of these devices. However, if the United States had faced defeat in the European theater in a Third World War, it is quite imaginable that the nuclear taboo would have unceremoniously expired. Any budding restraint in great power support for violent non-state actors would likely be roughly comparable to nuclear restraint over the last sixty years – there may be potent constraints operating on the particular states, but one should be cautious and not simply assume that a well-nigh unbreakable universal taboo exists.

166 However, interestingly, the CIA may have supported *Mujahadeen* operations on Soviet soil during the 1980s. See Steve Coll, *Ghost Wars: The Secret History of the CIA, Afghanistan, and Bin Laden, From the Soviet Invasion to September 10, 2001* (New York: Penguin, 2004), pp. 104–6.

167 It is, for example, most unlikely that China automatically would become the greatest power in the world if a terrorist group detonated a nuclear device on American soil, because such a strike probably would not massively and immediately degrade the overall power of the United States. While the US economy would be harmed (as, almost surely, would the economies of all the great powers – which itself would constitute "blowback" for China), its military likely would be able to rapidly adapt even if the Pentagon itself were the target of the blast, and Chinese leaders safely could presume that, if the terrorist group in question were seen as being their instrument, the United States would seek vengeance. Unlike a well-organized nuclear first strike by a state with a sophisticated intercontinental arsenal, such an attack probably would be the proximate cause of a nuclear war, but could not by itself *win* one.

168 The degree to which Pakistani support for terrorists operating in Kashmir has increased tensions between that state and India, and at least indirectly, led to the crisis that almost led to war between the two states in 2002, is instructive.

169 Ray Kurzweil, *The Age of Spiritual Machines: When Computers Exceed Human Intelligence* (New York: Viking, 1999), p. 26.

170 Ray Kurzweil, *The Singularity is Near: When Humans Transcend Biology* (New York: Viking, 2005), p. 105. However, Rodney A. Brooks makes the useful point that there is a very large and critical obstacle that AI researchers have not yet overcome: translating computing power into intelligence of a kind comparable to that which humans exhibit. "[Hans Moravec and Ray Kurzweil] rightly point out that no matter how much computation one estimates is going on inside a human, that will soon be surpassed by the computation available in a desktop machine. They assume that we will therefore soon have human-level equivalence in our computers and

robots. They are perhaps being slightly optimistic here – while both of them have worked on AI technologies for the last thirty years, neither is able to give a prescription for what new insights … will get us to human intelligence equivalence." *Flesh and Machines: How Robots will Change Us* (New York: Pantheon, 2002), p. 205.

171 See Kurzweil, *The Age of Spirtual Machines*, pp. 20–5.

172 For a detailed discussion of the possible potential of optical computing, see David D. Nolte, *Mind at Light Speed: A New Kind of Intelligence* (New York: The Free Press, 2001).

173 As Daniel and Mark A. Ratner note, "Various new approaches to computing will only be possible using nanotechnology. DNA computing uses DNA to crunch data as it now stores the formulae of life. Molecular electronics uses individual molecules as electronic computers. All-optical computing uses light instead of electrons for all functions of a computer. Perhaps most powerful of all, the quantum computer can compute problems using the quantum properties of matter. These advances have caused nanotechnology research pioneer Stan Williams of Hewlett Packard to suggest that, in spite of forthcoming limitations on current computer technology, 'It should be possible to compute one billion times more efficiently than is currently possible. That means you could hold the power of all earth's present computers in the palm of your hand.'" *Nanotechnology and Homeland Security: New Weapons for New Wars* (Upper Saddle River, NJ: Prentice Hall Professional Technical Reference, 2004), pp. 81 and 83.

174 For various critiques of Kurzweil's views on AI, and rejoinders to those critiques by Kurzweil, see Jay Richards, George Gilder, Ray Kurzweil, John Searle, William Dembski, Michael Denton, and Thomas Ray, *Are We Spiritual Machines? Ray Kurzweil vs. the Critics of Strong AI* (Seattle, WA: Discovery Institute Press, 2002).

175 For an overview of the progress in these fields and predictions on how they will shape the future, see Damien Broderick, *The Spike: How Our Lives are Being Transformed by Rapidly Advancing Technologies* (New York: Forge, 2001); Brooks, *Flesh and Machines*; Francis Fukuyama, *Our Posthuman Future: Consequences of the Biotechnology Revolution* (New York: Picador, 2003); William Kristol and Eric Cohen, eds, *The Future is Now: America Confronts the New Genetics* (Lanham, MD: Rowman and Littlefield, 2002); Jonathan Margolis, *A Brief History of Tomorrow: The Future, Past and Present* (New York: Bloomsbury, 2000); Jeremy Rifkin, *The Biotech Century: Harnessing the Gene and Remaking the World* (New York: Jeremy P. Tarcher/Putnam, 1998); and Gregory Stock, *Redesigning Humans: Our Inevitable Genetic Future* (New York: Houghton Mifflin, 2002).

176 This is no doubt at least partly explainable by the fact that most social scientists have little expertise in computer science, genetics, robotics, or similar fields. Moreover, many social scientists are uncomfortable speculating about the mid-to-long-term future, as this requires them to cut loose from the safe mooring provided by empirical evidence.

177 For example, viewed from a purely short-term perspective, many of President Franklin Roosevelt's actions in the months leading to December 1941 were foolish incitements that encouraged dangerous foes to declare war on the United States. From a longer-term perspective, however, Roosevelt's behavior not only was justified, but actually prudent, as the United States would face a grave long-term threat if Europe and the Far East were dominated by rapacious and ideologically hostile great powers.

178 See Gray, *Strategy for Chaos*, pp. 170–221.

179 Fred Charles Iklé offers– in his view – a very unattractive vision that appears to fall somewhere in between those of "soft" and "hard" AI advocates. He warns of the possibility that "an integrated brain computer system" whose "purpose would be greatly to enrich and expand what advanced computers can do by creating a symbio-

sis between, on one side, a computer system designed for this purpose, and on the other side, the judgmental capacities and essential emotive functions of the human brain" might be created. *Annihilation from Within: The Ultimate Threat to Nations* (New York: Columbia University Press, 2006), p. 32.

180 Of course, there always is the possibility that substantial resources secretly are being directed to develop such fully autonomous UCAVs, but given the dearth of available evidence for this, it is reasonable to assume that this is not the case.

181 See, for example, John Markoff, "In a Grueling Desert Race, A Winner, But Not a Driver," *New York Times* online edn, 9 October 2005.

182 One can imagine the reaction of the sort of individuals who are alarmed by such unexciting undertakings as the creation of genetically modified corn to the news that a computer program was empowered to make warfighting decisions. There would surely be no shortage of overwrought comparisons to the *Terminator* films, in which an AI computer program named "SkyNet" slips from the control of the US military and decides, as a first step in its vigorous campaign to eliminate humanity, to initiate a thermonuclear war.

183 This cautious course is counseled in, for example, Fukuyama, *Our Posthuman Future*, and Bill McKibben, *Enough: Staying Human in an Engineered Age* (New York: Times Books, 2003).

184 See Andrew Pollack, "Talks on Biotech Food Turn on a Safety Principle," *New York Times* online edn, 28 July 2000.

185 See Tom Wright, "Swiss Voters Approve Ban on Genetically Altered Crops," *New York Times* online edn, 28 November 2005 and Tania Ralli, "Modified Food Labeling Begins in Europe," idem, 21 April 2004.

186 See, for example, John Markoff, "Behind Bush's New Stress on Science, Lobbying by Republican Executives," *New York Times* online edn, 2 February 2006.

187 For an argument in favor of generous financial support for basic scientific research by two former high-level Defense Department officials, see John M. Deutch and William J. Perry, "Research Worth Fighting For," *New York Times*, online edn, 13 April 2005. Notably, the authors make specific reference to numerous RSP-related areas: "New threats, like catastrophic terrorism and the spread of weapons of mass destruction, urgently call for new technology. There should be no doubt that basic research will continue to make a contribution. Robotics, AI, biotechnology, brain and cognitive sciences, nanotechnology, large-scale modeling and simulation: all these fields can have a huge impact. If properly supported, basic technology work is likely to lead to unprecedented results."

188 For a very intriguing argument by one of the most thoughtful advocates of "technological primacy" see Martin Libicki, "The Emerging Primacy of Information," *Orbis*, 40:2 (Spring 1996), pp. 261–76.

189 For example, an average American can control the temperature of his or her home or automobile with the turn of a dial and thus can live and travel in much greater physical comfort than Alexander the Great or even Napoleon enjoyed. Technology has allowed individual humans to live ever less like their fellow mammals (aside from their canine and feline companions, who wisely hitched their fortunes to those of *homo sapiens sapiens* several millennia ago) and to create a sort of technological bubble around themselves that provides some protection from the less pleasant aspects of the physical world.

190 It is notable that the much-heralded "new" security studies areas, which focus on issues outside the realm of traditional strategy such as world overpopulation, poverty and social issues, and environmental matters like desertification and global warming, are explicitly geographical. Indeed, too many authors addressing these issues tend to err in the direction of geographical determinism, assuming all too readily that the pressures resulting from a growing overall world population and the increasing use of fossil fuels inevitably will cause a variety of cataclysms. A balanced assessment of

global challenges should take into account both the possible positive impact of technology on all manner of global problems. Even more importantly, the enormous number of variables relevant to these complex issues ensures that long-term predications cannot be made with any confidence. However, these "new security issues" indeed are all relevant to strategy and it is quite likely that they will play a major role in international political discourse, particularly in regard to those states that are too impoverished to cope effectively with environmental challenges.

191 Ostentatious phrases such as "ruling the sea" or "commanding the air" illustrate critical strategic goals, but they also mislead listeners because they imply control resulting from continuous occupation, even though the most puissant sea or air power will "occupy" only a tiny and ever-shifting fraction of the world's oceans or atmosphere at any given time.

192 "Cyberwar" has received – not undeservedly – a great deal of attention in recent years, but to assume that it will fundamentally alter the character of war exaggerates the importance of this form of warfare. Ultimately, the same question must be answered concerning cyber-attack, just as it would for any other offensive: What will it accomplish if it succeeds? Many observers have speculated about a possible cyber-attack intended to cause a massive temporary disruption of American life, but it is difficult to see how that would translate into military victory over the United States. (After all, the September 11, 2001 attacks enormously damaged the US economy, but certainly did not result in al Qaeda achieving its overall policy goals.) Moreover, there is reason to doubt that a truly massive interference with critical services throughout the United States is even plausible. Scenarios that conjure the image of hackers shutting down essential services throughout America, making most financial records inaccessible, and so forth represent conceivable, but not likely, events. Given the safeguards for critical data and systems that are in place and the fact that thousands – or even tens of thousands – of hackers would presumably have to work simultaneously to effect a massive disruption of US civil life, such scenarios seem highly implausible. A "technological Pearl Harbor" attack against a few critical military systems might be more practical, but that would hardly be an easy task, as it would be an attack on very well-guarded systems – and one of the characteristics of large computer networks is that they are robust. Perhaps a cyberattack could, for example, purchase a few critical days for the People's Liberation Army to undertake an invasion of Taiwan with minimal American interference, but cyber warfare ultimately would still be a complement to geographic forms of military power rather than a substitute for them. In isolation, cyberwar cannot win wars any more than the Ultra and Enigma codebreaking projects of World War II – "information warfare" efforts in the most literal sense of the term – could, but when used in concert with "hard" military power, it can be a useful and powerful tool.

193 See, for example, Robert B. Strassler, ed., *The Landmark Thucydides: A Comprehensive Guide to the Peloponnesian War* (New York: Touchstone, 1998), p. 43.

194 Strategy of course is not undertaken in a vacuum – states will not be competing against an abstract "Platonic great power" that makes no errors and experiences no Clausewitzian friction. They will all make mistakes and shackle their researchers, whether governmentally or privately funded, with constraints of various kinds. In regard to strategic success, the issue is, which states will be more competitive than their peers, but it would be most unwise simply to assume that democratic states will enjoy a natural advantage in technological research over their authoritarian counterparts. It certainly is true that, at least in recent decades, the leading states in most technological fields have been democracies. It is likely, however, that this was more the result of the fact that today's leading democratic states have relatively free markets than of democracy per se. As China is demonstrating, it is possible – at least for some period of time – to mix authoritarian government with a largely free market, thus partially or entirely negating the "capitalist incentive advantage" that

the democracies previously enjoyed. Also, as noted previously, undemocratic governments may – because they need not respond to the fears and moral/ethical preferences of voters – prove to have a key advantage over their democratic peers. If this proves to be the case, the Post-Columbian political environment may prove to be a very friendly one for authoritarian states, and the likelihood that the People's Republic of China will eclipse the United States as the preeminent global power would be increased considerably.

195 A classic study of the birth of the Congress system is Henry A. Kissinger, *A World Restored; Metternich, Castlereagh, and the Problems of Peace, 1812–1822* (Boston: Houghton Mifflin, 1973; originally published 1957). Today, the closest equivalent is the UN Security Council process, but the latter is wholly inadequate for serious great power deliberation, as it is warped by global media attention, confused by the presence of veto-holding medium and elected minor powers, and does not place Japan, India, and the EU in a permanent, co-equal position with China, Russia, and the United States.

Select bibliography

Books and monographs

Bacevich, Andrew, *American Empire: The Realities and Consequences of US Diplomacy* (Cambridge, MA: Harvard University Press, 2002).

Black, Jeremy, *Britain as a Military Power, 1688–1815* (London: UCL Press, 1999).

Blouet, Brian W., *Halford Mackinder: A Biography* (College Station, TX: Texas A&M University Press, 1987).

Broderick, Damien, *The Spike: How Our Lives Are Being Transformed by Rapidly Advancing Technologies* (New York: Forge, 2001)

Brooks, Rodney, *Flash and Machines: How Robots Will Change Us* (New York: Pantheon, 2002).

Brzezinski, Zbigniew, *The Grand Chessboard: American Primacy and Its Geostrategic Imperatives* (New York: Basic Books, 1997).

Bulliet, Richard W., *The Case for Islamo-Christian Civilization*, new edn (New York: Columbia University Press, 2006).

von Clausewitz, Carl, *On War*, ed. and trans. Michael Howard and Peter Paret (Princeton, NJ: Princeton University Press, 1984).

Diffie, Bailey W. and George D. Winius, *Foundations of the Portuguese Empire, 1415–1580*, Europe and the World in the Age of Expansion series, vol. 1 (Minneapolis: University of Minneapolis Press, 1977).

Fairgrieve, James, *Geography and World Power* (New York: E.P. Dutton, 1941).

Ferguson, Niall, *Empire: The Rise and Demise of the British World Order and the Lessons for Global Power* (New York: Basic Books, 2003).

Freedman, Lawrence, *The Revolution in Strategic Affairs*, Adelphi Paper 318 (London: International Institute for Strategic Studies, 1998).

Fukuyama, Francis. *Our Posthuman Future: Consequences of the Biotechnological Revolution* (New York: Picador, 2003).

Gernet, Jacques, *A History of Chinese Civilization*, 2nd edn (New York: Cambridge University Press, 1996).

Gray, Colin S., *The Geopolitics of the Nuclear Era: Heartlands, Rimlands, and the Technological Revolution*, Strategy Paper No. 30 (New York: National Strategy Information Center/Crane Russak & Company, 1977).

—— *Geopolitics, Geography, and Strategy* (London: Frank Cass, 1999).

—— *Strategy for Chaos: Revolutions in Military Affairs and the Evidence of History*, Strategy and History series (London: Frank Cass, 2002).

—— "In Defense of the Heartland: Sir Halford Mackinder and His Critics a Hundred Years On," *Comparative Strategy*, 23:1 (January–March 2004).

—— *The Sheriff: America's Defense of the New World Order* (Lexington, KY: The University Press of Kentucky, 2004).

—— *Another Bloody Century: Future Warfare* (London: Weidenfield and Nicholson, 2005).

Gregor, A. James, *The Faces of Janus: Marxism and Fascism in the Twentieth Century* (New Haven, CT: Yale University Press, 2000).

Hanson, Victor Davis, *Carnage and Culture: Landmark Battles in the Rise of Western Power* (New York: Doubleday, 2001).

Harding, Harry, "The Evolution of the Strategic Triangle: China, India, and the United States," in Francine R. Frankel and Harry Harding, eds, *The India–China Relationship: What the United States Needs to Know* (New York: Columbia University Press/Woodrow Wilson Center Press, 2004).

Harris, Lee, *Civilization and Its Enemies: The Next Stage of History* (New York: Free Press, 2004).

Haushofer, Karl, ed. and updated Lewis A. Tambs, trans. Ernst J. Brehm, *An English Translation and Analysis of Major General Karl Ernst Haushofer's Geopolitics of the Pacific Ocean: Studies in the Relationships Between Geography and History*, Mellen Studies in Geography series (Lewiston, NY: The Edwin Mellon Press, 2002; first German edn published 1924).

Hoffer, Eric, *The True Believer: Thoughts on the Nature of Mass Movements* (New York: Perennial Classics, 2002; first published 1951).

Huntington, Samuel, *The Clash of Civilizations and the Remaking of World Order* (New York: Simon and Schuster, 1996).

Ikle, Fred Charles, *Annihilation from Within: The Ultimate Threat to Nations* (New York: Columbia University Press, 2006).

Jenkins, Philip, *The Next Christiandom: The Coming of Global Christianity* (New York: Oxford University Press, 2002).

Kagan, Donald, *On the Origins of War and the Preservation of Peace* (New York: Anchor Books, 1996).

Kane, Thomas M., *Chinese Grand Strategy and Maritime Power* (London and Portland, OR: Frank Cass, 2002)

Kass, Leon, "The Wisdom of Repugnance," in Leon Kass and James Q. Wilson, eds, *The Ethics of Human Cloning* (Washington, DC: The AEI Press, 1998).

Knox, MacGregor and Williamson Murray, eds, *The Dynamics of Military Revolution, 1300–2050* (Cambridge, UK: Cambridge University Press, 2001).

Kristol, William and Eric Cohen, eds, *The Future is Now: America Confronts the New Genetics* (Lanham, MD: Rowman and Littlefield, 2002).

Kurzweil, Ray, *The Age of Intelligent Machines* (New York: Viking, 1999).

—— *The Singularity is Near: When Humans Transcend Biology* (New York: Viking, 2005).

Lawrence, Bruce, ed., *Messages to the World: The Statements of Osama bin Laden* (New York: Verso, 2005).

Levathes, Louise, *When China Ruled the Seas: The Treasure Fleet and the Dragon Throne, 1405–33* (New York: Simon and Shuster, 1994).

Lewis, Bernard, *What Went Wrong? The Clash Between Islam and Modernity in the Middle East* (New York: Perennial, 2003).

Libiki, Martin, *The Mesh and the Net: Speculations on Armed Conflict in the Age of Free Silicon*, McNair Paper #28 (Washington, DC: Institute for National Strategic Studies/National Defense University, 1994).

Lind, Michael, *The American Way of Strategy: U.S. Foreign Policy and the American Way of Life* (New York: Oxford University Press, 2006).

Love, James Trapier, *Geopolitics and War: Mackinder's Philosophy of Power* (Washington, DC: University Press of America, 1981).

Luttwak, Edward N., *Strategy: The Logic of War and Peace*, rev. and enlarged edn (Cambridge, MA: Belknap Press/Harvard University Press, 2002).

Margolis, Jonathan, *A Brief History of Tomorrow: The Future, Past and Present* (New York: Bloomsbury 2000).

Mackinder, Halford, *Democratic Ideals and Reality: A Study in the Politics of Reconstruction*, NDU Press Defense Classics (Washington, DC: National Defense University Press, n.d.; originally published 1919).

McKibben, Bill, *Enough: Staying Human in an Engineered Age* (New York: Times Books, 2003).

Mearsheimer, John, *The Tragedy of Great Power Politics* (New York: Norton, 2001).

Morgenthau, Hans J., *Politics Among Nations: The Struggle for Power and Peace*, 5th edn (New York: Alfred A. Knopf, 1978; first edn published 1948).

Mosher, Stephen, *Hegemon: China's Plan to Dominate Asia and the World* (San Francisco, CA: Encounter, 2000).

Mote, F.W., *Imperial China, 900–1800* (Cambridge, MA: Harvard University Press, 1999).

Nichols, Thomas M., *Winning the World: Lessons for America's Future from the Cold War* (New York: Praeger, 2002).

Nolte, David D., *Mind at Light Speed: A New Kind of Intelligence* (New York: The Free Press, 2001).

Ó Tuathail, Gearóid, Simon Dalby, and Paul Routledge, eds, *The Geopolitics Reader* (New York: Routledge, 1998).

Owens, William A., *Lifting the Fog of War* (New York: Farrar, Straus and Giroux, 2000).

Pagden, Anthony, "Heeding Heraclides: Empire and Its Discontents, 1619–1812," in Richard L. Kagan and Geoffrey Parker, eds, *Spain, Europe, and the Atlantic World: Essays in Honor of John H. Elliott* (Cambridge: Cambridge University Press, 1995).

Pape, Robert A., *Dying to Win: The Strategic Logic of Suicide Terrorism* (New York: Random House, 2006).

Parker, Geoffrey, *Geopolitics: Past, Present, and Future* (London: Pinter, 1998).

—— *The Grand Strategy of Phillip II* (New Haven, CT: Yale University Press, 1998).

—— *Success Is Never Final: Empire, War, and Faith in Early Modern Europe* (New York: Basic Books, 2002).

Paxton, Robert, *The Anatomy of Fascism* (New York: Vintage, 2005).

Ratner, Daniel and A. Mark, *Nanotechnology and Homeland Security: New Weapons for New Wars* (Upper Saddle River, NJ: Prentice Hall Professional Technical Reference, 2004).

Richards, Jay, George Gilder, Ray Kurzweil, John Searle, William Dembski, Michael Denton, and Thomas Ray, *Are We Spiritual Machines? Ray Kurzweil vs. the Critics of Strong AI* (Seattle, WA: Discovery Press Institute Press, 2002).

Rifkin, Jeremy, *The Biotech Century: Harnessing the Gene and Remaking the World* (New York: Jeremy T. Tarcher/Putnam, 1998).

Rosefielde, Steven, *Russia in the Twenty-First Century: The Prodigal Superpower* (New York: Cambridge University Press, 2004).

Schroeder, Paul W., *The Transformation of European Politics, 1763–1848*, The Oxford History of Modern Europe series (New York: Oxford University Press, 1994).

Schwartzenberger, Georg, *Power Politics: A Study of International Society*, 2nd edn (London: Stevens and Sons, 1951).

Scruton, Roger, *The West and the Rest: Globalization and the Terrorist Threat* (Wilmington, DE: Intercollegiate Studies Institute, 2002).

Spykman, Nicholas J., *America's Strategy in World Politics: The United States and the Balance of Power* (New York: Harcourt, Brace, 1942).

—— *The Geography of the Peace* (New York: Harcourt, Brace, 1944).

Stock, Gregory, *Redesigning Humans: Out Inevitable Genetic Future* (New York: Houghton Mifflin, 2002).

Strachan, Hew, *The First World War* (New York: Viking, 2003).

Treadgold, Warren, *A History of the Byzantine State and Society* (Stanford, CA: Stanford University Press, 1997).

Toffler, Alvin and Heidi, *War and Anti-War: Survival at the Dawn of the 21st Century* (Boston: Little, Brown, 1993).

Van Creveld, Martin, *The Rise and Decline of the State* (Cambridge, UK: Cambridge University Press, 1999).

Watts, Barry D., *Clausewitzian Friction and Future War*, rev. edn, McNair Paper #68 (Washington, DC: Institute for National Strategic Studies/National Defense University, 2004).

Weigert, Hans W., *Generals and Geographers: The Twilight of Geopolitics* (New York: Oxford University Press, 1942).

Whittlesey, Derwent, *German Strategy of World Conquest* (New York: Farrar and Rinehart, 1942).

—— "Haushofer: The Geopoliticians," in Edward Mead Earl, ed., *Makers of Modern Strategy: Military Thought from Machiavelli to Hitler* (Princeton, NJ: Princeton University Press, 1973; originally published 1943), pp. 388–411.

Zimmermann, Warren, *The First Great Triumph: How Five Americans Made Their Country a World Power* (New York: Farrar, Straus and Giroux, 2002).

Articles

Dodge, Paul, "Circumventing Sea Power: Chinese Strategies to Deter U.S. Intervention in Taiwan," *Comparative Strategy* 23:4–5 (October–December 2004), pp. 391–409.

Kane, Thomas M. and Lawrence W. Serewicz, "China's Hunger: The Consequences of a Rising Demand for Food and Energy," *Parameters*, 31:3, (Autumn 2001), pp. 63–75.

Krauthammer, Charles, "The Unipolar Moment," *Foreign Affairs*, 70:1 (Winter 1990/91), pp. 23–33.

Laqueur, Walter, "Postmodern Terrorism," *Foreign Affairs*, 75:5 (September–October 1996), pp. 24–36.

Libiki, Martin, "The Emerging Primacy of Information," *Orbis*, 40:2 (Spring 2006) pp. 261–76.

Odom, William, "Realism About Russia," *The National Interest*, 65 (Fall: 1991), pp. 56–66.

Saunders, Phillip C., "A Virtual Alliance for Asian Security," *Orbis*, 43/2 (Spring 1999), pp. 237–56.

Thayer, Bradley A., "Confronting China: An Evaluation of Options for the United States," *Comparative Strategy*, 24:1 (January–March 2005), pp. 71–98.

Walton, C. Dale, "The Decline of the Third Rome: Russia's Prospects as a Great Power," *Journal of Slavic Military Studies*, 12:1 (March 1999), pp. 51–63.

—— "Navigating the Second Nuclear Age: Proliferation and Deterrence in this Century," *Global Dialogue*, 8:1 (Winter/Spring 2006), pp. 22–31.

Index

Breinigsville, PA USA
18 August 2010
243782BV00007B/1/P